The Founding Fortunes

Also by Tom Shachtman

How the French Saved America

Gentlemen Scientists and Revolutionaries:
The Founding Fathers in the Age of Enlightenment

American Iconoclast: The Life and Times of Eric Hoffer

Airlift to America

Rumspringa: To Be or Not to Be Amish

Terrors and Marvels:
The Science and Technology of World War II

Absolute Zero and the Conquest of Cold

Around the Block: The Business of a Neighborhood

The Inarticulate Society:
Eloquence and Culture in America

Skyscraper Dreams:
The Great Real Estate Dynasties of New York

Decade of Shocks: Dallas to Watergate, 1963–1974

The Phony War, 1939–1940

Edith and Woodrow: A Presidential Romance

The Day America Crashed

The Founding Fortunes

How the Wealthy Paid for and
Profited from America's Revolution

TOM SHACHTMAN

St. Martin's Press ⚏ New York

First published in the United States by St. Martin's Press,
an imprint of St. Martin's Publishing Group.

THE FOUNDING FORTUNES. Copyright © 2019
by Tom Shachtman. All rights reserved.
Printed in the United States of America.
For information, address
St. Martin's Publishing Group, 120 Broadway,
New York, NY 10271.

www.stmartins.com

Library of Congress Cataloging-in-Publication Data

First Edition: January 2020
Names: Shachtman, Tom, 1942– author.
Title: The founding fortunes : how the wealthy paid for and
  profited from America's revolution / Tom Shachtman.
Description: First edition. | New York, NY : St. Martin's Press,
  2020. | Includes bibliographical references and index. |
Identifiers: LCCN 2019034040 | ISBN 9781250164766
  (hardcover) | ISBN 9781250170743 (ebook)
Subjects: LCSH: United States—Economic conditions—To 1865. |
  United States—Commerce—History—18th century. |
  United States—History—Revolution, 1775–1783—Finance. |
  Businesspeople—Political activity—United States—History—
  18th century. | Rich people—Political activity—United States—
  History—18th century.
Classification: LCC HC104 .S53 2020 | DDC 973.3/1—dc23
LC record available at https://lccn.loc.gov/2019034040

Our books may be purchased in bulk for promotional,
educational, or business use. Please contact your local
bookseller or the Macmillan Corporate and Premium Sales
Department at 1-800-221-7945, extension 5442,
or by email at MacmillanSpecialMarkets@macmillan.com.

First Edition: January 2020

10 9 8 7 6 5 4 3 2 1

For Leo, Giovanni, and Francesca

Contents

Part Four:

The Federalist Ascendancy, 1789–1796

Part Five:

Parties, Populism, and Striving for Economic
Independence, 1797–1813

Major Characters

John Adams (1735–1826). Lawyer, farmer, delegate to Continental Congresses, emissary to France, minister to Great Britain, vice president, president.

John Jacob Astor (1763–1848). Merchant, fur trader, real estate investor.

William Bingham (1752–1804). Philadelphia merchant, agent in Martinique, delegate to Continental Congresses, speaker of the Pennsylvania Senate, senator.

Tench Coxe (1755–1824). Merchant, author of economic tracts, delegate to Continental Congress, assistant secretary of the treasury.

Silas Deane (1738–1789). Hartford merchant, trader, delegate to Continental Congress, agent and envoy in Paris.

Elias Hasket Derby (1739–1799). Salem merchant and trader.

John Dickinson (1732–1808). Lawyer, farmer, delegate to Continental Congresses, president of Delaware and of Pennsylvania, delegate to Constitutional Convention.

William Duer (1743–1799). Merchant, provisioner, speculator, member of Continental Congress, assistant to secretary of the treasury.

Benjamin Franklin (1705–1790). Printer, scientist, agent for colonies in London, delegate to Continental Congress, emissary to France, delegate to Constitutional Convention, president of Pennsylvania Supreme Executive Council.

Albert Gallatin (1761–1849). Surveyor, developer, manufacturer, senator, representative, secretary of the treasury, minister to France and Great Britain.

Stephen Girard (1750–1831). Philadelphia merchant, trader, banker.

William Gray (1750–1825). Salem merchant, Massachusetts state senator, lieutenant governor.

Alexander Hamilton (1755–1804). Lawyer, banker, member of Continental Congress, delegate to Constitutional Convention, secretary of the treasury.

John Hancock (1737–1793). Boston merchant, trader, president of the Continental Congress, governor.

Thomas Jefferson (1743–1826). Delegate to Continental Congresses, Virginia governor, ambassador to France, secretary of state, vice president, president.

Henry Laurens (1723–1792). Charleston merchant, trader, planter, president of Continental Congress, minister to the Netherlands.

Benjamin Lincoln (1733–1810). Farmer, member of Massachusetts Provincial Congress, general, lieutenant governor.

James Madison (1751–1836). Virginia planter, delegate to Continental Congress, delegate to Constitutional Convention, representative, secretary of state, president.

Thomas Mifflin (1744–1800). Merchant, trader, president of Continental Congress, quartermaster, president of Pennsylvania Supreme Executive Council, delegate to Constitutional Convention, governor.

Gouverneur Morris (1752–1816). Lawyer, delegate to Continental Congress, delegate to Constitutional Convention, minister to France, senator.

Robert Morris (1734–1806). Philadelphia merchant, trader, delegate to Continental Congress, superintendent of finance, delegate to Constitutional Convention, senator.

James Wilson (1742–1798). Philadelphia lawyer, delegate to Continental Congress, delegate to Constitutional Convention, associate justice of the Supreme Court.

Jeremiah Wadsworth (1743–1804). Hartford merchant, trader, banker, agriculturalist, commissary, representative.

George Washington (1732–1799). Planter, member of Virginia House of Burgesses, delegate to Continental Congress, commanding general, delegate to Constitutional Convention, president.

Thomas Willing (1731–1821). Merchant, trader, banker, mayor of Philadelphia, delegate to Continental Congress.

Oliver Wolcott, Jr. (1760–1833). Hartford lawyer, banker, comptroller and secretary of the treasury, governor.

Part One

⸺❀⸺

Colonial Matters,
1763–1776

Offensive Acts

At sunset on May 9, 1768, the merchant ship *Liberty* sailed into Boston Harbor after a voyage from Portugal's Madeira Islands, with a cargo of the islands' fortified wine that the ship's owner, the thirty-one-year-old John Hancock, often drank: "I like rich wine" he had recently written to a friend. At the Hancock Wharf, the tidesman Thomas Kirk boarded the *Liberty* to ascertain the duty on the cargo. He was wary on several counts. Although among the wealthiest of Bostonians, Hancock was known for his radical sympathies, to the point that many other merchants considered him a traitor to his class. Also, as an experienced smuggler, he might dispute the relatively new import duty on Madeira not reshipped from Great Britain—previously he and a gang of seamen had blocked Kirk's fellow officers from access to the hold of his *Lydia*, suspected of containing dutiables, and when a lone officer sneaked aboard at night he was surprised below by men demanding to see his writ of assistance or search warrant. He had neither. Hancock had him seized, held over the side, and asked whether he really wanted to search the vessel. He said no, well aware of recent incidents in which customs officers were tarred and feathered, and Hancock advised that he was free to inspect but not to linger. He left the ship.

Regarding the *Lydia,* the colony's attorney general had ruled: "Though Mr. Hancock may not have conducted himself so prudently or courteously as might be wished . . . it is probable that his intention was to keep within the bounds of the law." On boarding the *Liberty* a month later, Kirk made sure to have proper papers. Hancock was not there, either attending to his duties for the town council or provincial congress, or at his palatial home atop Beacon Hill, or traveling in his gilded carriage. Aboard the *Liberty* Hancock's representative offered Kirk a bribe to report fewer casks of Madeira. When Kirk did not accept, he was locked in the steerage. During the night he "heard a noise as of many people upon deck at Work hoisting out goods." Released, he was warned not to say a word, and he didn't: He reported the *Liberty* as carrying just twenty-five pipes (casks of 125 gallons each), a quarter of its capacity; Hancock paid the duty and that seemed the end of it—business as usual. Collusion was rife: In an article Stephen Hopkins, former governor of Rhode Island, accused Massachusetts officials of "shutting their eyes or at least of opening them no further than their own private interest required."

A month later, as Hancock's *Liberty* was being readied for another voyage, the HMS *Romney* entered Boston Harbor, and everything changed. The fifty-gun warship had been sent "to over-awe and terrify the inhabitants of this town into base compliance and unlimited submission," according to a Boston newspaper. Its presence emboldened Kirk to recant his twenty-five-pipes report and to charge that Hancock had evaded import taxes. This gave the port commissioner reason to have a broad arrow painted on the *Liberty*'s mast, a sign of imminent seizure. The *Romney*'s marines approached in small boats and prepared to haul the *Liberty* away.

Hancock was not there, but three hundred to five hundred other men gathered at the pier to protest the seizure.

Revolutions that produce lasting change, rather than just disruptions, cannot succeed without the participation of both the rich and the poor. The British seizing of the *Liberty* provided Americans with a specific object on which to act in unison, a rich man's ship that poor men decided to defend. They ripped up paving stones and threw them at the marines.

They did so in part because Hancock had proved himself to be on their side when few other wealthy merchants were, and in part because of fear for their livelihoods—half the jobs in Boston depended on the foreign trade being carried on by Hancock and other merchants. Critics then and since have dismissed the pavestone throwers on the Hancock Wharf as a mob. But they were not the same sort of unruly group as those that sprang up in Europe and in Great Britain, those masses of the unemployed and the destitute who regularly rioted to obtain food. The American port protests of the 1760s, as documented in letters, diaries, and newspaper reports, reveal the participants as overwhelmingly from the working classes. The protesters did include black slaves and white indentured servants, but many more of them had some money or property. In terms of income the lowest members were the occasionally employed—the sailors, dockworkers, and manual laborers. Above them in income were the regularly employed craftsmen such as shoemakers, tailors, coopers, and weavers. The protests also usually included some who were even higher in income—what passed then for the middle class—artisan makers of cabinets, instruments, silverwork, and houses, and small entrepreneurs such as bakers, distillers, and chandlers.

Also of note is that these pavestone throwers were not knee-jerk antitaxers whose anger might purposefully be misdirected by a politician. They had long since acknowledged the need for taxes to fund such activities as keeping Native Americans at bay and constructing better roads. Their beef was with Great Britain for its attempt to once again levy taxes on Americans without American consent and despite American objections, for they believed that they had settled this matter by their 1765 protests against the Stamp Act, which had resulted in its rescinding.

Back in 1765 the Boston-based protesters of the Stamp Act could have more accurately been called a mob, as they burned a few mansions of the wealthy and threatened to torch fifteen more. Even then, however, their rage had not been inchoate but based on their realization that the purpose of the Stamp Act was not the regulation of commerce, the ostensible aim of all previous Navigation Acts. They saw the Stamp Act as an attempt to force the colonies to pay retroactively for the British having provided military protection during the French and Indian War.

It is a characteristic of the arrogant—and in that era the British were routinely in-your-face arrogant—to believe that anyone opposing them is dumb, incompetent, or has a short memory. The American colonists who actively opposed the Stamp Act and the Townshend Acts, named for Charles Townshend, the chancellor of the exchequer, who fashioned them for Parliament, were neither dumb nor ignorant, and they did not need very long memories to recognize that their difficulties had begun with the accession to the throne of George III in 1760. The end of the French and Indian War in 1763 had exacerbated those problems, as had the British government's realization that it had expended a great deal of money on that war and needed to recoup £2.5 million. Americans had already laid out plenty in property and poll taxes to fund American militias' operations, taxes that had been kept in force after the war to defray their allotted share of Great Britain's prior military expenses. By 1765, Americans had paid in so routinely and in so stalwart a manner that they had already retired £1,765,000 and were on schedule to retire the remainder of the £2.5 million. A British MP had even cited their terrific repayment record to justify enacting the Stamp Act, arguing that the payment record was evidence of Americans being prosperous enough to bear additional taxes.

Prosperous enough? Today we do not generally think of our colonial forebears as having been prosperous, certainly not when their lives are juxtaposed to our own luxury-filled lives, but in the 1760s, and in comparison with most of Europe, they were. Nor do we think of them as willing to be taxed—but the slogan "No taxation without representation" did not mean that the protesters were antitax; rather, it meant that they wanted a say in what taxes were levied. Massachusetts' colonists, for instance, paid property taxes that were several multiples more than comparable ones in Great Britain, which were themselves higher than all others in Europe.

It is when the arrogant think they are being the shrewdest that they are the most oblivious to reality. The British MPs believed they had been very canny in structuring the Stamp Act so as to avoid an

American backlash against their port officials, the usual collectors of taxes: The Stamp Act would be administered by the colonists themselves—they would need to buy stamps to make legal all their commercial documents, including newspapers. The MPs omitted from their calculations that the need for colonial cooperation in administering the Stamp Act gave the colonists leverage to resist it.

John Hancock's understanding of that vulnerability changed his life, commencing his transformation from an ordinary, if quite wealthy, colonial merchant into a leader of the resistance. News of the act's impending imposition came to him while he was still in mourning for his uncle and mentor, who had died just a year earlier. His response was immediate, and it went against his economic interests: "I have come to a Serious Resolution not to send one Ship more to Sea, nor to have any kind of Connection to Business under a Stamp," he wrote to his firm's London supplier. "I am Determin'd . . . to Sell my Stock in Trade & Shut up my Warehous Doors & never Import another Shilling from Great Britain. . . . I am free & Determined to be so & will not willingly & quietly Subject myself to Slavery." He appended a note to a copy: "This Letter I propose to remain in my Letter Book as a Standing monument to posterity & my children in particular"—just then, he had no children—"that I by no means Consented to a Submission to this Cruel Act, & that my best Representations were not wanting in the matter." His ensuing actions spoke as forcefully: He made common cause with the leaders of the resistance—lawyer James Otis, brewer and former tax collector Samuel Adams, and physician Joseph Warren, men whom most Boston merchants considered below them socially.

But then, those other wealthy merchants were almost all Tories, as were most of the wealthy throughout the colonies in 1765. In every age the wealthy tend to be fundamentally conservative, in the sense of opposing any alteration of the pattern that has made and is sustaining their fortunes. In Boston this fundamental truth became apparent as some of the merchants warned the would-be resisters against making the sort of over-the-top protests of the Stamp Act that London might deem too rebellious.

Hancock was then just as loyal a British subject as his more Tory-minded commercial colleagues, and as well aware as they of having benefited from the status quo. But along with a few other fairly wealthy merchants in port cities up and down the American Atlantic coast, he did become involved in active resistance to the Stamp Act, uniting with considerably poorer neighbors against the status quo to a degree that only a few years earlier even the most fervent of rabble-rousers had not imagined would be possible.

Underlying the status quo in the 1760s in America was the hundred-plus-year-old system of commerce created by and still regulated by the British Navigation Acts. The original 1651 act had been fashioned to prevent France, Spain, and the Netherlands from poaching on Great Britain's colonial markets and from destroying the fledgling colonial economies. Judging that initial intent admirable, the colonists did not protest when additional acts were promulgated. These included a decree that goods entering or exiting a British colony could only be carried in British or British colonial ships, and others that specified which goods the colonists could and could not export, what they could and could not manufacture, and that they must pay for British imports only in specie or in bills of exchange.

What props you up is often what holds you down. The Navigation Act regulations did foster the growth of America's economy, but only in narrow configurations. American trees suitable for ship masts, potentially worth a great deal to a Europe almost denuded of such trees, could be sold only for British use and at a low price; American indigo, rice, and livestock could not be sent to Great Britain, which had plenty from its own farms, but could profitably be sent to British Caribbean colonies, which because of the same regulations were not producing enough food of their own; and American wheat and tobacco, although craved by Europe, had to first be taken to Great Britain for reexport. (A later tweak to this law allowed direct shipping of such crops from America to Europe if carried in a British vessel.)

Among the Navigation Acts system's most detrimental effects was embedding slavery into the American economy. In the 1760s two-thirds of American exports consisted of tobacco, rice, and indigo—crops that were profitable only with slave labor. One of every six Americans was a slave. Virginia's ratio of slaves to free people was 1 to 1, and South Carolina's was 2 to 1. Beyond slavery's exploitation and degradation, it exacted less obvious costs. As Virginia planter and slave owner George Mason was contending, just then, America's over-dependence on slave labor was diminishing the number of skilled whites coming to America, resulting in lands west of the Alleghenies remaining unproductive.

Peyton Randolph was the king's attorney general for Virginia, and led the Virginia House of Burgesses when its speaker was absent. He was the scion of a family that had been at the forefront of Virginia affairs for generations, and that included Thomas Jefferson, a recent graduate of William & Mary, and the equally young John Marshall, another lawyer. Randolph had been in the House of Burgesses since 1748, and in 1765, while he did not like the Stamp Act, he was not inclined to take too radical a stance against it. At the request of like-minded colleagues he introduced a rather mild set of objections to it for the burgesses to send to London. But to Randolph's surprise and dismay, the young lawyer Patrick Henry outmaneuvered him. Henry introduced a far more fiery set of resolutions and, taking advantage of a mostly empty chamber, managed to get them passed. Randolph, temporarily in the chair, fumed, but then began to see the necessity of a more potent protest against British overreaching. Shortly Randolph resigned as the king's attorney, was elected speaker of the House of Burgesses, and became increasingly radicalized.

Farther south, in Charleston, South Carolina, another longtime loyal British subject and beneficiary of the Navigation Acts system, merchant and plantation owner Henry Laurens, mused on his situation: "I go to church and come home again, to the House of Assembly and return to my habitation, avoiding disputes about tenets, refined politics, and party. At home I am always cheerful and never sad."

Although he shared with Hancock, Washington, and Randolph a love of luxury, wine, and the esteem of fellow citizens rich and poor, he saw no need to seek political power or be more involved in governance than was needed to maintain his social station. Charleston's aggregate wealth was then greater than that of any other American city. "In grandeur, splendor of buildings, decorations, equipages, numbers, shippings, and indeed in almost everything, [Charleston] far surpasses all I ever saw or expected to see," Bostonian Josiah Quincy, Jr., John Adams's law partner, would shortly write home.

Laurens was the son of a saddle maker and tack seller who had died in 1747. Expanding a modest inheritance into a substantial fortune—four plantations, merchant enterprises, and the like—he became quite a character; even an admiring biographer admits that Laurens was too "cocksure about the rightness of his contentions, and his egoism was something a little too much in evidence." After amassing considerable wealth from selling slaves, he stopped slaving in the mid-1760s and concentrated on his plantations, which were doing well enough to enable him to send his sons to be educated in London and to make plans to follow them there. His detractors included Christopher Gadsden, a middling-successful merchant who was among the most radical men in South Carolina. But while Samuel Adams and Hancock had become allies, and Randolph and Patrick Henry were beginning to see more eye to eye, Gadsden and Laurens were not yet on the same side. Their differences came to the fore as they awaited the arrival of the stamps: While Gadsden exhorted the mechanics and dockworkers to resist unloading these when they arrived, Laurens expressed dismay at Stamp Act riots in Boston and New York and touted the stamps' imminent arrival in Charleston as "a glorious opportunity of standing distinguished for our loyalty" while awaiting the act's inevitable rescinding. The stamps reached the city, and the governor sequestered them. A Gadsden-inspired crowd thought Laurens had the stamps and came angrily to his door. Laurens said he did not have them and would not sign an oath that he did not know who did. "I am in your power," he advised the visitors. "You are very strong and may if you please barbicu me—I can but die." After the visitors found no stamps, they left, giving him three cheers. Nine days of rioting followed, and the stamps were returned to London. Gadsden then led the call to convene the Stamp Act Congress, the first attempt to coordinate colonial action. Laurens did not attend.

In the wake of the repeal of the Stamp Act in early 1766, Baron Johann de Kalb was sent by France to America to reconnoiter the British colonies' readiness to revolt; he reported an uprising as unlikely since the repeal had taught the Americans that "their value to the mother country is their best safeguard against any violation of their real or imagined privileges."

That fall thirty London merchants signed an open letter to Hancock and Boston's merchants, warning them not to further bite the hand that fed them, since the Navigation Acts system, "framed on liberal principles," was still working to "reciprocal advantage." On that point the addressees might have agreed. But then the writers contended that the system was "relieving the colonies from injudicious restrictions and severe duties," so Americans should "prevent, by every possible means, foreign states from sharing in the advantage of your commerce and thereby depriving Great Britain of the means to afford you instances of her paternal protection." Americans should also not interfere "with the manufactures of the mother country, either by furnishing her rivals with raw materials, or by the encouraging of similar manufacturing among yourselves."

Just then, sales in America of British-manufactured clothing, furnishings, ceramics, woolens, hats, and complex iron tools were so lucrative, and American addiction to these products was so strong, that Parliament viewed the connection as infinitely exploitable. But its limits were rapidly being approached. Jefferson would shortly write that an American was "forbidden to make a hat for himself of the fur which he has taken perhaps on his own soil [which constituted] an instance of despotism to which no parallel can be produced in the most arbitrary ages of British history." And William Pitt the

Elder warned the Commons: "The kingdom . . . has always bound the colonies by her regulations and restrictions in trade, in navigation, in manufactures—in every thing except that of taking their money out of their pockets, without their consent." With the Stamp Act, it was doing that, too.

The Scottish economist Adam Smith realized that such rapacity would lead to an American revolt and eventually to independence. As he was writing in *An Inquiry into the Nature and Causes of the Wealth of Nations*, which would not be published until 1776, he labeled the system produced by the Navigation Acts mercantilism, and asserted that the American part of it had brought Britain's trade to a "splendour and glory which it could never otherwise have obtained." American colonial trade produced five million pounds a year, one-third of Great Britain's total foreign trade, and its cargo-carrying businesses employed forty thousand British seamen in two thousand ships.

Smith's confidence that America would become independent was based on American colonists' having already surpassed Britons in per capita income—seventy-eight pounds per year compared with the British fifty per year—and on their being more regularly employed and their earnings able to purchase more of the necessities of life. The labor market was one key to this prosperity, Smith asserted, as the paucity of skilled labor in America forced up wages, and the other key was the remarkable fecundity of Americans' farms and fisheries. As a result there were proportionately fewer poor people in America. In Boston 7 percent of the populace was deemed poor, while 29 percent owned no taxable property, but in London and in Paris the figures were twice that, a third of these cities' populations being deemed poor and an additional third hovering on the edge of poverty.

Still, America had plenty of poor people. The truly impoverished included the half million black slaves and a quarter of all whites, those who possessed little or no property and had only enough food to prevent starvation. Then there were the working poor, such as sailors and fishermen who were seldom on land, dockworkers who lived in rented barracks, and itinerant laborers who had no income when the weather shut down their work. Yet the lives of America's poor were closer in character to the lives of their richer neighbors than were those of the European poor to the château dwellers along the Loire and the Rhine. In New Jersey the wealthiest 10 percent of the populace held six times the amount of property as the lowest 10 percent, but in Europe that ratio was forty times as much. Significant wealth in America was in the hands of about fifteen thousand out of three million people—that is, given an average family size of five, in the hands of three thousand wealthy men—the 1 percent of that era.

The biggest gulf in wealth in America was between the coastal cities, which contained nearly all the wealthy colonists, and the vast interior sections, where 90 percent of the populace lived and were poorer—although they were not as poor as American mythmaking has characterized them. The majority of American rural residents engaged in subsistence-plus farming, a term that does not mean existing on the edge of poverty but rather farming that produces enough for the resident family plus a bit more that can be sold or bartered. In northern areas, the surplus was 16 percent more than subsistence, and in southern ones, 30 percent more because slaves did the labor. And as a scholar of the period writes, except in the South the surplus "was based to a great extent on the ability of women in the household" to produce it. In the Northeast that meant dairy production, and in the Mid-Atlantic, spinning and weaving. Since rural communities lacked currency with which to make transactions, surplus could not be turned into cash; instead it was manufactured into goods for barter. That system was so advanced that in a western Massachusetts hamlet on the eve of the Revolution, regularly bartered products included rye, corn, flaxseed, lambskins, firewood, shoe-leather, butter, straw hats, shingles, hemlock boards, soap, cider, vinegar, cheese, oats, mutton, beans, tallow, lard, veal, flour, and honey.

None of these lightly manufactured products could be exported because the Navigation Acts prohibited exporting any processed farm product. Through the decades this prohibition had forced farmers in Virginia and Maryland to be overreliant on planting tobacco, to the point that by the 1760s its quality had deteriorated, causing a fall in prices for the crop and consequent financial instability for the planters. In 1766 George

Washington, George Mason's tobacco-planting neighbor, after years of receiving alarmingly low prices, stopped raising tobacco at Mount Vernon. He was good at farming—a British agrarian expert would later call him the most scientific farmer in America. He had inherited wealth and had become much richer by marrying one of the wealthiest widows in Virginia, twenty-seven-year-old Martha Custis, and adding her 17,500 acres on five farms to his. Washington then had enough income to forgo the British tobacco subsidy. He essentially agreed with the American pamphleteers who were just then writing that the subsidies on tobacco granted by the British were more than offset by the prohibition on selling tobacco to anyone other than a London factor, who would then resell it in France for three times the price paid to the grower. Daniel Dulany, the mayor of Annapolis, a British-trained lawyer and a scion of one of the families that had controlled Maryland's commerce for generations, contended that the combination of having to sell tobacco only to Great Britain and of having to buy all manufactured goods from Great Britain was "effectually a tax" of 65 percent on American crops. James Otis echoed this, charging that as a result of the lopsided exchange, "many of the little villages and obscure Boroughs in Great Britain have put on a new face, and suddenly started up and become fair markets and manufacturing towns and opulent cities." As Adam Smith would assert, the more products manufactured, the more liquid capital was produced.

Liquid capital! Great Britain's wealthy had it and America's wealthy did not, and that was why American wealth had not soared as British wealth was doing. Liquid capital was what allowed Britons to commission the new factories and advanced machinery that would shortly push Great Britain to the forefront of the Industrial Revolution and lead to the immense profits accruing from it. American colonists lacked not only the liquid capital but the scalable enterprises in which to invest—there were hardly any manufacturers, wholesalers, international traders, or insurers, and there were no banks.

Today banks are so integral to our society that it is hard to imagine life without them, let alone a financial system. Banks are a way of aggregating a community's wealth and using it as collateral to lend larger amounts to individuals and companies to underwrite the growth of their operations and holdings. No wonder then, that to limit the expansion of colonial enterprises, the British had expressly prohibited banks in America as well as manufacturing entities. Great Britain did not even permit more than six Americans to invest together in any entity without written permission from Parliament, which was seldom granted.

The absence of banks, writes the financial historian Edwin J. Perkins, forced colonists to hold their wealth in "land, livestock, inventories, slaves, personal items, [and to send] coinage overseas to buy goods they could have gone without if building up the stock of money had been a high priority." In earlier colonial days small American "land banks" had made short-term loans of up to one hundred pounds apiece to farmers and artisans. Land banks were so successful in Pennsylvania that for years the interest they paid to the provincial government allowed the colony to avoid imposing additional property taxes. Yet in Massachusetts, when a land bank was set up to tide farmers over from one harvest to the next and enable small retailers to expand, it was opposed by "principal Merchants, Factors, & rich Usurors," according to a pamphleteer, and soon Great Britain outlawed land banks too: "You have given the inhabitants [American colonists] only a limited and circumscribed form of acquiring wealth," said a leader of the Opposition Party in Parliament. He was echoing the argument in Sir James Steuart's influential 1767 book, *An Inquiry into the Principles of Political Oeconomy*. Steuart's research showed that in countries where trade was in its infancy and credit scarce, the rich had "the greatest difficulty in turning [their property] into money, without which industry cannot be carried on . . . and consequently the whole plan of improvement is disappointed."

But Great Britain did not want America to improve, it wanted the colonies to remain fragmented and near-primitive, able only to raise crops and send them, unprocessed, to the mother country and its Caribbean isles, and with the proceeds from those sales to buy ever-larger quantities of British-manufactured goods. Through the 1760s this system continued to work, and the American colonies continued to be economically infantilized, with very little liquid capital yet with resources enough to sustain a population that was doubling every twenty years due to high birth, fecundity, and longevity rates.

The splendid manors of Boston, Newport, New York, Philadelphia, Baltimore, Williamsburg, Charleston, and Savannah showcased American fortunes and their owners' slavish copying of the London originals, including the ways in which Britons vied with one another in conspicuous consumption. Both British and American merchant traders believed themselves to be a breed apart from their poorer neighbors, but in America such snobbism entailed deliberately ignoring that the system enriching them was simultaneously impoverishing their neighbors born to small-acreage farmers, artisans, tradesmen, enslaved blacks, or Native Americans.

The few American thinkers who regretted that inequality and sought to elevate the bottom tier had no other solution in the 1760s than to plead for the elimination of British restrictions on trade, so that a rising economic tide would float all boats. Thus Otis defended high levels of imported goods as a stimulus for the American wealthy to commission products from local craftsmen: "I should be glad to see here as in England, tradesmen and yeomen worth their tens and their hundreds of thousands of pounds." So he, along with Stephen Hopkins, George Mason, and most other critics of Parliament, rejoiced when that body repealed the Stamp Act.

Boston's merchants eagerly resumed their regulated transatlantic trade. Hancock certainly did, but he also took the opportunity to distance himself further from his fellow merchants by using his wealth to achieve greater political power. For generations in America, service in town- and colony-wide councils had been viewed by the wealthy mainly as an obligation. Hancock saw it as a route to fulfillment, and cultivated the taxpayers who would assure him of power in those councils. By inventing jobs to construct ships he did not need, homes he did not plan to live in, and retail shops that did not do enough business to justify their staffing, he made certain that in subsequent public elections for various posts he always received the most votes. John Adams estimated that a thousand families depended on Hancock for their livelihood and voted for him regularly.

Hancock cultivated those votes without pandering to the voters' worst instincts and without toning down his inventive flaunting of wealth. He was a peacock, his wardrobe the equal of a London gentleman's—dozens of red, blue, and lavender coats trimmed with gold lace, velvet breeches in matching or contrasting colors, and shoes with silver or gold buckles—and he rode about in a gilded carriage. But he was keenly aware, from previous sojourns in London, that he might never be as wealthy as his London factors because his capital was mostly tied up in his ships, wharf, warehouses, and inventory. So was the capital of the wealthiest man in the American colonies, the Charleston merchant, plantation owner, lawyer, and sometime partner of Henry Laurens, Peter Manigault, whose estate at the time of his death would be £33,000, equivalent to $5,000,000 today, a minor fortune in our age of billionaires.

The belief that things had returned to normal after the rescinding of the Stamp Act was shattered by the 1768 Townshend Acts. Conceived as a way to avoid colonial objections to imposts but still generate money, the Townshend duties were touted as indirect—a distinction rejected by the pavestone throwers defending Hancock's *Liberty*. When British marines moved the *Liberty* out of range, the crowd turned on the customs officials, badly beating one and chasing another to his home and smashing its windows. Hancock, Adams, and Warren appealed to the crowd to stop. It did, demonstrating that appeals to reason could sway crowd members. Yet the Massachusetts governor beseeched Gen. Thomas Gage in New York to send troops to protect Boston from anarchy.

Anarchy was not threatening the colonies: subjugation was. The shift toward extracting tax moneys from Americans had begun with the 1760 ascension to the throne of George III. To date the colonists had avoided blaming him; they attributed the Stamp Act and the

Townshend Acts to his malevolent counselors. Benjamin Franklin, in London, traced them to the "extream Corruption prevalent among all Orders of Men in this old rotten State [and the] Numberless and needless Places, enormous Salaries, Pensions, Perquisites, Bribes, groundless Quarrels, foolish Expeditions, false Accompts or no Accompts, Contracts and Jobbs [that] devour all Revenue and produce continual Necessity in the Midst of natural Plenty." He and the British Whigs—members of the Parliamentary Opposition—blamed the corruption on the nouveau riche who used their wealth to influence legislation. That, to Franklin and friends, signified a government drained of all civic and personal virtue, a potent reminder of what had caused the declines of ancient Greece and Rome.

The *Liberty* was seized on a Friday. Over the weekend Otis and Adams pressured Hancock to use the incident to reinflame the populace; but he was also importuned by fellow merchants to simply pay the arrears so that he, and they, could resume profitable trade. The British port commissioners agreed that Hancock could post a bond, retrieve the *Liberty*, and sail it until a court resolved the issue. On Saturday, Hancock said he would go along with the merchants, but on Sunday, Otis and Adams persuaded him to leave the *Liberty* in British hands as a symbol for resistance. He would lose a substantial sum, in addition to the nine-thousand-pound fine, but he had five other ships for trade.

In this period, Hancock, as well as the Manigaults and Laurens and many other wealthy American merchants, reluctantly reached the conclusion that the mercantile system was slowly digging them deeper and deeper into debt. To obtain British goods to sell in America, these merchants had to borrow from their British suppliers, at 2.5 percent for a year; and then had to extend their own credit to retailers and artisans. American export-crop farmers had become similarly overdependent on British credit. Washington had sizable debts to the London factor who handled his tobacco, most of the debt attributable to bad trade balances but some of it stemming from his luxurious tastes. Even before marrying Mrs. Custis, Washington had purchased through his factor a fancy coach emblazoned with his coat of arms, a sword, ceiling ornaments, brass fittings, bed linens and matching wallpaper, tailored suits, and statuary for Mount Vernon's entrance hall. But three years later Washington had to beg an American court to extend a ninety-pound debt he owed a fellow Virginian because he did not have the cash to pay the man. The historian T. H. Breen argues that Virginia's tobacco planters were troubled by their debt, not because they were afraid of insolvency but because it "threatened to undermine the Virginians' personal autonomy. [And so] to achieve personal independence—indeed, to restore personal honor and virtue—they had to break with the economic and political system that threatened to enslave them."

The British repurposed Hancock's *Liberty* as a government revenue cutter and sent it to patrol Long Island Sound. Hancock sued for compensation in a vice-admiralty court, and hired as his attorney Samuel Adams's cousin John, whom he had known since childhood. In researching, John Adams came across a precedent of ships arbitrarily seized, and a useful polemic written about the cases by the ships' owner, Charleston merchant Henry Laurens.

After the repeal of the Stamp Act, Laurens had remained willing to obey British law. In this he mirrored his city's commerce, for while Boston's depended on smuggling, Charleston's did not. Thus it was doubly galling to Charlestonians when a new port collector seized Laurens's intercoastal schooner the *Wambaw* after it arrived from his Georgia plantation with tools, provisions, and "unenumerated goods"—those not on a proscribed list—but without the right travel papers. A deputy collector confided that "the charity of the vessel" might be preserved if it would "slip away in the Dark," but Laurens refused. Shortly word came that the applied-for papers had arrived. "No fraud had been committed" ruled a vice-admiralty court judge married to Laurens's niece, but Laurens still had to repurchase his ship. Then a second Laurens ship was seized on a spurious charge; this time the same judge awarded Laurens fourteen hundred pounds. The port collector was recalled to London. In June 1768 the deputy, promoted to collector, seized a third Laurens intercoastal. The same judge rejected that claim and gave Laurens permission to write a pamphlet about the cases. It took everyone to task, including the judge. When the judge penned his own pamphlet lambasting Laurens, the merchant responded with a second, chastising "those who call truth 'Virulence,' and whose mistaken policy and unbounded ambition lead them to act as if they thought the interest of Great Britain would be most effectually promoted by the distress of her colonies."

Laurens's pamphlets were just what Adams needed to buttress his court arguments on Hancock's behalf. By then the government cutter that had been the *Liberty* had been destroyed in Newport's harbor by men incensed because its captain "behaved more like a pirate, than like one appointed or commissioned to protect our trade." By then too, Gage's troops were making their presence felt in Boston. Adams later recalled the trial period as one of "painfull Drudgery," purposefully dragged out by the prosecution. He did a good job in court while outside the matter was kept in the public eye through newspaper articles, likely written by cousin Samuel, exposing the venality of the customs men and the arbitrary injustice of the court. The articles also made Hancock a national figure as a patriot and patrician injured by unjust proceedings.

In March 1769 the charges against Hancock and his codefendants were mooted.

The underlying acts that had prompted those charges were not repealed, however, and to exert economic pressure on Great Britain to withdraw the Townshend Acts, Americans had to find a new tactic. Massachusetts and other colonies decided on a radical one, "nonimportation," a consumer boycott of all imported British goods.

2

Resistance Becomes Rebellion

Attempts to understand the past cannot escape the influ-ence of the present in which they are composed. This chronicle of the founding fortunes is written during the presidency of Donald J. Trump, by some measures the wealthiest man ever to hold that office, and whose cabinet consists of other extremely wealthy people. His and their governmental decisions have been criticized for favoring themselves and those on their elevated income level. By contrast, one obvious characteristic of that handful of the colonial wealthy who took leading roles in the growing resistance to British rule in America was that they made decisions that went flagrantly against their immediate financial interest, and which they knew would disrupt the system that had enriched them.

That was certainly the case with another important wealthy pamphleteer, John Dickinson of Delaware and Pennsylvania, who in 1768 considered himself to be a good British citizen when he lit up the resistance with his pen. The scion of a family owning several thousand acres in the area, he had followed a then-usual route to comfort and productivity, studying law in London, then returning home to practice it, expand his father's holdings, and marry a wealthy woman. Dickinson's wife, Polly Norris, had been managing her late father's estates for five years, and owned a home containing Philadel-phia's largest private library. He expressed his distaste for the Town-shend Acts in ways that appealed to people well beyond his social circle—a series of articles, initially printed in a Philadelphia paper, that achieved enough popularity to warrant reprinting as *Letters from a Farmer in Pennsylvania, to the Inhabitants of the British Colonies.* Dickinson was particularly effective in identifying British attempts at hoodwinking. Of a clause that obligated New York to provision that city's British garrison, he asked: "What is this but *taxing* us at a *certain sum* and leaving us only the manner of *raising* it?" He contended that the colonists had consented to earlier Navigation Acts because they fostered trade and were revenue-neutral, but could not consent to the new ones because, as the Stamp Act had, they sought only to extract money from the colonies. He encapsulated his ideas in a song that boosted their popularity:

> *In Freedom we're born, and in FREEDOM we'll live.*
> *Our Purses are ready;*
> *Steady, Friends, Steady,*
> *Not as SLAVES, but as FREEMEN, our money we'll give.*

As the lyric implies, Dickinson believed that the quarrel between America and Great Britain could be resolved by a reconfigured relationship in which Americans' autonomy would be acknowledged in exchange for Americans voluntarily paying a fair share of Britain's tax burden.

Dickinson embraced nonimportation as a nonviolent strategy aimed at hastening that realignment. His *Letters* were influential during the debate in Massachusetts over a Sam Adams–proposed nonimportation pact. Hancock and most Boston merchants signed on to it, some because they agreed with the idea, but the bulk of them because they knew that not signing would risk condemnation from their neighbors. Other colonies drew up similar measures. In Virginia those two moderate-minded plantation-owners, Mason and Washington, discussed the issue for months before Washington introduced Mason's nonimportation bill in the Virginia House of Burgesses. It echoed Pennsylvania's and contained apocalyptic language similar to Hancock's, such as, "dreading the evils which threaten the Ruin of themselves and their posterity, by reducing them from a free and happy people to a Wretched & miserable State of slavery." When the burgesses adopted the measure, along with another that asserted their right to levy taxes on Virginians without obtaining the royal governor's consent, the governor disbanded them.

How do the rich sell a self-sacrifice idea to the poor? By emphasizing that they too will be subject to it. The writers of nonimportation's to-be-forbidden lists included on it silk garments, jewelry, clocks, chaises, and carriages—only eighty-five families in Philadelphia had carriages—to balance the larger number of imported items that were routinely bought by almost all colonial homes, from loaf sugar, mustard, and linseed oil to gloves, shoes, starch, stays, and pins and needles. The Puritans had once decried these as luxuries. The definition of luxury shifts with time, place, and context, often transforming what was once opulence into necessity. So an attack on "extravagance" in a Boston newspaper had to concede "*a certain Degree* to which *Luxury* may be tolerated [as] it contributes its Part toward Happiness and Support of the State, especially a trading one; and it may perhaps be difficult to . . . determine exactly . . . where it becomes exorbitant and dangerous."

American public acceptance of nonimportation was deepened by coupling nonimportation with voluntary restraints on consumption and with increased support of local manufacture. Heretofore home-spun clothing had been shunned by the wealthy as an indicator of poverty. Suddenly they became fashionable. Most homes already had spinning wheels, and more now acquired looms to weave cloth. Home weavers were celebrated as Daughters of Liberty. The social historian Barbara Clark Smith writes that in Connecticut's program of boosting local manufacture:

Cabinetmakers, spinners, weavers, hatters, tailors, dressmakers, shoemakers, tatters, goldsmiths, brewers of cider, and growers of apple trees all had a stake. . . . Now their purchasing neighbors would patronize their shops, keep them and their journeymen employed, and help members of the trade cancel debts of their own. . . . The effect was also a modest redistribution of wealth.

Added income was sorely needed by those on the lower rungs, since, as a New York newspaper put it, most of the American colonists "facing ruin [were] the poor industrious tradesman, the needy mechanic, and all men of narrow circumstance."

The change to manufacturing of goods in America rather than importing them began an emancipation of the American working classes. Previously most of them had earned their livings by servicing the needs of the wealthy, but that tether was loosened by nonimportation and homeland manufacturing, which created new paths to earning a living. In turn, the ability of urban artisans and mechanics to work independently of the patronage system strengthened their willingness and their ability to resist British colonialism.

For families nonimportation became a test of fealty: Are you with your neighbors in the agreed-upon task of refusing to buy British manufactured goods? Or are you defying the majority's desires by continuing to buy imports? Women made most of these familial decisions because they were in charge of household-staple purchases. Nonimportation became a litmus test: Families that readily adopted the strictures became more rapidly and more thoroughly convinced of the need for a revolution, while those who balked at nonimportation or devised ways to evade the strictures became more confirmed in their Loyalist ways. James Bowdoin, a third-generation merchant in Boston who was wealthy enough to use his fortune and leisure to undertake scientific projects, became integral to the Massachusetts nonimportation effort. But once the pamphleteer Dulany had declared he would have nothing to do with Maryland's nonimportation council, he lost public influence. Samuel Chase, a firebrand Maryland lawyer, came to the fore. Laurens, who had been as loyal a subject of the Crown as Dulany, decided that nonimportation was less a disobedience to British law than a flexing of American muscle, and chaired the proceedings of the South Carolina Association, held under Charleston's Liberty Tree, a council that became the most effective of all those throughout the colonies.

In chairing that council—a task he could have avoided—Laurens was acknowledging an unwritten rule for the wealthy, one that continues to resonate today: that in a society aspiring to republicanism and in which the opinion of the multitude bears considerable weight, the wealthy must not use their riches to evade restrictions placed by common consent on everyone in the community. Hancock and Jefferson came perilously close to breaching that unwritten rule. When a newspaper claimed that Hancock had imported a carriage, he could legitimately protest that it was within the nonimportation regulations since it was for personal use and not for resale—but to salvage his integrity he had to urge the rewriting of the regulations so that even such importations were illegal. He did not, however, resist the urge to strike back at the newspaper; when it continued to assail him he had its editor chased out of the country and an editorial assistant tarred and feathered. Soon Jefferson, after a similar error in luxury importing—fourteen pairs of sash windows—apologized to Virginia's nonimportation association, surrendered the windows upon arrival, and was forgiven. These were crucial moments: Had Laurens, Hancock, and Jefferson not recognized that they must subsume personal interest to the general good, their public careers would have been fatally tarnished.

In December 1769 a Philadelphia merchant prophesied the impending death of nonimportation, because "Romans we are not, as they were . . . when they despised Riches and Grandeur, abode in extreme poverty and sacrificed every pleasant enjoyment for the love and service of their Country." Mason and Washington also predicted nonimportation's demise, but from a more sensitive reading of human nature: They understood that while they and other wealthy colonists were able to live well enough under the restrictions, the vast majority of the populace could not, being more directly dependent on imported basics such as tea, salt, sugar, rum, woolens, and pins and needles. The differential between the wealthy and the nonwealthy on nonimportation became evident in 1770 in Boston, when men from Glasgow arrived to commission four ships and asked for an exception to nonimportation to import materials for the task. Seventy artisans, then out of work, were ready to agree to the exception. They were dissuaded only by the Boston merchants' committee's promise to replace the lost business by commissioning three new ships.

Nonimportation did wind down, but while in force it produced important side effects. Town meetings held to implement it drew the populace closer, and the need for those meetings spurred the resurgence of the Sons of Liberty and a broadening of its leadership to include moderates such as John Adams and his law partner. Nonimportation also energized previously complacent merchants to become politically active, such as Benedict Arnold of New Haven, a pharmacist, bookseller, and international shipper, and John Brown of Providence. As important, nonimportation forced Americans to become acutely aware that the British Navigation Acts were violating their rights as British citizens, and to edge toward cherishing one particular right, not in the British canon, that was of increasing importance to Americans—equality of opportunity, the right of an individual, regardless of the accident of birth, to have as much of a chance as any other to climb the ladder of success.

"There are not five Men of Sense in America who wou'd accept of Independence if it was offered," Mason wrote to a friend in early 1770. The reason was that he, as well as many other Americans engaged in overseas commerce, could not then imagine an American economy existing without a continuing, visceral tie to Great Britain's. Colonial objectors to the Navigation Acts sought only a loosening of restraints on trade, to enable American ships and cargoes to be sent to all parts of Europe, free of limitations. And so in April 1770, when Parliament repealed the Townshend Acts, most Americans were happy, believing it meant a return to economic normal. They did not mind that Parliament left in place the duty on tea, as it would be easy to avoid because smuggled-in Dutch tea was readily available.

News of a potential repeal of the Townshend Acts did not reach Boston by February 22, when a crowd trying to enforce nonimportation put a nasty sign on the shop of a man suspected of violating it. A local busybody tried to use his cart to knock over the sign. A melee ensued; in it, an eleven-year-old boy was killed. His funeral, choreographed by Sam Adams and attended by thousands, spurred minor clashes with the British regulars. These matters were still simmering on the evening of March 5, when a British soldier had a very public disagreement with a colonial wigmaker—the soldier bashed the wigmaker for contending that he had not paid his bill. This escalated into a confrontation between locals and the resident British garrison, whose Redcoats, in response to being attacked with sticks, stones, and snowballs, fired into the crowd, killing five people. John Adams, who would successfully defend the soldiers indicted for the Boston Massacre, would later assert that the "foundation of American independence was laid on March 5, 1770." The official report on the massacre, written by Bowdoin, emphasized British bad actions and was a major piece of propaganda, useful in fomenting further rebellion.

Prosperity in the American colonies returned after the repeal of the Townshend Acts. One effect was to muddy the radicals' issues and sow dissension in their ranks, notably bringing about a split between Hancock and Sam Adams. But British arrogance seemed incapable of permanent restraint. It undercut the repeal by egregiously traducing American rights: Army units in New York and Boston, and naval personnel in Providence and Baltimore bashed, robbed, and clapped into irons various colonists. Reported in the newspapers, these incidents spurred colonists to defend their neighbors' actions and to rekindle their animosity toward the British. Eighteen months of prosperity ended abruptly once British merchants, caught in a credit crunch, demanded immediate reimbursement from American consignees for goods that had been advanced, rather than waiting for payment until the goods had been sold. Credit crunches had happened before and Americans had grudgingly paid up. Not this time. Now they bristled at having to make forced sales and take losses just to rescue British factors. Hancock was joined in his refusal to comply with the factors' demand by dozens of his fellow Boston merchants and by their counterparts up and down the Atlantic coast.

For years these merchants had been resistant to what Adams, Gadsden, Patrick Henry, and other radical leaders had been shouting: that the British were abrogating Americans' rights. Now the merchants' London factors' overreaction to the credit crunch forced the traders to realize the truth of the radicals' charge. Action followed. In June 1772 John Brown led a group from Providence and Newport to attack and burn the British *Gaspee*, which had been raiding American shipping on the pretext of enforcing the supposedly relaxed Navigation Acts. By November 1772 British arrogance and abridgement of rights had convinced enough of Boston's merchants to agree to Sam Adams's request for the city's Committee of Correspondence to "state the rights of the colonists and of this Province in particular, as men and Christians, and as subjects; and to communicate and publish the same to the several towns and to the world."

Parliament did worse than dismiss these warning signs of American unrest; in May 1773 it yielded to pressure from the country's largest overseas enterprise, the British East India Tea Company, to make up for its losses elsewhere by soaking Americans. The Tea Act gave the company the sole right to sell tea to Americans. The MPs presumed that Americans would accept this arrangement because henceforth tea was going to be less expensive for Americans than it had been, even with the tax. They ignored that Americans could buy inexpensive, smuggled-in Dutch tea, and might resent a plan that prevented their neighbors from selling tea while being made to pay a tax to drink it.

American reaction to the Tea Act was immediate, near-universal, and in evidence in every port from Boston to Savannah, its intensity varying with the degree of a port's dependence on British trade. The mildest involved the use of peer pressure. In New York, Philadelphia, Wilmington, and Charleston the preponderance of the merchants persuaded their colleagues who were the consignees of the tea not to accept the shipments. In some instances peer pressure escalated into bullying and threats, but not into overt violence. Boston's consignees readily professed to their merchant colleagues and to the Sons of Liberty their willingness to turn around the tea-bearing ships, but

Massachusetts's governor foiled that by forbidding the ships to leave the harbor until all the taxes on the cargoes were paid, an edict he could enforce by cannons controlling the harbor.

The stalemate in Boston continued until December 16, 1773, when a Sam Adams–chaired meeting rejected last-minute proposals by the governor, shipowners, and consignees because none would result in sending the tea back. Then seven thousand mostly young men from the Boston area, including silversmith Paul Revere (a Hancock tenant), gathered at the pier. In groups of fifty, their visages blackened and dressed as Mohawk, they boarded the ships and tossed overboard 342 chests holding 92,600 pounds of tea.

Parliament did not learn of the Boston Tea Party until January 1774. After comparing Boston's violent refusal of the tea with the gentler resistance of New York, Philadelphia, and Charleston, the MPs passed what they called the Coercive Acts and that colonists soon labeled the "Intolerable Acts." The Boston Port Act forbade the entrance or exit of vessels engaged in foreign or domestic trade; as Jefferson would write of it: "A large and populous town, whose trade was their sole subsistence, was deprived of that trade, and involved in utter ruin." Other Coercive Acts enhanced the Massachusetts governor's power to appoint and remove colonial officials, prohibit town meetings, choose juries, and make Bostonians pay to house British troops. As Joseph Warren put it, the Coercive Acts displayed "the power, but not the justice, the vengeance but not the wisdom of Great Britain."

The acts could not have been more perfectly designed to enrage Americans by attacking their basic rights to property, autonomy of governance, and judgment by peers and neighbors. In reaction, in nearly every town in Massachusetts, including those in the remote Berkshires, the populace confronted newly appointed British supervisors and tax collectors and forced them to resign or leave town. Militias closed many courts. Also in reaction, an even larger number of Hancock's fellow Boston merchants now agreed with the radicals' accusations against British bad behavior. The Boston Committee of

Correspondence easily found enough backing to call on all the colonies to completely boycott British goods.

Some colonies agreed to that without ado. Others voted on the matter. After observing the voting in New York City, the well-born law student Gouverneur Morris wrote, "On my right hand were ranged all the people of property, with some few poor dependents," who were against the boycott, "and on the other all the tradesmen," whom he thought of as "reptiles" crawling out from under rocks for their moments in the sun. The tradesmen lost; New York did not back a boycott. But the Philadelphia committee requested that all colonies send representatives to a congress there, to "clearly state what we conceive as our rights and to make claim or petition of them to his Majesty, in firm, but decent and dutiful terms."

On September 5, 1774, fifty delegates from eleven colonies crowded into the long room of Philadelphia's City Tavern to commence a Continental Congress. The attendees were among the wealthiest men in America, and for the most part their wealth had come to them through inheritance. It is important to note that in America just then, almost no one had gone from rags to riches—the mythological, latterly celebrated "self-made man." More delegates were like the Livingstons, one from New York and another from New Jersey, whose family fortune dated back a hundred years, than resembled Thomas Johnson of Maryland, a lawyer whose modest fortune was of more recent vintage. The Boston Sons of Liberty, understanding that this would be the case, had had tailored for Sam Adams, a relatively poor man, a bespoke suit with gold knee buckles to prevent his congressional colleagues from dismissing his ideas because he might appear impecunious. Patrick Henry's plain clothing, which was compared by other delegates to those of a threadbare rural minister, predisposed the Congress's secretary not to expect much from Henry in the way of eloquence. Soon the secretary was pleasantly surprised. Patrick Henry, Sam Adams, and Christopher Gadsden were the most radical of the delegates. Analysis of the attendees' backgrounds reveals that they shared several attributes with other wealthy Americans of that time: a practiced ability to use state power, a consciousness of themselves as a breed apart, and social behavior patterns copied from those of the British gentry. The delegates also shared the presumption, gained from their near-universal prior service in provincial assemblies, that they were the proper arbiters of governance. Despite that snobbish attitude, in the coming months the wealthy delegates' actions did properly reflect the will of most Americans, even if the delegates did not actually represent their poorer neighbors.

Three absent men influenced the delegates by written thoughts. Jefferson had returned home because of ill health but had sent along "A Summary View of the Rights of British America," which, together with Warren's "Suffolk Resolves" and Dickinson's *Letters from a Farmer*, provided philosophical underpinning. All three documents shared two core beliefs: that the colonies were of supreme economic importance to the British Empire, and that the colonists were entitled to all the rights of British citizens.

Jefferson's "Summary," intended as instructions to the Virginia delegation, had not been adopted. Circulated to the larger assembly, it nailed the Navigation Acts' abrogation of the colonists' rights: "A view of these acts of parliament for regulation . . . of the American trade, if all other evidence were removed out of the case, would undeniably evince the truth of th[e] observation [that] bodies of men, as well as individuals, are susceptible of the spirit of tyranny." Free trade, Jefferson asserted, was a "natural right." Slavery, he further asserted, was one malicious result of British regulation, and so "the abolition of domestic slavery is the great object of desire in those colonies where it was unhappily introduced." Warren's "Suffolk Resolves" (the Massachusetts county of Suffolk included Boston), which arrived a fortnight after the Congress began, delivered by Paul Revere, called for the ousting of all royal appointees and jailing of those who refused to resign. Almost as an afterthought, it endorsed nonimportation and nonconsumption of everything from the East Indies, especially rum. Congress approved the "Resolves" and applauded the conduct of the Bostonians in the face of British oppression.

Independence was briefly considered. Patrick Henry was its most vocal champion. But independence was rejected as too radical—as was Henry, put only on secondary committees to prevent him from impeding the main discussion: Should the colonies accept the legitimacy of earlier Navigation Acts while seeking repeal of later ones, or should they reject them all? Since five colonies wanted to accept all and five to reject, no congressional vote was taken on the matter.

Nonimportation, as less controversial, rose to the top of the agenda. Its failure in the recent past spurred the delegates to create a better structure for compliance: This time nonimportation rules would be uniform throughout the colonies, express provision would be made for their enforcement, and nonimportation would be accompanied by nonexportation. The radicals Gadsden and Sam Adams wanted nonexportation to be really punishing, Adams seeking to cease export of lumber, livestock, and grain to the British West Indies, so as to wreak havoc there, and of flaxseed to Ireland, to idle thirty thousand spinners. But Virginian delegates argued that tobacco should not be on the list to prevent their neighbors from being hurt by it; a New Hampshire delegate asked for an exception for lumber, a New Yorker for fish; and the South Carolinians walked out to emphasize that a proposed ban on exporting rice and indigo would ruin their colony. Although nonimportation would start soon, nonexportation was put off for a year, to afford American farmers time to sell their current harvests—and the British, to come to their senses.

The Continental Congress's passage of nonimportation, nonexportation, and nonconsumption, Breen writes, was "a brilliantly original strategy of consumer resistance to political oppression." A Continental Association of seven thousand locally elected men, far more than had ever served in colonial legislatures, and most of them from the less-well-off classes of society, would enforce the program.

While the delegates were deliberating in Philadelphia, Gage's troops seized gunpowder from a storage depot in Somerville, a Boston suburb. News of this traveled quickly in New England; militia companies were mustered, equipped, and made ready to deploy if the British struck again. A Tory newspaper heightened the likelihood of a debacle by advocating that if rebellion began, the soldiers should immediately put Hancock, Adams, and others "to the sword, destroy their houses, and plunder their effects." Hancock was certainly to the fore: When the Massachusetts Assembly decided to buy cannons, rifles, and war matériel for twelve thousand minutemen, he had the assembly mandate that provincial tax collectors turn over their receipts to underwrite the purchases. Some of them did, in order to escape tarring and feathering. When he realized that the resulting revenues could not pay for all the needed matériel, Hancock bought some himself.

This time nonimportation was very effective: In one year, non-importation reduced British imports by more than 90 percent, from £2,843,469 to £220,555, producing consternation in London commercial circles. The operations of Continental Association committees were also an important precursor to democratic rule. After returning home, John Adams exulted to a fellow congressional delegate:

> We are trying by a Thousand Experiments, the Ingenuity as well as Virtue of our people. . . . Imagine 400,000 people [in Massachusetts] without Government or Law, forming themselves in Companies for various Purposes, of Justice, Policy, and War! You must allow for a great deal of the ridiculous, much of the Melancholly, and Some of the Marvellous.

High among the reasons that nonimportation worked the second time was an even higher participation rate among women, who controlled household purchasing and were also privy to what their friends and neighbors were and were not buying. Restraint in consumption by ordinary citizens also provided a stark contrast to the high living engaged in by congressional delegates riding to sessions in carriages, attending sumptuous dinners, and often exhibiting flamboyant garb similar to that of the MPs they were excoriating. These displays of privilege, a historian of symbols suggests, were intentional, since "opulence, grandeur, and refinement were technologies of governance in the eighteenth century." But after such displays provoked a near-riot in Philadelphia, Congress reduced its ostentation.

The delegates issued three proclamations, one to the people of Great Britain, a second to the colonists, and a third to the king: "A Declaration of Rights and Grievances" that declared null and void thirteen recent acts of Parliament. At Dickinson's insistence the petition to George III was couched as being from his majesty's loyal subjects. After loosing this hail of arrows at London, the delegates adjourned and made plans to reconvene in May 1775, by which time the arrows would have hit and the British would either have yielded or refused to, making obvious the American need to take more drastic action.

In the meantime, in a New York paper a writer calling himself Massachusettensis labeled the participants in nonimportation committees "disaffected" and "likely to introduce perpetual discord." And the Reverend Samuel Seabury, writing as "A W [Westchester] Farmer"—a conscious mocking of Dickinson—called them "a venomous brood of scorpions." John Adams answered under the name Novanglus, championing Americans' right to resist and for the non-affluent to lead that fight, celebrating the nonimportation committeemen as upholders of an "advoca[cy] for liberty . . . a resentment of injury, and indignation against wrong [and] a love of truth and a veneration for virtue." Seabury's other antagonists were the playwright Mercy Otis Warren, who wrote a satirical play about him, and Alexander Hamilton, then a sophomore at King's College. In anonymous articles later known as "The Farmer Refuted," Hamilton upheld the correctness of the boycott, directed farmers to grow flax and hemp to sell locally, to be less dependent on crops for export, and pointed out the stupidity of British attempts to stifle the economic growth of a continent whose natural resources "will infinitely exceed the demands, which Great Britain and her connections can possibly have for them. And as we then shall be greatly advanced in population, our wants will be proportionably increased."

For the first time in America, adherents of the British Crown were so actively harassed for their views that they fled in droves to the protection of the British army in Boston. Gage's troops had recently been augmented to nine regiments, one Redcoat for every five civilians in Boston. Shortly, emboldened soldiers ran their sabers through the fence bordering Hancock's home, and others barged in to determine if his stables could be used as a barracks. The residents' safety committee, which Hancock led, countered by stealing some British cannons.

King George III ignored the congressional petition's grievances but took them as a basis to conclude: "The New England governments are now in a state of rebellion [and] blows must decide whether they are to be subject to this country or independent." In what a London correspondent labeled "the death warrant against the Colonies . . . both the House of Lords and the House of Commons vowed to Support the King against the Colonies with their Lives & Fortunes [and troops were ordered] to Seize [Hancock's] Estate, & have his fine house for Genl Burgoyne." Gage's military orders, which arrived on April 14, 1775, instructed him to make a show of force and seize rebel leaders. Earlier, in London, Gage had argued that the best way to end the crisis was to rescind the Coercive Acts; nonetheless, on April 19 he dutifully followed his orders and sent troops to arrest Hancock and the Adamses and to seize an arms depot in Lexington. The Adamses and Hancock were out of town, preparing to depart for the Continental Congress. They hid in a field while Gage's troops fought with minutemen at Lexington and Concord, producing casualties on both sides. As the British were retreating at day's end, additional rebel militia units were already en route from as far away as Connecticut.

News of the actions at Lexington and Concord drastically changed the purpose and the urgency of the spring 1775 session, known as the Second Continental Congress. As one American near the action on the battlefields wrote to a friend about the "skirmish" in a widely circulated and copied letter: "This is a Prelude to a Tragedy of a most unnatural kind. The Sword is drawn & when it will be sheathed again God only knows."

3

Pledging Lives and Fortunes

Throughout his life Benjamin Franklin had a knack for fortuitous timing. The prime exemplar of the American rags-to-riches story, then sixty-eight, arrived home to Philadelphia just after Lexington and Concord, in time to be appointed a delegate to the spring 1775 Continental Congress. Until a year ago he had shared with most of his peers the belief that the colonies must remain within the Empire. For more than a decade in London he had worked toward that end, until pilloried in front of an audience of MPs. Their refusals to accede to any suggestions for reconciliation with the colonists forced him to conclude that America must break with the mother country.

The majority of his fellow delegates in Philadelphia had not yet reached that point, but the American blood shed at Lexington and Concord had convinced more of them that doing nothing to halt the British would bring increasing indignities and an eventual loss of their honor as well as their fortunes. Those who recognized that the only alternative to submission was independence were still in the minority, but they, as well as all the others, accepted the need for more active resistance to Great Britain, and plunged into the tasks of defending America: summoning an army and deciding how to pay for it.

American mythology has glossed over their decision to finance the war. Even at the time there was remarkably little discussion of it: Taxation being the bone of contention with Great Britain, not for an instant did the delegates consider direct taxes to finance the war; and anyway, Congress had not been specifically granted the power to tax American citizens. Options for obtaining money for the war had been further narrowed by the absence of a national bank. While in 1694 Great Britain had established the Bank of England primarily to finance wars in exchange for first call on future British tax receipts, in America there were no banks and no federal tax receipts to promise. So the delegates adopted the financing method used by provincial legislatures, the printing of money, known as making an emission. They authorized a two-million-dollar one; by fall they would approve another six million, and before the end of 1776 a total of twenty-five million.

They could not guarantee the value of the currency in which these emissions were made, even though the Continental dollar certificates said that they were redeemable for gold or silver, because without actual future tax receipts, the value of the paper currency would vary according to the whim of the market. To back the Continental dollar, the Continental Congress could only hope that the colonies would honor their pledges to pay into the central government on a regular basis, enabling the central government to sink (redeem) the new currency—as individual colonies had done in the past with their own emissions. The delegates decreed a four-year payment schedule, based on each colony's percentage of the overall population. They believed that the thirteen colonies would not have much difficulty in meeting the schedule since the amounts requested would be less, per capita, than what the colonies had recently been collecting in taxes. Hancock, Washington, and a few other wealthy delegates supplemented the first emissions by themselves paying to outfit soldiers, although they knew that repayment might well have to wait until war's end.

There was similarly not much discussion on choosing a commander in chief. While Hancock thought he was perfect for the job, those who knew him best did not. His dismay was visible as John

Adams nominated Washington—a French and Indian War veteran and colonial legislator who had recently raised and outfitted a thousand troops—and as Sam Adams then seconded his cousin's motion, which carried easily. Thereafter Hancock had little to do with the Adamses; instead, a biographer writes, he "developed increasingly warm friendships with Southerners, who like him were wealthy, well-educated, cultured men who appreciated fine clothes, foods, wines, and other luxuries."

Part of Washington's attractiveness to Congress lay in his presumptive immunity to bribery due to his significant wealth. They had all heard how Washington's British military-leader counterparts enriched themselves through their service or by accepting rewards after it, and they did not want that to happen in America. An equal part of Washington's appeal for Congress lay in his extraordinary willingness to abide by republican ideals and to subsume his authority to civilian control. He raised no objections when Congress chose his subordinates, one general from each colony. Two were fellow wealthy delegates, John Sullivan of New Hampshire and Philip Schuyler of New York. In June 1775 Washington traveled with them, and with rifle companies from Virginia, Pennsylvania, and Maryland, toward Boston, to take over the command.

While Congress had been meeting, several generals had arrived in Boston from Great Britain, accompanied by more troops and bearing cash for those already there. These new officers had previously served in America, and their leader, William Howe, as an MP had opposed the Coercive Acts as counterproductive; he was returning to America only at the personal request of King George III. Howe and his colleagues hatched a plan to break the British troops out of rebel encirclement. But their plan was based on the assumption that the rebels did not possess the discipline to withstand a coordinated frontal assault by seasoned Redcoats. On June 17, 1775, while Washington was still in transit, the British charged the most heavily defended rebel points, Breed's Hill and Bunker Hill. They eventually took both hills but suffered twice as many casualties as the defenders, and had a third of their men wounded—and then did not pursue the rebels. For allowing that, General Gage was recalled to London. Among the American dead was military leader Joseph Warren, author of the "Suffolk Resolves."

"The burthen [of military service] falls chiefly on the poor and the middling sort of the inhabitants, whilst the more opulent are, for the most part, exempt," not by fiat but by choice, future brigadier general Anthony Wayne was explaining to the Pennsylvania Assembly. Wars, even revolutionary wars, are convened by the rich and fought by the poor. Washington had acknowledged as much in his recruiting posters in Virginia, which promised each enrollee one hundred acres of land at the conclusion of service. He also found that the rich were not as willing as he was to take up arms. While Sullivan, Schuyler, and a few others among the wealthy joined him on the front lines, most did not. Forty percent of the wealthy were Loyalists who would not take up arms against the British. Of the remainder who were with the radicals in spirit, some could not envision submitting themselves to the discipline of the army or committing to three-year hitches, others decided to do their patriotic duty by serving in provincial assembles, and the rest simply chose to stay home to protect their own interests.

Later there arose the myth of the Continental soldier as American yeoman—the small farmer/landowner who grabbed his rifle from above his fireplace and marched willingly to war. Not so, according to the enlistment rolls studied by the social historian Charles Neimeyer: Most of the two hundred thousand men who served during the war were "young, landless, and unskilled." Many were also what today might be termed undesirable aliens, a quarter of them Irish and another eighth German, many of whom had come to America as indentured servants to avoid or to shorten prison sentences. Of the 396 men in several Massachusetts regiments, less than 10 percent owned any property; all 28 members of the Middlesex County (New Jersey) unit were substitutes who had been hired hands or indentured servants. As the historian Gregory H. Nobles points out: "Yeomen successfully pressured members of the gentry to keep the burden of military service on the poor and landless men who constituted the lowest stratum of whites."

Two weeks after the battle of Bunker Hill, when Washington arrived in Cambridge, the Continental army was beset by smallpox, starvation, and shortages of guns, ammunition, and powder. The camp in Cambridge was divided into various colony-by-colony contingents, each colony's men having their own supply chief, all of whom were encountering difficulties: "Butter, butter, butter is the cry, and none to be had," wrote the Hartford, Connecticut, merchant Joseph Trumbull, son of the governor, to his subordinate back home, Jeremiah Wadsworth, who was trying to obtain tents to replace the makeshift barracks that left the troops overexposed to disease. Washington was impressed enough with Trumbull to hire him as commissary general, to operate in tandem with the new quartermaster general, Thomas Mifflin, a well-to-do Philadelphia merchant, Quaker, and former congressman who had been serving as an aide-de-camp. Mifflin longed to be in battle but agreed to take charge of obtaining everything other than food because Washington needed someone he trusted in that position. The commander soon expanded Trumbull's shopping list to include requests for chocolates for his officers and for hunting shirts to induce sharpshooters to remain in New England in winter.

Congress required from Mifflin and Trumbull much more than their expertise—it desperately needed their private credit. Without the willingness of these leaders and of their immediate purchasing-corps subordinates to risk their personal credit in the nation's service, either the troops would continue to be hungry and unclad, or there would have to be wide-scale confiscations of food, horses, clothing, and other supplies that could rile the populace and undercut prorevolutionary zeal. The wealthy delegates in Congress, in relying on the credit of these purchasing agents were summoning the resources of a system they knew well. Built up over the years, this merchant community system obligated the farmer, the wholesaler, the wagoneer, the trader, and the shipper to trust one another and to grant credit to one another: Credit was an extension of mutual trust. Indeed, potential partners in the system had long been evaluated on the basis of trustworthiness, and those judged as wanting—for such sins as tardy repayments or short-weighting or squeezing extra profits at others' expense—dropped from membership.

Then too, Mifflin, Trumbull, and their immediate subordinates such as Wadsworth construed as a patriotic duty the extending of their personal credit for the benefit of the army and the country. This was the new, wartime iteration of the individual economic patriotism that American merchants had earlier adopted in eschewing their own mercantile interests to support the resistance. In Washington's camp near Boston, the commissaries continued to extend their own credit even after learning that some Massachusetts, Connecticut, and Rhode Island farmers and merchants did not share their patriotic fervor. Wadsworth fretted to Trumbull that these current suppliers were less reliable than those they had regularly dealt with before the war: "I am tired of trying to Please every Body. Am haunted to death [and] obliged to be concerned with all sorts of Creatures—am under Necessity of Advance of Money to men with [whom] I would wish not to invest." Washington, too, soon complained, to the colony of Massachusetts, of an "artificial scarcity" of firewood and forage created "by some persons who are monopolizing those Articles, in order to advance the Price, and . . . those in the Neighbourhood of the Camp who keep them up . . . to profit by our distress." That invidious spirit was not confined to suppliers near Cambridge. "After Lexington and Concord," according to a biographer of the Brown brothers of Providence, they "were alert to every opportunity which the situation offered. They combined service in the common cause with advantage to themselves, and on occasion they allowed their own business interests to take precedence."

Civilian patriotism was also being put to the test in the form of loyalty oaths of nonimportation and nonexportation charters. Those who signed them and abided by the charters were cheered, while those who did not became pariahs. In South Carolina the need to sign occasioned a moral crisis for Laurens, then the head of the provincial assembly: As a still-loyal British subject he did not want to sign, but as an American public official he felt forced to, and he did.

In Congress, Hancock got his chance at leadership. Peyton Randolph, who had become almost as radical as Patrick Henry, and who was the first president of the Congress, took ill and was given a leave. Hancock became temporary president of the Congress in 1775, a position made permanent when Randolph died. Hancock's tasks were more managerial than presidential, chairing congressional sessions and handling the paperwork. His wife would later recall "trimming off the rough edges of the bills of credit . . . and packing them up in saddle bags to be sent off . . . for the use of the army."

Jefferson replaced Randolph as a delegate and was asked to compose a "Declaration Setting forth the Causes and Necessity of Taking up Arms" for the generals to read to the troops. His draft was so strong that Dickinson toned it down. "We are reduced to the alternative of chusing an unconditional submission to the tyranny of irritated ministers, or resistance by force. The latter is our choice," the joint effort began, and asserted: "Our cause is just. Our union is perfect. Our internal resources are great." Only in its final paragraph did it declare: "We mean not to dissolve that union which has so long and so happily subsisted between us." Dickinson also composed, without Jefferson, a last plea to King George III, the so-called Olive Branch Petition, beseeching the king to heal the breach and stanch "the further effusion of blood, and . . . avert the impending calamities that threaten the British Empire."

As the delegates returned to Philadelphia in the fall of 1775, hopes for the Olive Branch Petition were dashed by the arrival of "A Proclamation for Suppressing Rebellion and Sedition," in which George III declared the colonies to be in revolt and labeled its leaders traitors. This rejection of any path to reconciliation but total submission undercut the moderates among the delegates. And it did so at a particularly poignant juncture, the arrival of new delegations from New York and Virginia that had been specifically enlarged to slow the radicals' rush toward independence.

Those colonies' new delegates, and others from Pennsylvania were even wealthier than the earlier set. Notable among them were Robert Morris, who in two decades as a merchant had made a lot of money and was "a man on the rise, but not quite arrived," as a biographer wrote, and James Wilson, who emigrated from Scotland in 1765 and since completing his law studies with Dickinson had become sought after for his legal sense. Wilson, Morris, and Dickinson all opposed immediate independence.

Yet they and their compatriots still had to deal with the growing headaches of the undeclared war. How should they treat a request from Trumbull to pay commissions to purchasing agents? Everyone agreed that Trumbull was doing a fine job; he had recently displayed his ingenuity in saving ten thousand pounds by buying pigs on the hoof and having them slaughtered close to encampments rather than paying more for prepared pork. Nonetheless Congress had refused immediate repayment for what he and his subordinates had advanced, even though Washington had urged Congress to do so. Taking ill, Trumbull returned to Hartford and petitioned Congress to change the remuneration structure so that supply agents worked on commission, as they routinely did in private business, rather than for their current meager salaries. But Congress was simultaneously being petitioned by female nurses who did not want to continue working for fifty cents per week, and by other underpaid functionaries. The wealthy delegates, who seemed to lump together all such pleas as moneygrubbing by the working classes, granted slightly increased salaries to nurses and other vital employees but refused commissions to agents.

Some frontline procurement agents then quit, although Trumbull and Wadsworth continued in harness, their patriotism not yet sapped. Wadsworth, son of a noted preacher and grandson of a governor, had inherited at the age of four. Apprenticed to an uncle, he had gone to sea, soon became a captain and began trading on his own, and by 1775 was among Connecticut's wealthier men. He had been host to Washington on the commander's trip north, lending him a horse when the general's regular mount was indisposed. At Trumbull's request Washington gave Wadsworth a warrant for $120,000 to pay past bills and to buy provisions for the winter. Wadsworth took it to Philadelphia where he got it cashed and tarried for a while with his fellow Hartford merchant, delegate Silas Deane.

Wadsworth's extended visit to the seat of government was testament that no set of circumstances ever really disrupts the iron law of supply and demand. Indeed, back then that law seemed to operate more rigorously than it does today. Because of the large distances and poor communications involved in transporting goods in 1775, should a shipload of a commodity or of a manufactured good arrive at a destination when and where it was desperately wanted, the cargo could be sold for triple or quadruple the investment, and for far more than what had been offered for a similar cargo a month earlier when the need had not been so great; but should a cargo arrive during a supply glut, it would sell for less than the costs of production and transport, and sometimes not sell at all and have to be dumped. Just a single cargo load that made it into Philadelphia in wartime, writes Thomas Doerflinger, historian of the city's merchants, "could exceed in value the total imports received by a major firm during three years of peace." On the downside the punishment for delivering the wrong stuff at the wrong time could as often be bankruptcy and disgrace.

No wonder, then, that so many American merchants concluded that the most reliable and least hazardous opportunities for profit during an undeclared war lay in meeting urgent military needs. As the biographer of Elbridge Gerry, a minor international trader and congressional delegate from Massachusetts, writes: "Being at the seat of government, [Gerry] was privy to information not available to outsiders and, as a result, became heavily involved in both public and private business," amassing a fortune in the dozen years between 1776 and 1788. Congress's ability to enrich a merchant was why Wadsworth tarried in Philadelphia, and why John Brown of Providence did too, leaning on his friendship with delegate Stephen Hopkins, a partner in his ironworks, and why William Duer of Saratoga, after failing three times to obtain a contract to furnish supplies to the British army, was courting contracts from Northern Army Department chief Schuyler.

Two important committees of Congress had been formed to exploit the old-boy networks of the wealthy for the benefit of the united colonies, and they were led by experienced participants in such activities, Benjamin Franklin and Robert Morris. The brief of Franklin's Secret Correspondence Committee was to get in touch with "friends" abroad for aid, and that of Morris's Secret Committee was to obtain large quantities of war matériel. Franklin, after twenty years in Great Britain and France, knew who in the Old World would respond to a New World appeal; and Morris, having spent those decades establishing his credit abroad, could use his regular overseas suppliers and cachepots to obtain and forward goods to America. Franklin and Morris became friends and often acted in tandem, for instance in the effort to obtain gunpowder for Washington, the shortage of which, in the commander's view, had forced the retreat at Bunker Hill. Washington had been so afraid that his troops might find out how little powder they possessed that to mislead them he partially filled powder barrels with sawdust. Separate attempts by Nicholas Brown and Elbridge Gerry to obtain powder for the troops had failed. In Morris's effort, he too used deception—false shipping papers, orders, and cargo lists—to lessen European and Caribbean powder sellers' fear of British reprisal for vending contraband to the American rebels. In August 1775 Morris and his private partners requested repayment of twenty-five thousand pounds that they had advanced for gunpowder. Since some powder had arrived, Congress paid up, and a month later, in a deal signed on Congress's behalf by Franklin, advanced Morris eighty thousand pounds to buy more. In these deals Congress also became the insurer, accepting responsibility for repaying the merchants' losses should the ships be sunk or captured.

Congressional delegate–merchants regularly purchased war matériel for the troops from one another's companies, and sometimes from their own. Such arrangements were not then illegal. Only one delegate, from Connecticut, grumbled that there were not ten men in his colony whose net worth amounted to as much as the Morris firm (Willing & Morris) would make from their gunpowder contract. A Pennsylvania delegate set him to rights by declaring that the comparison proved only that "there are no men [in Connecticut] whose capital or credit are equal to such contracts. That is all." Congress also permitted other practices later made illegal: shipping private cargoes on public vessels, and temporarily tapping into public funds to complete private purchases. As the historian Elizabeth Nuxoll writes in her study of the Secret Committee: "There was substantial conflict of interest. . . . The members were free to carry on private trade ventures, along with their public ones, as were the committee's agents." These were standard practices throughout Europe as well; as the historian Pierre Gervais notes: "Insider trading, buyer and seller cartels, price-fixing, speculation, [and] market cornering . . . were not bugs, they were fixtures" of the system. As Morris informed one of his committee agents: "I have much in my power or under my influence both Public and private. My desire is to serve justly and faithfully every interest I am connected with."

The general public is always willing to believe that merchants do not act out of concern for the public good but for private profit. And as the Revolution began they found ample evidence for that belief in the actions of America's international trader-merchants. As the deadline approached for the beginning of nonexportation, merchants filled and sent out every available vessel—on the very last day, fifty-two from Philadelphia, denuding the port of masts. The traders' avidity angered the working classes: The public was constantly exhorted to sacrifice, but what sacrifices did the rich make?

Congress exacerbated the problem by giving in to requests for exceptions to nonimportation. Initially it had refused to agree to allow merchants to send out American produce to be exchanged abroad for munitions. But when Morris informed his colleagues that those merchants had told him they would no longer do business with the Secret Committee, Congress caved, ceding to the committee the power to make exceptions to nonexportation. A big one was for Bermuda, the largest British Caribbean colony, after Bermuda's representatives pleaded with Congress to dispatch livestock and flour for their starving inhabitants, pledging to pay for that with salt and munitions. The Bahamas was next to apply, and plenty of American merchants stood ready to send foodstuffs there. Such exceptions, while humanitarian, eviscerated nonexportation, since ordinary merchants could not be expected to hold back when exceptions were being so readily obtained. Loud charges of favoritism further undercut public confidence in the government's fairness.

Near the end of 1775, Franklin met in Philadelphia with an unusual visitor from the court of Louis XVI, Julien-Alexandre Achard, Chevalier de Bonvouloir, who had come—not in an official capacity, but close enough—to tell America that France might be willing to join them against their common enemy, Great Britain. Franklin and those delegates who became privy to this information realized that a future alliance and substantial aid from France or Spain depended upon those kingdoms being able to deal with an independent American country, since the European sovereigns were understandably reluctant to provide overt aid to the rebellious colonial subjects of a fellow king.

In early January 1776, a copy of George III's annual December speech to Parliament arrived in America. It contained his vow to crush the revolt by any means necessary, including the use of foreign mercenaries, and his offer of amnesty to colonies and individuals that would return to the fold. Combined with the news of a devastating defeat of American forces at Quebec; a counterattack at Norfolk by Virginia's governor; and intimations that New York might accept the amnesty, the king's speech deflated American hopes for a peaceable reunion with Great Britain and heightened the need for a declaration of independence.

Multiple rationales for such a declaration were provided by a bombshell of a pamphlet, *Common Sense,* that exploded into the American consciousness in February.

Initially unattributed, it was written by Thomas Paine—a British-born rope maker, civil servant, failed businessman, and, since coming to Philadelphia, magazine editor. *Common Sense* raised the stakes for immediate American independence with its contention that "the cause of America is, in a great measure, the cause of mankind." Paine led his list of reasons for independence with the charge that Great Britain had already acted so dishonorably that Americans had no choice but to sever ties. Less moral but more practical was an economic reason that posterity does not usually ascribe to Paine: that independence would allow America to conduct its own trade. In a passage that could as easily have been written by Adam Smith, Paine wrote that to a trading country, freedom of trade was

> of such importance, that the principal source of wealth depends on it; and it is impossible that any country can flourish . . . whose commerce is engrossed, cramped and fettered by the laws and mandates of another. . . . A freedom from the restraints of the Acts of Navigation I foresee will produce such immense additions to the wealth of this country that posterity will wonder that ever you thought your present trade worth its protection.

Most other American pamphlets had been composed to sway the elite; Paine deliberately addressed his to what were known as the "people out of doors," the farmers, artisans, and mechanics seldom heard in America's corridors of power, yet who, as the historian Craig Bruce Smith documents in a monograph on American honor in the Revolutionary era, were as fully concerned as the elite with personal and national honor. The split between pamphlet audiences occasioned a public fight in Charleston, between Gadsden, brandishing a copy of Paine's pamphlet, and Laurens, who cursed its call for independence, although he privately admitted that "the Author's reasoning, tho not all original is strong & captivating & will make many converts to Republican principles." Only after *Common Sense* quickly sold one hundred thousand copies did legislators become enthusiastic about a call to arms that resonated so deeply with the majority of Americans. John Adams would cavil that *Common Sense*'s argument was "hackneyed in every Conversation private and public" of previous years, but had to concede that its passionate eloquence moved rich and poor toward independence.

Paine was not an enemy of wealth per se, only of the privileges of inherited wealth. Other rabble-rousers saw no distinction, with "A Watchman" in the *Pennsylvania Packet* warning: "Remember the influence of wealth upon the morals and principles of mankind. Recollect how often you have heard the first principles of government subverted by the calls . . . to make way for men of fortune . . . as if a minority of rich men were to govern the majority of freeholders in the province"; and "A Tradesman" in the *Evening Post* asserting that merchants feared independence would upset their monopolies: "They get all the profit and will soon reduce and control the people [of America] as the East India Company controls Bengal."

For years the antipathy of the poor to the wealthy had been one of the factors preventing the latter from seeking leadership roles in the rebellion. But by the spring of 1776, many more of the wealthy, including merchants, had become as enraged as the poor by British arrogance, as expressed by the British wanton destruction of American towns and shipping. Shortly Parliament pushed additional wealthy Americans toward independence by enlarging the Coercive Acts to encompass all the colonies, and by declaring its right to seize any ships trading with the rebels "as if the same were the ships and effects of open enemies." Several congressional fence-sitters now announced for independence. Indiscriminate British shelling of Norfolk, Virginia, which burned eight hundred buildings, further increased the number in favor of independence.

To move a majority of a populace from resistance to rebellion requires victories as well as outrages. Washington provided a victory in ousting the British from Boston. In November 1775 he had dispatched Col. Henry Knox to Fort Ticonderoga, in northern New York, closer to Canada than to Manhattan, to bring its captured cannons to Boston. Knox and his men accomplished this Herculean task, and on the night of March 4, 1776, Washington moved cannons and troops to Dorchester Heights, a commanding point above the harbor.

General Howe planned an attack on the heights for the next day, but it was frustrated by a sudden snowstorm. He then changed his mind and made Washington an offer: The British army would leave Boston unburned if permitted to depart without a battle. Washington agreed, since his troops had less than thirty rounds of ammunition apiece. On March 17, 1776, Howe, eleven thousand soldiers, and eleven hundred Loyalists evacuated Boston in seventy-eight ships.

This American victory emboldened Congress to decree that private vessels could arm themselves as privateers, and to declare all American ports open to commerce from anywhere except Great Britain. John Adams wrote to a friend: "The Ports are open you see, and Privateering is allowed. Is this independency?" In many ways it was, for these edicts completed the severing of the colonies' former commercial ties to the British Empire.

Political decoupling from Great Britain took another three months, part spent awaiting a nebulous British peace commission, and part the outcome of a British attempt to invade Charleston. The British had imagined Charlestonians to be mostly Loyalists who would welcome them, but the attempted assault produced the opposite effect, galvanizing more South Carolinians to embrace independence. A similar effect on wavering Philadelphians was created by the appearance of British warships at the Atlantic edge of the Delaware River, threatening the city.

Two days later Congress formally advised each colony to form its own government. Most had already done so. But on May 15 a vote in Congress on heading toward independence passed only narrowly, an indication that many delegates were still undecided. Three committees were appointed, one to design a bare-minimum central government, and a second to write potential treaty terms for foreign alliances. The third was a declaration-writing committee of John Adams, Franklin, Robert R. Livingston of New York (a cousin of the other Livingstons), Roger Sherman of Connecticut, and Jefferson as designated penman.

The Virginian's majestic preamble aimed at uniting all Americans by their hopes for the future—in Jefferson's enigmatic phrase, "the pursuit of happiness." During revisions by the committee and then by the whole Congress, his preamble remained remarkably intact. The rest of Jefferson's draft was mostly a list of grievances, many of them economic. Congress toned down the accusatory rhetoric aimed at king and Parliament, added a few extra references to God, and deleted Jefferson's excoriation of slavery.

As the delegates wrapped up work on the Declaration, British troops began landing on Staten Island. That news spurred the last holdout colonies into the independence camp. The Declaration was signed by Hancock and issued. Shortly most other delegates signed as well. It was indicative of the cooperative attitude of the wealthy delegates that those opposed to the will of the majority avoided getting in its way. Dickinson and Thomas Willing, who did not want to sign, "withdrew behind the barrier"—absented themselves—to allow their replacements to sign, and Morris, who had voted against independence, decided to sign anyway. Similarly, some South Carolina delegates, either opposed to independence or believing the Declaration to be premature, signed because they too were not about to counteract the judgment of the majority of South Carolinians.

They took such actions because they, along with the other signers, were acutely aware of signing not as individuals but as representatives of their states—on the document their signatures are grouped by states—and of signing as much on behalf of the people out-of-doors as for those insiders who had selected them as delegates. They embraced the Declaration's lofty preamble and assertion of inalienable rights, and its equally fervent and powerful conclusion that the "united States of America," as "free and Independent States," had "full power to levy War, conclude Peace, contract Alliances, establish Commerce, and to do all other Acts and Things that Independent States may of right do." Toward those ends the delegates mutually pledged to each other "our Lives, our Fortunes, and our sacred Honour."

Part Two

⸺⊷⊶⊷⸺

The Revolutionary War,
1776–1781

4

Blood, Property, and Profit

*T*he Declaration of Independence asserted the idea that all people possess certain "inalienable rights," including "life, liberty, and the pursuit of happiness." English philosopher John Locke's list of inalienable rights had included the possession of property. Jefferson's omission of property from the Declaration's list was startling to those who believed, as many of the wealthy did, that the only essential function of government was the protection of private property. Though Jefferson believed that the right to own property was implicit in the Declaration, he left it unstated for three reasons.

First, while life, liberty, and the pursuit of happiness were shared by all, property was not. Second, to include property would roil Congress, since southerners considered slaves as property and northerners did not. Third, that the declaring of independence was in effect a promise to those Americans who possessed little or no property that a new country's rules of governance would help them acquire some. Independence would bring a new legal system that overrode the old concepts of entail and primogeniture, which for generations in Great Britain and most of Europe had dictated that real property could be inherited only by the eldest son, serving to keep ownership of most property in the same families' hands for generations, dooming the poor to perpetual poverty because they could never acquire property. Jefferson had already attacked these concepts in the Virginia legislature for enabling "a distinct set of families [that] being privileged by law in the perpetuation of their wealth, were thus formed into a patrician order," introducing a bill to "annul this privilege, and instead of an aristocracy of wealth . . . make an opening for an aristocracy of virtue and talent."

The new Pennsylvania constitution pursued both goals: to protect private property and to coax into being an aristocracy of talent. The document did unequivocally uphold the right of "acquiring, possessing and protecting property," but its path toward an aristocracy of talent was circuitous, to be achieved by heightened democracy. While other constitutions were being written by lawyers and large property owners, Pennsylvania's constructors, Robert Whitehill, Timothy Matlack, and James Cannon were neither: They were militia members. Whitehill was a small farmer. Matlack had owned a steel furnace, then gone to debtors' prison and become a brewer; as a staff member of Congress, his job was to write out documents in a beautiful hand. Cannon was a mathematics professor. He warned:

> It is the Happiness of America that there is no Rank above that of Freeman existing in it, and much of our future Welfare and Tranquility will depend on its remaining so forever; for this Reason, great and over-grown rich men will be improper to be trusted [with writing the state constitution]. They will be too apt to be framing distinctions in society, because they will reap the benefits of all such distinctions.

So they chose not to consult Pennsylvania's reigning legal experts, the patricians Dickinson and Wilson. Dickinson pressured the writers anyway, in a pamphlet entreating them to formulate the new constitution "in such a manner as will . . . secure the State from the fatal influence of hasty, incorrect, passionate, and prejudiced determination." Then and since, the adjectives "hasty," "incorrect," "passionate," and "prejudiced" have been regularly applied by certain minorities to actions by majorities that are not to their liking.

The anti-wealth-holder aims of Whitehill, Matlack, and Cannon shone through virtually every choice they made, starting with the definition of eligible voters. Most colonial plebiscites had been restricted to Protestant white male adult property owners whose rents yielded the equivalent of one month's wages for a laborer, or mechanics or artisans who could show that they had paid a certain amount in taxes. The New England colonies' many small farms made eligible 50 to 70 percent of the area's white males; in Pennsylvania, however, higher property-ownership requirements had kept eligibility to 10 percent of white males, producing legislatures mainly attuned to the needs of significant property holders. The new Pennsylvania suffrage still excluded women, blacks, children, Jews, Catholics, and Native Americans—as would other states' rules—but did enfranchise the 87.5 percent of adult white Protestant Pennsylvanians who had paid any amount in taxes. It also trimmed the overweighting of Philadelphians, which had contributed to the continued dominance of the wealthy in the legislature.

To further undercut the influence of the wealthy, the unicameral assembly was to be elected annually, and its edicts to become law only after being discussed openly for a year and reratified by the next assembly. "The mob made a second branch of the legislature," a North Carolinian sniffed: "Laws subjected to . . . a washing in ordure by way of purification. Taverns and dram shops are the councils to which the laws are referred for approbation before they possess a binding influence." Still more causes for alarm among the wealthy: The chief executive had little power, the judiciary could easily be replaced by the legislature, and imprisonment for debt was abolished. In an early draft there was a line, believed to have been written by Franklin, "That an enormous Proportion of Property vested in a few Individuals is dangerous to the Rights, and destructive of the Common Happiness, of Mankind; and therefore every free State hath a Right by its Laws to discourage the Possession of such Property." That idea was discarded, but still Pennsylvania's constitution was the most radically democratic, anti-wealth-holder official document ever produced in America. "Of all the radical steps taken in the bright light of early revolutionary enthusiasm," writes the historian Gary B. Nash, "this was the most significant: the insistence . . . that ordinary men struggling for a foothold on the ladder of property-owning status had just as much right to inclusion in the political community as the wealthiest shipowners, plantation proprietors, money lenders, and slaveholders."

One of the new assembly's first acts realized the doubters' fears by taxing previously exempt speculative holdings of unimproved land, much of it in the western part of the state and owned by Philadelphians.

New York's Congressional delegates wrote home: "We ardently wish that in our own state the utmost caution may be used to avoid a like calamity" to Pennsylvania's. But New York as well as four other states followed Pennsylvania in drastically redefining the suffrage, and five more widened it. Only Virginia and Delaware retained the old property qualifications for voters. At the outset of the United States of America, the will of the people was to encourage voting by those who had never before enjoyed that privilege.

Perhaps because of our justifiable celebration of the Declaration of Independence, our mythology has forgotten the problems associated with another congressional committee-written document presented just a week later, the Articles of Confederation. Its major flaw—known at the time—was that it reserved taxation power solely to the states. That could hardly have been otherwise, since British taxation was the triggering issue of the Revolution, and no congressman would dare argue in favor of a central government's right to directly tax the citizenry. Even so, the delegates did nearly come to blows over what today seems a statement of the obvious, the proposed Article XI: "All charges of war & all other expenses that shall be incurred for the common defence, or general welfare . . . shall be defrayed out of a common treasury, which shall be supplied by the several colonies in proportion to the number of inhabitants of every age, sex & quality." The sticking points were that each colony should pay on the basis of its share of the national population, and that "inhabitants" meant free whites. Northerners wanted slaves counted as taxable inhabitants. Southerners did not want slaves counted for tax purposes, as that would mean that their colonies owed more, but they did want slaves counted toward total population, to give their colonies greater clout in Congress. Dickinson initially proposed changing the arrangement that currently permitted Rhode Island, with a small population, to have a vote in Congress equal to that of highly populous Virginia or Pennsylvania. But the southern colonies threatened to pull out of the confederacy if slaves were counted toward tax obligations; and the small colonies, if their power was lessened.

Congress then had to cease discussing the Articles to deal with renewed British military attacks.

After the British had evacuated Boston in the spring, America's generals and congressional delegates knew they would return and try to take New York, and prepared for such an attack. But when Howe landed in Staten Island in July 1776, his 32,000 men and many ships were more numerous than the American forces, and their military superiority soon became evident. For weeks Howe maneuvered on Long Island before fully engaging the American forces in a pitched battle that ended disastrously. Only Washington's skill in extracting his forces from Brooklyn prevented a disaster that could have ended the Revolution.

Washington's actions in saving his army were masterful and heroic, but the speed and totality of the evacuation also had an unfortunate consequence that would plague the war effort for years to come: the abandonment of enormous amounts of military supplies. That occasioned a rush to replace them, which set off a vicious cycle of currency depreciation. Trumbull and Mifflin, to obey instructions to quickly acquire new supplies, had to pay more per item than they had done for the initial batches. And as they made the new purchases, the worth of the Continentals, the currency issued by the Continental Congress, decreased. During the purchasing agents' next buying spree, the same amount of Continentals fetched even fewer supplies. Depreciation of the Continentals, and the shortages that ensued when the armies bought up a large proportion of the available staples, raised the prices of those staples in the private sector, which hit hardest the poor, who could least afford to pay more for the basic necessities of life.

The citizenry's loud objections to raised prices and accompanying shortages brought the matter to the attention of state assemblies. Some quickly enacted price controls. Rhode Island's edict, for example, announced its intent: "An act to prevent monopoly and oppression, by excessive and unreasonable prices for many of the necessaries and conveniences of life, and for the better supply of our troops in the army." Connecticut's edict charged that the rise in prices was "chiefly occasioned by Monopolizers, the great pest of Society, who prefer their own private Gain to the interest and safety of their country." These state laws were based on a new, unwritten but widely accepted code of individual economic patriotism: Merchants and farmers were not to take advantage of the crisis of war to sell their goods at inflated prices. Plenty of them tried to do so anyway, and thus became targets for anger, especially those merchants who had earlier been against independence. Now they were accused of gouging, not only to make a profit but also to deliberately undermine the Patriot economy. A Maryland legislator's response to plantation owners' hoarding of salt was to ask rhetorically: "Was they real friends to their country as they stile themselves, would they ingross that necessity article salt, and keep it from the necessitous as they do . . . for no other purpose than to distress the needy (for what end?) to make the war in which we are engaged more irksome, occasion the people to mutineer and create divisions among them."

Depreciation's deeper source was identified in a pamphlet whose anonymous author was soon revealed as Pelatiah Webster, a former Philadelphia merchant whose business had been forced to close by the advent of war, and who was now serving as an assistant quartermaster. Having spent most of his life, as he later explained, with his nose in a book, he now with more leisure was using his book learning to elucidate the "natural and original principles" of money and finance. He identified as the source of depreciation the government's printing of money without gold and silver to back the notes, and—even more basic—the government's inability to levy direct taxes. Politicians were impressed with the pamphlet but they ignored his recommendations: Direct taxation was still politically out of the question.

Washington believed that in a democratic society, supply for the military ought not to be coerced. He did not want to use confiscation even if some states were already doing so. Yet by December 1776 his army's needs had become so desperate that he directed William Duer, then supplying Schuyler's army, to have cattle driven the two hundred miles from upper New York to lower New Jersey because he could not locally obtain enough beef for the troops. Camped at the Delaware River, opposite Hessian troops guarding Trenton, the commander in chief knew that if the Continental army did not have a success soon, most of his troops, their enlistments scheduled to be up at the end of the year, would likely just return home. Desertion was already a significant problem, and executing a few caught deserters did not completely deter the practice or aid troop morale. To boost his soldiers' willingness to remain in arms, Washington had the officers read to them Paine's new, stirring call to courage, *The American Crisis*, which celebrated the "winter soldier" who stayed the course and would eventually reap greater glory over the "sunshine patriot" who stayed for a season and then retired. On Christmas night 1776, Washington and his men daringly crossed the ice-choked Delaware and attacked the Hessian camp. They produced a much-needed victory. Further victories at Trenton and at Princeton also boosted morale.

Morris, who once had objected to the Declaration as premature, had become so thoroughly converted to the cause that he remained in Philadelphia when other congressmen fled, and he had been helping Washington. Excited to learn of the victories at Trenton and Princeton, he dispatched fifty thousand dollars of his own to Washington so that the commander could reward each of the troops with a bonus, telling him: "If further occasional supplys of Money are necessary, you may depend on my exertions either in a publick or private capacity." Whether due to the added cash or the victory, desertions ceased to be as much of a problem. Washington's esteem for Morris grew, and they became close friends.

Two weeks later Congress decreed reprinting and wide distribution of the Declaration. Many printers declined the task because the British still threatened to overwhelm the United States; should the British prevail, whoever printed what the British considered a treasonable document would be targeted for arrest. Mary Katherine Goddard of Baltimore—that city's postmaster as well as publisher of the *Maryland Journal and the Baltimore Advertiser*, operator of a bookstore, and printer of an almanac and other materials—took the chance. She reprinted the Declaration. The "Goddard Broadside" was bought widely enough that Goddard's success irked her brother William, with whom she had been operating the press. He had been away from Baltimore promoting other trade, and when he returned he devoted himself to taking back control of the business.

One of war's benefits, a modern adage holds, lies in its creative destruction. That had occurred in Philadelphia in 1775–76, when the Quaker merchant elite was forced into exile by their opposition to the Revolution, giving opportunity to newer entrepreneurs such as Morris. In Boston, after March 17, 1776, when eleven hundred Tory Loyalists departed with the British, the disappearance of 213 merchants and their families—70 percent of the area's merchants—made room for growth by such men as Elias Hasket Derby of Salem, son of a sea captain and owner of a handful of vessels.

At the time of his death in 1799, Derby would be the wealthiest man in the United States of America. Since he never held public office, and his life was free from scandal, he has been overlooked in most histories, including financial ones. But his rise to the top of the wealth pyramid reflects the tenor of his times. His initial motivation was prior British bad behavior. The British had captured his *Jamaica Packet* and brought it into the harbor. But after the Admiralty Court acquitted the ship of breaking any laws and Derby sought to have it leave, he was unable to sell the cargo to post the required bond. He would have settled for the *Jamaica Packet* departing with the evacuation fleet, but British sailors cut down its sails, took the hoops from its hogsheads, and stole the cables tying it to the wharf, causing it to go aground and burn, "by which," Derby wrote, "I lost £3,000 Sterling." He continued to instruct his ships in the Caribbean to be carefully laden with "cotton, cocoa, sugar, molasses, duck, cordage, powder" from approved ports, so they would not run afoul of the American nonimportation council. The British seized the ships anyway, and in reaction Derby obtained privateering licenses for the remainder of his fleet.

Privateering was legal armed robbery; but even those Americans who were just a generation beyond Puritanism could embrace such a morally ambiguous activity, since British sea power was preventing them from plying their prior, honorable trade. Derby did resurrect a Puritan practice that has been forgotten in our rush to distance ourselves from those stern forebears: a share-the-rewards system for collaborative enterprises. Sharing profits was already out of fashion, but in his privateering Derby, who habitually closed his letters to his captains with the salutation, "Your friend and employer," emphasized both his friendship and his status as employer by splitting the spoils not only with captains and officers, which was standard, but also with crews, and in a larger proportion than he had done during peacetime commercial voyages. Since ordinary and able seamen now risked capture and imprisonment if caught by the British, to induce them to sail Derby offered them partial shares "of all the Prizes and Plunder [resulting from a] Cruise against the Enemies of the United States," as his printed form put it. Within months, his *Revenge, Dolphin*, and other ships captured nineteen prizes, whose profits catapulted him to the upper tier of wealth in the country: The sale price for the first dozen of those ships was £37,500, more money than the estate of Manigault had been worth just three years earlier. However, Derby decided to buy the seized goods himself for later resale—knowing, for instance, that beeswax was so scarce that a captured ton of it could fetch £5,000. Shortly he would send out ships whose cargoes mixed New England and captured goods; one, destined for Guadeloupe, carried New England salt fish, shingles, whale oil, spermaceti candles, tallow, staves, and barrels, and privateer bounty of Irish linens, silks, and British white lead, used for paint. Derby poured the profits from those voyages into constructing new privateers; the smallest, the forty-five-ton *Centipede*, took eleven prizes.

Derby's fellow Salem shipowners got into privateering almost as quickly, and with similar results: Forty and fifty years later, at the time of their deaths, they would be among the wealthiest men in the country. The Cabot brothers used their father's ships; Israel Thorndike, who had gone to sea at seventeen, then partnered with Moses Brown in the Caribbean trade before returning home to privateer; Joseph Peabody, a cobbler's apprentice in his youth, who sailed for both Derby and Cabot; Asa Clap; Thomas Russell; Cyrus Butler; and William Gray, known in Salem as Tertius Gray because there were two other William Grays, a militiaman and the son of a shoe-factory owner.

The actual extent of American privateering in the Revolutionary War remains hazy, with estimates varying from the capture of 600 British commercial vessels to 3,386 of them, and their worth from eighteen to sixty-six million dollars. The United States of America received a quarter of the sales at auction, and the country also benefited from privateers providing crucial war matériel. In a typical venture the Browns of Providence sent out the *Diamond*, which took five prizes that included a thousand hogsheads of sugar and large quantities of rum and coffee. "Even after splitting the proceeds with the government," a Brown biographer writes, "there was bounty enough to enrich the Browns, [their captain], and all of the *Diamond*'s crew." Washington, Knox, Franklin, and Hancock also invested in privateers.

Derby, more so than other privateer owners, understood that to make a bigger profit he did not need to overly rein in labor costs, especially since his tars, by sailing in his ships, were exposing themselves to considerable danger from a British act decreeing that captured privateers were to be treated as pirates. So Derby arranged that an experienced crewman's partial share of a single Derby privateering voyage could bring fifty pounds, at a time when the average family income was still eighty pounds a year—and his ships sailed four to six times a year. Some hands sold their shares back to Derby prior to departure in exchange for his provisioning their families during their absence.

Shipbuilding by Derby and other privateer owners furnished income for thousands of land-based carpenters, blacksmiths, rope makers, warehousemen, clerks, and the makers of casks, sea chests, rum, cider, flour, lumber, and pitch. The extensive employment commissioned by the owners' enterprising activities reinforced the then-held view that wealth was better situated in the hands of the wealthy, who would spread it around by providing work for others, rather than in the hands of the poor, who would spend it on themselves.

The high remuneration offered by the privateers lured so many rural workers that it soon caused problems for agriculture: "The farmer cannot hire a labourer for less than 50 or 40 dollars per month, and difficult to be had at that. This naturally raises the price of provision," observed a New Hampshire delegate.

The Continental Congress "sits at the fountain Head of Welth," Nicholas Brown wrote in acknowledgment of a generally held view among the merchants at the time: The surest path to wartime profits was a government contract. He persuaded Congress to buy some of his eight hundred unsold boxes of spermaceti candles, warehoused because of prohibitions placed on Americans' purchases of luxury goods. Spermaceti candles were prized for burning brighter and lasting longer. Congress kept some for its own use and authorized him to send others overseas to exchange for war matériel. In Martinique one batch was valuable enough to buy 117 casks of gunpowder, 129 small arms, 60 pistols, 11,000 flints, 48 cutlasses, 4 swivel guns, and 1,900 pounds of shot. But another cargo of candles, salt pork, flour, oil, and 350 bunches of onions could not purchase the ordnance sought in the Caribbean, so the captain sold the cargo and with the proceeds bought Russian canvas duck, useful in making sails. On the way home he had to scoot into an out-of-the-way harbor to avoid capture. Delay and red tape ensued, to the point of sapping the Browns' eagerness to be provisioners.

Since other vendors were also having fulfillment problems, Franklin and Morris decided to make provisioning more attractive by introducing the profit motive. Morris's Secret Committee then offered commission deals to businessmen who would act as purchasing agents abroad. Silas Deane, an international businessman and former member of Congress (and of the committee), would go to Paris, and young William Bingham, the inheritor of a modest fortune who owned several ships and had been secretary to the committee, would go to Martinique. In both places they were to buy goods for America, not as government employees but as private citizens (Deane) or in partnership with Willing & Morris (Bingham): "We shall be ready to transact rich business," the firm wrote to Bingham. Other Secret Committee agents included Morris's brother. In a typical purchase one agent sold American flour in Portugal, and from the proceeds of that sale bought rope and duck in Germany, Sweden, Holland, and Poland, then shipped it all home in vessels financed by French bankers.

Bingham in the Caribbean also commissioned privateers. At first Morris did not participate, yielding to Willing's caution that privateering could hurt their former trading partners. But within the year he could write to Bingham: "My scruples about Privateering are all done away. I have seen so much rapine, plunder & Destruction [by the British] that I join you in thinking it a duty to oppose and distress so merciless an enemy." He also saw large profits: From one privateer he reaped £43,994, Bingham £29,329, and its captain £14,664. Bingham had assured success by promising the governor of Martinique a small percentage on all trades and prizes brought in by American privateers. Shortly Bingham had as many privateers operating as Derby and his Salem neighbors, and was conducting as much international business as Morris and the Philadelphia-based merchants.

Morris and Franklin dreamed of a metaswap: of American tobacco, rice, indigo, lumber, furs, and meat for European war matériel. Seeking to shift the balance of world power, Louis XVI and his foreign minister, Charles Gravier, comte de Vergennes, had already decided that the easiest and cheapest way to diminish Great Britain's clout was to tie down its military in a prolonged North American conflict. So they backed the American rebels, but initially through third parties, so as not to give the British an excuse to declare war on France. Vergennes introduced Deane to playwright-businessman Pierre-Augustin Caron de Beaumarchais and international trader and banker Jacques-Donatien Le Ray de Chaumont. They bought the French military's outmoded cannons and rifles, a clearing out of old inventory that allowed France to commission newer arms. A second plus was that the Americans wanted to pay in crops such as tobacco, which were in demand in France but previously only obtainable through the British at exorbitant prices. Now they would be shipped to France more directly, and at a far lower price, saving money for France while depriving Great Britain of profit.

Global thinkers often get tripped up by local actors. The French-American tobacco swap fell victim to Gallic red tape, so it was the cash and credit of Chaumont and Beaumarchais (to whom the kings of France and Spain each extended a million *livres*), and the prewar resources of Deane and Morris in such ports as Bilbao, that obtained the much-needed munitions. Aboard just one Beaumarchais-Deane ship, the *Amphitrite*, which would land in Portsmouth, New Hampshire, were fifty-two cannons, plus cannonballs, 250,000 bullets, rifles, tents, pickaxes, and clothing.

The United States was still unaware of the forthcoming Deane-Beaumarchais ships, when in late October of 1776, to assist Deane in obtaining the much-needed French help Congress dispatched to France its most experienced diplomat, Benjamin Franklin. He arrived in Paris just after Christmas. For this visit he had decided not to wear the fine tailored suits he had sported in 1773, when he was inducted as a member of the French Academy of Sciences. Now, to emphasize that he was an official ambassador of the new United States of

America, as well as the quintessential American, he would present himself in provincial American garb, complete with coonskin cap.

As the Revolutionary War dragged on, the killer edge of the law of supply and demand became sharper. The acuteness of demand arose from the American and British armies on American soil requiring as much food and clothing as the populations of Philadelphia and New York, thereby restricting supply for everyone else. Then too, as Washington wrote his brother: "There is such a thirst for gain, and such infamous advantages taken to forestall, & engross those articles which the army cannot do without, thereby enhancing the cost of them to the public fifty or a hundred prCt, that it is enough to make one curse their own Species, for possessing so little virtue & patriotism." (Forestalling was refusing to sell until buyers became willing to pay more, and engrossing was creating a monopoly so as to charge high prices.)

Congress lacked the statutory authority to prevent seller-based abuses. They could do more to rein in buyers, and opened corruption investigations into the Quartermaster, Commissary, and Medical Departments. These uncovered minor criminality and led to rule changes, but as a historian of supply observes, Congress's real effort was "not to control day-to-day management, but to control fraud [and] achieve . . . public accountability."

The phrase "not worth a Continental" came into use around this time and has survived as a handy one believed to encapsulate America's economic troubles back then. Depreciation of the currency, however, was more a symptom than a cause of the distress. Much more disruptive was the upending of prior import and distribution patterns. The British naval blockade and occupation of New York City forced Americans to cart overland the goods formerly moved by intercoastal shipping, for instance from the breadbasket of Connecticut to mid-Pennsylvania. To do so during the blockade required crossing five major rivers whose ferries could operate only when the rivers were not at flood stage or iced over. The increased need for oxen for those trips had farmers breeding them and neglecting beef cattle and grains; to halt this practice, the state of Connecticut decreed that only one pair of oxen could be used to transport private property in the state, on pain of confiscation. The food and goods shortages, the blocking of exports, and the British marauding and destruction of towns combined to wrench the American economy into a severe depression. The drop in personal income was as precipitous, as widespread, and as persistent as that of the Great Depression in the twentieth century.

That Revolutionary America's state governments continued to institute price controls reflected the degree to which those legislatures had become republicanized—responsive to the will of the majority rather than solely to the elites, as they had been in colonial times. The controls had a further republican aim, according to a delegate to a convention on controls, to "fix the price of goods at a due proportion of soldiers' wages, [to honor those who] are continually taught to believe this, as an encouragement for enlisting. While they are fighting in defence of our liberties . . . they may reasonably expect, that we who remain at home, will exert ourselves in support of a law made to realize [the buying power of] their wages."

The merchants' plaint that controls sapped profit from their enterprises and did not provide better prices for customers, nor avail the merchants in state assemblies in the late 1770s, but it did in Congress. John Adams (lawyer, farmer) and Benjamin Rush (physician, educator) contended that merchants and farmers who refused to sell their goods to civilians for mandated prices should not be punished because they were only obeying the dictates of the law of supply and demand. Sam Adams disagreed: "I think every Step should be taken for the Downfall of such Wretches, and shall be ready to join in any Measure within Doors or without which shall be well adapted to this effect." The without-doors response was soon in evidence in Boston: When Thomas Boylston, a prominent merchant, did not want to sell his coffee and sugar for what the state said he must charge, a hundred women forced him to give up the keys to his warehouse, carted off its wares, and sold them for "fairer" prices. Abigail Adams reported to John "a great cry against the merchants, against monopolizers, etc., who, 'tis said, have created a partial scarcity." In Longmeadow, a female-led crowd donned blankets and face paint to combine the tactics of the Boston Tea Party and the Salem witch trials. They confronted a merchant couple who had overly raised the prices on imported Jamaican rum and molasses:

> Sirs: it is a matter of great grief that you Should give us cause to call upon you in this uncommon way. . . . We find you guilty of very wrong behaviour in selling at extravagant prices. . . . This conduct plainly tends to undervalue paper Currency which is very detrimental to the Liberties of America. We therefore as your offended Brethren demand satisfaction of you the offender by a confession for your past conduct and a Thorough reformation for time to Come.

This appeal to Matthew 7:12, "Do unto others as ye would have them do unto you," persuaded the errant couple to immediately lower prices, publicly accept their guilt, and offer an apology. The historian Barbara Clark Smith found reports of thirty other such incidents, in which participants expressed "the conviction that a fundamental relationship existed between these incidents and the patriot cause. . . . Rioters and their allies claimed that confronting merchants in their shops was a patriotic action, much like facing redcoats on the battlefield." Even so, Robert Abraham East, a historian of business in that era, concludes that while states did take action against some hoarding merchants, "the great merchants were seldom interfered with."

Commissary General Trumbull, blaming price controls for hampering his purchasing, and Congress for oversupervision, readied his resignation. Wadsworth, too, quit his Connecticut supply post but agreed to become deputy to Quartermaster Mifflin, who was busy scouting potential battlefields and bivouac sites. Washington insisted that he also ensure Philadelphia's bakeries keep supplying the army with bread while he did so, since "in our desultory state we shall have the greatest occasion for it, & shall feel much inconvenience if we don't have it."

Washington was rightly alarmed: British forces were at the mouth of the Delaware River, whence they could try to overrun Philadelphia, and a second large British army under Burgoyne was threatening to course down from Canada and take control of the Hudson Valley. The British plan was for the Howe and Burgoyne armies to meet and split the radical northeastern colonies from the moderate southern ones and end the rebellion. In the summer of 1777, the first parts of this plan were working. Bad news reached Congress from the Northern Department: In July, Burgoyne's troops retook the linchpin site of Fort Ticonderoga, its defending army only narrowly escaping. Congress then wrested command from Schuyler and returned it to Horatio Gates. Although Washington believed that Gates was trying to replace him as commander in chief, he dispatched to the Northern Department his most enterprising general, Benedict Arnold, as well as a sharpshooter battalion and the cannons from the *Amphitrite*. These turned the tide: Gates's forces prevailed in battles at Bemis Heights, winning Burgoyne's surrender at nearby Saratoga, with five thousand British and Hessian troops.

This was a huge triumph and a vitally important American victory. But it had not yet become known to Washington as he tried to prevent the British from taking Philadelphia. Forts on either side of the Delaware protected the city from a British riverine invasion, but the British could overwhelm it by land. On September 11 the armies clashed in the Battle of Brandywine Creek. American troops were outnumbered, and Washington was outgeneraled. His army suffered significant losses and was unable to keep Howe's from Philadelphia. The United States survived only because a few hundred troops, led by French engineer volunteers, were able to defend those Delaware forts successfully until the river iced over, which prevented Howe from augmenting his forces by sea and capturing the American army before it ever saw Valley Forge.

The Continental Congress moved to York. Hancock returned

home; his only child had died, and his businesses were so strained that his agent could collect less than 2 percent of what was owed. Morris continued to be involved from a home near York, while his partner, Willing, remained in British-occupied Philadelphia, to attempt to collect from those who owed the firm. Willing soon sent distressing news: Morris's half brother's "dissipation, extravagance, and total neglect . . . of all business" had made messes in France and Spain that so compromised the firm that it might have to be dissolved. In December 1777, Washington moved his forces to Valley Forge, eighteen miles northwest of Philadelphia. As he did, the British stole two thousand of his cattle. The absence of food was felt even more keenly because the winter was so cold that the Schuylkill River froze solid, making it unsuitable as a supply route. On December 23, 1777, Washington wrote to the new president of Congress, Henry Laurens: "Unless some great and capital change suddenly takes place . . . the Army must inevitably be reduced to one or the other of these three things. Starve—dissolve—or disperse, in order to obtain subsistence"; and to the governors: "We had in Camp . . . not less than 2898 Men unfit for duty by reason of their being bare foot and otherwise naked."

The army had not been fed in three days. The camp had no cattle, no soap, no vinegar, and only twenty-five barrels of flour. Washington pledged to the governors, though, to continue to "conceal the true state of the army from public view" despite that bringing him "calumny," because the British must not find out how vulnerable the Continental Army was at Valley Forge. The commander could only hope that his soldiers would have enough victuals, clothing, firewood, and shelter to survive until the spring, and that by then the American representatives in Paris would have succeeded in obtaining considerable help from France.

5

Valley Forge Dreams

The image of the starving, shivering troops at Valley Forge has been rightfully seared into Americans' understanding of the Revolutionary War, but we have little conception that ample food was available beyond Valley Forge. Not enough of it was brought to camp, and while responsibility for that lapse did rest in part, as Washington often groused, on the greed of some merchants and farmers, it was equally attributable to congressional intransigence. Refusals to pay going market rates to wagon owners and drivers, ostensibly to keep costs down, resulted in wagons sitting idle; and overdeference to former member Mifflin in not swiftly replacing him as supply chief allowed Mifflin, who was annoyed at Washington for spurning his military advice, to get away with doing almost nothing to relieve the army's suffering.

Several state governors, surprised to learn from a Washington circular letter of the shortages at Valley Forge, did dispatch supplies. Money to buy more was still lacking, however, and as Gen. Nathanael Greene wrote to Washington:

Money is the sinews of war, and an army cannot be supported without magazines, for its subsistance, and military Stores for it's appointments. I confess I think there is more reason to fear our funds and military stores will fail us than the want of [soldiers]—but the present plan for carrying on the war is ruinous to our funds—destructive to our magazines—& fatal to our men.

Laurens, now fully privy to such problems, during that harsh winter had an idea for rescuing America's finances: Mobilize the wealth of the wealthy. Used to luxury and comfort, he had been putting in eighteen-hour workdays in small quarters, lame from gout and subsisting on Valley Forge–type rations, bread, cheese, and grog. He outlined his idea in a letter to his son, John, an aide-de-camp to Washington. Since three million pounds were needed to properly fight the war and retire the debt, Laurens wanted five hundred wealthy Americans to start a pot of loans to the government. He would "subscribe to morrow five or Ten thousand Pounds Sterling & if these were found insufficient, all my Estate shall be given for saving the public." He believed that the example of the wealthy would inspire men of lesser means to buy in.

The notion was not unreasonable. There were several thousand wealthy heads of households in America, and although many were cash poor, there were perhaps a thousand who also had stashed away, as Laurens had, five to ten thousand pounds. But they did not rush to participate, for several likely reasons: Many of them were Loyalists—quite a few wealthy Loyalists were just then coming out of hiding in Philadelphia to fawn over Howe—and even the more Revolution-minded wealthy had a justifiable fear of an eventual American loss of the war, and with it, their fortunes. Then too, not all merchants were doing well: Thomas Doerflinger's study of the records of Philadelphia merchants found that while during the war traders "did enhance the efficiency and increase the diversity of the economy, the mainspring . . . was not general prosperity. Despite the rise of a few great fortunes, the capitals of many merchants shrank or stagnated."

Even such proven patriots as Wadsworth, who had advanced fifty thousand dollars for the cause and had not yet been reimbursed—in Continentals or in any other currency—were not inclined to risk more. "The want of this Money much retards my accounts," he wrote, "as it is in vain for me to call on People [to obtain new supplies] when I can't pay them." A Wadsworth friend at Valley Forge similarly advised that that he had lost "two or three thousand pounds" advanced for the public interest, "and I think I have done my part that way."

Laurens also wanted Congress to cut back on public expenses, institute "taxation in each Colony . . . clear the States of enemies—sell vacant and forfeited estates—encourage manufactures . . . and do a thousand other things which . . . we would do, if luxury and avarice were discountenanced."

Another quite reasonable idea for rescuing the country was birthed during this period by Laurens's son, John: mobilizing a different facet of its wealth, America's slaves. He and his young officer friends at Valley Forge—Lafayette, Hamilton, François Louis de Fleury, and Pierre L'Enfant—sought to double the size of the Continental army by enlisting slaves in exchange for their freedom. Free blacks were already serving in the army, and had shown their worth in every important battle so far, from the earliest skirmishes to the most recent. The British had mustered thousands of black soldiers by such promises—could Americans do less? Henry Laurens, who owned hundreds of slaves, would have objected had the idea come from anyone but his son; he did raise the caveat that slaveowners would need to be compensated for loss of manpower. Washington agreed. The young officers had an answer: Slaves would be freed only if their service was satisfactory, and in the interim owners would be given money to hire other workers. There was even precedent: Rhode Island, unable to raise its allotment of troops from the state's white males, had let slaves enlist in exchange for freedom.

Congress was not ready to tackle so thorny an issue.

Actually, Congress tackled almost no thorny issues. Where Henry Laurens called for cutting back on public outflow, the delegates warmed to a bill that would mean an even greater outflow and the future obligation—with Washington's approval—to award to the army's officers, currently earning only a third of what British officers did, half pay for life after the war. Dozens of officers were resigning every week, and as many line soldiers were deserting. Greene explained:

[They] compare their condition in the field with that at home—
the situation of their famelies, & their future prospects grow
into objects of importance. to return into private life with a

ruined fortune—with a broken constitution, after years of hard servitude—there to sink into neglect & almost contempt, are comfortless considerations.

To resist privilege is to uphold republican values, and the denial has the greatest effect when coming from one who is privileged. Laurens charged that half pay for officers would create an aristocracy that would rule America just as surely as Great Britain's did that country, and would make of retired officers "drones and Incumbrances of society, pointed at by Boys & Girls—there goes a Man who robs me every Year of part of my pittance." His principled opposition led to a compromise, half pay for officers for seven years after the war. He and Washington disagreed on little else. When Laurens received an unsigned letter accusing Washington of incompetence, he figured out that the writer's plan was to force him to read it aloud to Congress—as all such incoming letters to the president of Congress were to be—and for it to provide reasons to sack Washington and replace him with Gates, the victor at Saratoga. So Laurens announced that since the letter was anonymous, it need not be read; and then enclosed it in a missive to his son, knowing that John would show it to Washington, who would use it to prepare to counter all such accusations.

Those accusations came to Valley Forge in the form of a committee of legislators in late January 1778, a committee configuration we would recognize today: a set of critics whose real agenda was to assign blame for any shortcomings to the chief officer, as a prelude to replacing him. This 1778 committee visiting Valley Forge was led by Francis Dana, a Sons of Liberty lawyer, and by Joseph Reed, a former Washington aide who had become aligned with opponents of the commander. Washington had invited such a visit, so he could clear up misconceptions. Upon the visitors' arrival he handed them a fifteen-thousand-word report, composed by Hamilton from briefs by the commanders, specifically addressing all the problems, and he escorted them on a warts-and-all tour. To the credit of Dana, Reed, and their fellow committee members—and in contrast to modern committees that never let facts alter their preexisting conclusions—they soon confessed to Congress that they had had their minds changed by "the inevitable Force of Evidence," and now felt that "every nerve should be strained" to obtain meat to feed the army, since "the very Existence of this Army depends on its resources. . . . Should we neglect any prudent Precaution in providing . . . we very much fear [that] General Howe with his collected Force will ravage the middle States with Impunity." For several more weeks, the committee remained at Valley Forge, working out the details of the reorganization of supply with Washington's staff and senior commanders, while becoming convinced that congressional interference had been a significant contributor to the supply mess.

Commissary General Trumbull's resignation underscored that. He had earlier advised Washington: "I am willing to do & to suffer, for my Country and it's Cause, but I cannot Sacrifice my Honor & Principles." At Washington's request he had stayed on, fighting the system from within, but by early 1778 he'd had enough. To Congress he cited his ill health—indeed, he would die within a few months— but the underlying causes of discontent were lack of latitude in choosing his subordinates, and rules requiring those subordinates to post five-thousand-dollar bonds and to be responsible for what they could not control—food rotting and soldiers stealing. Prior to the war, the merchants and traders system relied on mutual trust and generally did not ask for or post bonds; but most members of Congress refused to believe that people poorer than they would operate honestly without the restraint of a posted bond. The insulting regulation provided experienced traders with a reason to refuse to continue in the supply cadre; they resigned and were replaced by grifters who conjured new ways to skim and to demand kickbacks. That transformation of the commissariat was why the visitors' committee to Valley Forge, known as the Committee at Camp, wrote that "The number of little, piddling, pilfering, Plunderers in the Character of Deputies and Deputies Assistants is sufficient almost to form an Army."

It should be noted that those deputies were also legitimately hampered by having to compete for scarce resources with British commissaries in Philadelphia, who willingly paid high rates to farmers and merchants, as they had in New York. "Almost open Trade is carried out from [New York] with the rebels," a Hessian officer wrote, adding: "Passionately anxious for gold and silver, [farmers and merchants] constantly brought us cattle and other provisions."

Many merchants in Philadelphia dealt with the British but concealed the transactions in the hope of avoiding later condemnation for consorting with the enemy. One was Tench Coxe, scion of a Philadelphia merchant family, who had been in exile in New York until he reentered Philadelphia with Howe, acting as guide to Gen. Charles Cornwallis. Although Coxe would later avow: "I never was in any employment whatever under Great Britain or her Governors, Generals, Admirals," during British control of Philadelphia he sold not only his own goods but also those of New Yorkers who shipped him their excess, and he acted as agent for New York shippers to obtain Royal Navy clearances to send their cargoes to the Caribbean.

Men such as Coxe and Duer throughout their careers played the angles and shifted allegiances, excusing their dalliances with the enemy as necessary to making money. The financial historian Tom Cutterham writes that "a knack for rhetoric, for speculation, and for promises" eased such men's interchanges with fellow merchants in a commercial community built on an honor code that included an admiration for risk taking.

That code now spurred Henry Laurens, himself a successful merchant, to question the previous activities of Morris with the Secret Committee. The South Carolinian had not been in Congress during that committee's most active period, but had heard and read enough about them to become incensed at Morris's having overly intertwined private and public businesses and possibly made undue profits. "You plead in excuse many other avocations," Laurens wrote Morris. "But why did you engage in so much more business than you were competent to? If private affairs would not admit of a close attention to your Public Duties . . . you should have relinquished in time and delivered up the Books in good order." Thus goaded, Morris finally compiled reports on the failed French tobacco trade and the successes with Beaumarchais and Deane. He offered again to turn over the books. But Laurens had no time to audit them and Congress no capable personnel, so Morris was told to keep the books, Congress begging leave to consult him "whenever we find ourselves embarrassed."

In March 1778 Congress, after receiving the Committee in Camp report and the demands of Greene and Wadsworth as conditions for acceptance of the posts of quartermaster general and commissary general, finally wrote the profit motive permanently into the supply equation. Henceforth all agents would earn commissions. The Hartford merchant had also insisted on being reimbursed for the now-$75,000 advanced to the government, and on the right to hire and fire subordinates, because, as he confided to a Connecticut delegate: "To undertake what I could not execute would be worse to me than Starving—indeed I had rather die." A tough-minded delegate wrote: "We have got Col. Wadsworth at the Head of the commissariate *unfettered* strictly so. Had the same steps as now been taken with Trumbull a year ago, amazing Sums would have been saved."

Wadsworth was also tougher on the states, warning Massachusetts that someone was buying up all their cattle, possibly with intent to sell them to the British: "I am persuaded You will not let the Cattle . . . depart out of Your State as it may be attended with the most fatal Consequences." He hired his longtime deputy Peter Colt, and others who had worked for him in the past. In short order the commissary was spending four million dollars a month, from which he and his subordinates were to split forty thousand dollars in commissions—in Continentals or in warrants that were likely to be redeemable only after the war ended, and then only if America was victorious. The huge amounts of provisions to be purchased and properties and personnel to be managed made for on-the-job training for a next generation of entrepreneurs. A typical third-tier commissary official, in charge, say, of the area west of Philadelphia, had more to buy, warehouse, and distribute than Hancock at the height of his prewar trading, and employed a greater number of men than Greene at his prewar ironworks.

It is doubtful that Congress and the armies could have continued the war without this new supply system in place, and as doubtful that the procurers would have worked as assiduously had potential profit not been embedded in the system.

After a year of delay France finally hurried up and negotiated two treaties with the United States, signed on February 6, 1778, a commercial pact and a military alliance that committed France to guarantee American independence. The latter was to be kept secret until Great Britain provided France with a casus belli. Both were sent to America with Silas Deane's brother Simeon, but his ship was delayed.

On March 4, while Silas was preparing to be formally presented at court, he was flabbergasted to receive from Congress a summons home. It had been spurred by the campaign of his colleague in negotiating with the French, Arthur Lee, to fault Deane for possible fraud and mingling private and public business, and to implicate in such endeavors the third commissioner, Franklin. Deane made plans to return to America aboard the French fleet then being readied, under the command of Adm. Charles Hector, comte d'Estaing.

Simeon Deane and the treaties reached York at the end of April. Congress immediately ratified the treaties despite the competing arrival of a British "peace" delegation that offered almost everything Americans had sought prior to the war, short of independence: very light import duties, representation in Parliament, and freedom to trade. The British commissioners even dangled the capital to establish a national bank. The acceptability of a bribe depends more on its timing than on its size: Had the British offer been made two years earlier, it might have been taken, but in 1778 Congress, French alliance in hand, dismissed it without discussion.

Before d'Estaing's fleet had reached the mouth of the Delaware, the British reacted to its rumored approach by abandoning Philadelphia. Departing with them were Tories who feared retaliation for cooperation during the occupation. Some who remained, such as Coxe, were put on trial, but most of the well-connected, including Coxe, avoided punishment.

Among the one hundred ships leaving Philadelphia with the British was a brig seized from Stephen Girard. In that seizure the French émigré lost almost his entire fortune; but that had happened several times already and, as with Derby, after this British bad behavior Girard became more American and more wrathful. He signed the new loyalty oath, becoming a citizen, and fitted out a new boat—as a privateer.

On July 4, 1778, French commercial agent John Holker met Morris at a celebratory dinner in Philadelphia and tried to persuade him to manage the "large Concerns and important Business" that French businessmen had committed to Holker's care. Morris demurred, but Holker and the French emissary, Conrad Alexandre Gérard, kept pressing, and shortly Morris was quite involved with Holker, whose mixing of private and public business was more blatant than his own.

By then d'Estaing's fleet was at Sandy Hook, the entrance to New York Harbor, waiting for a favorable tide to clear the sandbar. His provisions were exhausted. Washington sent him a herd of cattle. D'Estaing had difficulty obtaining other necessities, for instance fresh water. John Laurens, visiting the admiral, in a report to his father stated that the "disaffected inhabitants either refused their wagons [to haul the water], or granted them only at an exorbitant price." However, the admiral's money—a reputed £150,000 was offered—was not enough to persuade experienced pilots to guide his ships over the sandbar and face the myriad cannons of the British. Frustrated, d'Estaing took sail to Newport, the secondary target to which he and Washington had agreed.

The Franco-American Newport adventure took up many weeks in the summer of 1778, and was ultimately a fiasco brought on by several factors: d'Estaing's caution, based on his instructions and his decades of service; American general John Sullivan's questionable tactics and daredevil attitudes; and a natural disaster. Units from several American sources, including six thousand Massachusetts militiamen led by Hancock, readied for battle, but the joint Franco-American assault was aborted when a British fleet appeared, d'Estaing sailed out to meet it, and a hurricane severely damaged both fleets. The American land attack afterward was ineffective, and to Hancock's dismay the troops ostensibly under his command then deserted: The British garrison at Newport remained in place.

After d'Estaing's forces had removed to Boston to repair their ships, Wadsworth was chagrined to learn that some contracts for those forces had been awarded to suppliers outside the normal army chain, and warned his superiors: "If the French are not supplied I shall not think myself blameable whilst thus prevented by the interference of others." The more basic problem of supplying the armies lay in some of these merchants' lack of sensitivity to the notion that in a democracy all citizens were expected to act in more socially responsible ways than did their counterparts under autocratic regimes. Notable among the flaunters was Maryland delegate Samuel Chase. Back in July, while d'Estaing was idling off Sandy Hook, when Chase learned from a letter to Congress of an alarming scarcity of flour—a letter deliberately kept secret by Congress to prevent speculation—he conspired to corner the flour market. The next time Wadsworth visited Baltimore, to buy twenty thousand barrels of flour, he found prices wildly inflated and the future output of nearby mills already spoken for. This he reported to Congress, which then accused the Maryland delegation of revealing secret information. All the Marylanders but Chase denied involvement; he kept silent. Shortly Hamilton echoed the public's anger at speculators by pillorying Chase in the *New York Journal*. Chase lost his seat in the next Congress; but then as now, public dismay over politicians' licentiousness is often no more to them than a temporary inconvenience. Within a few years Chase would be back in favor.

Wadsworth had to feed four armies—Washington's, Sullivan's, d'Estaing's, and the captured Burgoyne's—and this necessity changed his prior free-marketeer stance of being against price controls. Now he pleaded for their reinstatement so that his budget would stretch far

enough to buy the needed supplies. Peter Colt reported to him some
of the difficulties attendant on buying the supplies:

> A great Number of unprincipled men are . . . engrossing, &
> buying up, on *Speculation*, every Article that the Country af-
> ford for the Subsistence of the Army—and then sell them again
> to the stationed Commissary—or transport them out of State,
> as best suits their interest—as these people are always in Cash,
> and are under no controuls, they have the advantage of those
> who are employed to purchase for the Army.

It was not the greed of merchants per se that alarmed the chron-
ically impecunious Thomas Paine; rather, what galled him was that
Morris, Wilson, and friends were using the war and the public's worries about shortages to try to regain control of Pennsylvania's government. Writing once more as Common Sense, Paine published in
the *Pennsylvania Packet* a series of articles on "a serious matter," the
Morris group's assaults on Pennsylvania's constitution. He warned
that if the wealthy managed to "expel the poor" from the state by
laws forcing them out,

> the rich will soon supply their places by becoming poor
> themselves, for where there are none to labor, and but few
> to consume, land and property is not riches. . . . I have heard
> it advanced, by those who have objected against the present
> [state] constitution, that it was a good one for a poor man. I
> reply, that for that very reason it is the best government for a
> rich one, by producing purchasers, tenants, and laborers, to the
> landed interest, and consumers to the merchants.

Paine left unfinished this series of articles to turn his attention
to Silas Deane, whom he viewed as the epitome of crooked insider
merchants. The Lee-Adams faction of Congress also tarred Deane
through guilt by association with other former congressmen's malfeasance, Mifflin's fraud as quartermaster, and a chief medical officer for

selling the army's medical supplies to civilians. As time would reveal, the sins of all three were either inadvertent or minor. But just then the general public, watching merchants throw lavish parties and import French furniture, was quite willing to believe that too many wealthy were profiting from the war.

Deane threw no parties and had nearly become impoverished while doing far more for his country than any of his congressional accusers, having obtained the munitions that assured the American victory at Saratoga and negotiated the alliance with France that maintained American independence. But the greater the problems facing a legislative body, the more acute its need for a scapegoat. In this instance, unable to solve the military supply problems, Congress yielded to the Lees and Adamses faction's antipathy to Deane, Morris, and Franklin, and for six months hammered at Deane on the floor of the House while refusing to allow him to speak in his own defense. When he finally published his explanation in the *Packet*, Laurens wanted Congress to condemn Deane officially for it, but the motion failed by one vote. Laurens took that as occasion to resign as president and return home. Then Paine, secretary of the Secret Correspondence Committee, citing committee records, accused Deane of fraud in an article that targeted the lack of patriotism and inherent greed of all merchants doing business with the government, including Morris, who was also mentioned by name. Paine, the Lees, and the Adamses wanted every man in government service to be as selfless as Washington and themselves, even though Lee family members had also mixed public and private business. Almost instantly the tables turned: Paine's disclosures of secret information subjected him to the same treatment as Deane—accusations in Congress while he was not permitted to refute them—and he was forced to resign.

Deane refused a settlement of ten thousand dollars, labeling that a small percentage of what he was owed, and unduly vindictive. His charge appeared all the more realistic when Congress approved an arrangement, suggested by Beaumarchais's agent, to delay paying him an owed two hundred thousand pounds until 1782 and to do so then by sending produce to France. The bad treatment of Deane discouraged other American merchants from devoting their energies and credit to the cause.

The marquis de Lafayette, to best serve that cause, had decided to return home and lend his now-resplendent prestige to the American request to Louis XVI for additional money, troops, and ships. D'Estaing, a distant cousin of Lafayette's, after repairing his ships in Boston, obeyed orders and sailed to the Caribbean. Once the British commander in New York realized that the d'Estaing fleet was leaving North America, at the end of 1778 he dispatched three thousand British, Hessian, and Loyalist troops to Savannah, to launch a "Southern Strategy" to separate the southern colonies from the northern ones to end the war. Continental forces under Benjamin Lincoln did not arrive in Savannah in time to prevent the British from capturing the city.

It was a low moment for the new country, Washington thought:

> The common interests of America are mouldering & sinking into irretrievable (if a remedy is not soon applied) ruin. . . . Speculation—peculation—& an insatiable thirst for rishes seems to have got the better of every other consideration. . . . Party disputes & personal quarrels are the great business of the day whilst the momentous concerns of an empire—a great & accumulated debt—ruined finances—depreciated money—& want of credit (which in their consequences is the want of every thing) are but secondary considerations & postponed from day to day.

Washington's point of view on these matters was shared by many of the poor. To them it seemed that the divide in the country between rich and poor, which had been superseded at the time that independence was declared, had since reemerged and widened. On one side were those on the front lines, the laborers, mechanics, indentured servants, and small farmers risking their lives in battle; and on the other side were merchants and farmers, managing to remain at home, not risking combat but making money from wartime scarcity. That this white-and-black portrait was not entirely accurate did not deter such thoughts.

The reemergence of the split between rich and poor was made manifest in Massachusetts in its wealthier citizens' response to a draft of a proposed state constitution that too closely resembled Pennsylvania's in its provisions for protecting debtors from creditors, for enfranchising voters who did not own property, and for a unicameral legislature. In reaction to it, in April 1778 businessmen and lawyers convened at Essex, debated the issues, and summed them up in a report known as the Essex Result. Its stunning central tenet: "The legislative body should be so constructed [that] every law affecting property, should have the consent of those who hold a majority of the property." To achieve that end the Result recommended adding a senate comprised of large property holders, to balance the popularly elected house. Conceding that "the bulk of the people," as reflected in a lower house, were the best source of "political honesty, probity, and a regard for the interest of the whole," the Essex Result nonetheless asserted the need for a senate of "men of education and fortune" who would provide "the greatest wisdom, firmness, consistency, and perseverance." The Result also advocated property ownership requirements for candidates for state office. Its recommendations were Puritanism redux, the conflating of commercial self-interests with the conceit that wisdom was reserved for a select few. John Adams had embraced that combination in 1776, writing that men without property were "too little acquainted with public Affairs to form a Right Judgment, and too dependent upon other Men to have a Will of their own." But Adams was also in favor of providing the poor with ways to accumulate the needed property:

> The balance of power in a society accompanies the balance of property in land. The only possible way, then, of preserving the balance of power on the side of equal liberty and public virtue, is to make the acquisition of land easy to every member of so-

ciety; to make a division of land into small quantities, so that
the multitude may be possessed of landed estates. If the multitude is possessed of the balance of real estate, the multitude
will take care of the liberty, virtue, and interest of the multitude
in all acts of governance.

Shortly, enough voters agreed with the Essex conveners to reject
the proposed constitution, and chose delegates to a convention that
would write a replacement.

Both Commissary Wadsworth and Quartermaster Greene were doing superb jobs, according to Washington and Congress, but within
months of appointment they considered resigning because their salaries, paid to them in Continental dollars, were so rapidly losing value.
Commiserating, they became friends, and in an attempt to preserve
the value of their incomes, secretly capitalized a new supply firm,
to be headed by Barnabas Deane, another merchant brother of Silas
(and a privateer owner). Greene cautioned Wadsworth not to publi-
cize their participation, because "however just and upright our conduct may be, the World will have suspicions to our disadvantage. . . .
By keeping the affair a secret I am confident we shall have it more in
our power to serve the commercial connection than by publishing
it." Wadsworth was adamant that nothing in the establishing or operating of the enterprise would be contrary to law or morality, but he
yielded to Greene's caution.

Bingham in Martinique, similarly having advanced money to underwrite privateers, and having sent home scads of war matériel, was
nearly bankrupt because Congress was so slow to pay yet was insistent that he continue to shell out for repairs and for the outfitting of
American vessels arriving in the Caribbean. Because he hadn't been
able to pay some of his bills, he faced confiscatory judgments from St.
Eustatius to Boston, notably from George Cabot. One of Cabot's privateers, the *Pilgrim*, had captured a ship named the *Hope* and brought
it into Martinique for Bingham to sell. The captain of the *Pilgrim*

asserted that the *Hope* was British, but its captain told Bingham he was Danish and that all of the crew spoke Danish. Bingham therefore concluded that the *Hope* was a protected neutral; he sold its perishable cargo of flour, and from that sale gave the captain some money for repairs and held the rest in escrow for the U.S. government. The Cabots then sued him for taking away the *Pilgrim*'s lawful prize. In a Boston court Bingham was capably defended, yet lost in a rigged proceeding. The Cabots' judgment against him allowed them to place a lien on Bingham's property in Philadelphia. Only the indulgence of the Martinique governor prevented Bingham from being imprisoned.

When Congress awarded Bingham a partial bill of exchange, drawn on the Paris commissioners, he cashed it in Martinique and obtained a brief respite from some of his debt—but not of that to Cabot. His obligations and outgo soared again after the Franco-American pact, when even more vessels arrived with instructions that Bingham should pay for repairs and outfitting. It was still an open question whether, when he returned home, he would be poorer and indebted or Congress would pay up and make him far wealthier.

6

Interlude: Assault on Fort Wilson

When the British evacuated Philadelphia in June 1778, supporters of the new nation were joyful. However, in the ensuing months prices and supplies did not improve, roiling the city. Flour became a flashpoint: Angry citizens assaulted a merchant who held a contract to provide flour for the military and would not sell any of it to civilians. In January 1779 an event took place that presaged an open clash of civilian rich and poor: The Pennsylvania Supreme Executive Council issued an order to prosecute price gougers for "most heinously criminal [acts] ruinous to the industrious poor."

As with many supposedly populist decrees, this one was spurred into existence by arrogance and faulty information. Robert Morris and partners, among them the French commercial agent Holker, had a ship full of flour in the Philadelphia harbor but would not acknowledge ownership nor sell the flour, which was consigned to the d'Estaing fleet that had not yet returned to the United States from the Caribbean.

Morris was himself a flashpoint, so unpopular that his presence on a political slate, or his known backing of one, was enough to sink it. That had happened recently when he and Wilson had attempted to elect enough of their wealthy colleagues to the assembly to amend the Pennsylvania constitution, and failed to win. In reaction, in March 1779, Morris and friends decided to form a Republican Society, touting it in a newspaper advertisement as a haven for "moderates" such as Mifflin and Richard Bache, Franklin's son-in-law. The Republican

Society also laid claim to being more patriotic than others, asserting in the advertisement that some members had served in Congress and in state councils, "and in the darkest seasons . . . neither betrayed nor deserted our trusts, when we sat with halters around our necks." Benjamin Rush described his eighty-four fellow members as "distinguished for their wealth, virtue, learning, and liberality of manners."

In opposition to the Republican Society, a Constitutional Society was formed by those who had written the state constitution, plus Paine, and the painter and militia leader Charles Willson Peale, and Joseph Reed, the current president of the state's Supreme Executive Council. The Constitutionalists pledged resistance to "the whole country [being] imposed on by forestallers and monopolizers."

Then, overnight between May 22 and 23, the price of flour doubled. The next morning, a broadside summoned an assembly: "In the midst of money we are in poverty and exposed to want in a land of plenty. You that have money and you that have none, down with your prices, or down with yourselves." A speaker at the meeting charged: "The tax laid on us by monopolizers and forestallers amounts to more money than would carry the war on twelve months to come." The attendees formed a committee to force the rollback of prices. Its members were mostly militiamen. Its justification, printed in the *Pennsylvania Packet* and influenced by or directly written by Paine, was a precise statement of the perceived need for intervention in a free market, one that still resonates today:

> The social compact or state of civil society, by which men are united or incorporated, requires that every right and power claimed or exercised . . . should be in subordination to the common good, and that whatever is incompatible therewith, must, by some rule or regulation, be brought into subjection thereto. . . . [The merchants'] idea of a free trade is, for every man to do as he pleases . . . which . . . is repugnant to the very principles on which society and civil government are founded.

During the following week, as the militia continued to seize warehouses and jail their owners, a subcommittee fixated on Morris's flour ship in the harbor, and demanded to see Morris. He received a delegation that included Paine and let them in on the secret that the flour was for the French. They still saw fit to publicly accuse him, in the *Packet,* of engrossing and monopolizing. He then published his own account in the *Packet.*

Prices continued to rise. On July 1 the militia warned: "We have arms in our hands and know how to use them. . . . If . . . your [price control] Committee find themselves inadequate to the task, *our drum shall beat to arms.*" A few days later, a town meeting featured the Republican Society's Morris, Wilson, Rush, and Deane. The next day the committee read out the names of merchants believed to be price-fixing. Holker came in for abuse; French plenipotentiary Gérard, upset over that and the seizing for public use of flour consigned to the French, threatened to move the legation out of state.

Pennsylvania then held elections to choose price-fixing committees. Morris headed a Republican Society slate in Philadelphia pledged to abolish controls. It was rejected, 2,115 to 281, an indication of how oblivious the wealthy were to the desires of the vast majority. The radicals similarly triumphed in Lancaster and Reading. Price controls would continue. But Pelatiah Webster now made his objection to them on principle known in a new pamphlet. His explanation for why price controls never accomplish much was as powerful, and as relevant today, as the price-control committee's on the other side. Contending that the restricting of prices hurt farmers and merchants and resulted in fewer supplies for everyone, he wrote that:

Trade should be as free as air [and as] uninterrupted as the tide. Every limitation on prices . . . checks the circulation of money, than which nothing can be more dangerous. . . . Business immediately stagnates, goods can't be had, people can't purchase with their money the necessaries they want, they begin of course to think that their money is worth nothing, and refuse to take any more of it, and grow willing to part with what they have of it for a depreciated value, so that the certain [result] of a limitation of prices is a further depreciation of the money instead of the contrary.

After another month, with prices continuing to rise, the people's committee ceded back to the state the fixing of prices. However, the militiamen still wanted to enforce controls, and on October 4 gathered at Paddy Byrne's Tavern. They asked Commander Peale to lead them, but he refused, so a few announced a plan to "drive from the city" British supporters, forestallers, and monopolizers. They arrested four merchants and paraded them about town.

Wilson, Mifflin, Morris, and friends, reasoning that the militia would next come after them, took preparatory action. Mifflin convened the First City Troop, had them issued rifles, and went to Wilson's house to drill him and twenty friends in defensive skills. Wilson barricaded himself in with Morris, Mifflin, and a few other Republican Society members. The "mob"—militia members—approached. Shots erupted from both sides, barrages following. The only casualty in "Fort Wilson" was the man who loosed the first shot. But four militiamen and a young black bystander lay dead, and seventeen others were badly wounded, most from the militia but including Mifflin's brother. The firefight lasted until Reed arrived with the First City Troop and ended it.

The incident was over but its effects lingered on. To prevent further violence, flour was given free of charge to the families of those serving in the military, and Morris and Reed sent messages to merchants to avoid gouging the public and to work harder to curry its favor. The plea did not avail, for in the November 1 elections the reinvigorated militia and its allies turned out of state office many Republican Society stalwarts.

This electoral defeat of the Republican Society slate only reinforced the belief of Morris, Wilson, and friends that the poor not only rejected their sensible notions but were dismissive of their substantial contributions to the war effort. Their generosity ignored and their ideas rejected, Morris and friends decided to push harder to replace Pennsylvania's anti-wealth-holder constitution and its irresponsible assembly with the kind of governance more attuned to creating conditions that would enhance their economic activities and be less inclined to blame the wealthy for the country's ills.

7

Bricks Without Straw:
The Path to Yorktown

*W*e can no more support the Army without cash, than the Israelites could make bricks without straw," Nathanael Greene wrote to Washington around the time of the Fort Wilson incident, and he accompanied the observation with a letter to Congress urging a redoubling of efforts to supply the army and resigning as quartermaster general. The states' response to renewed appeals for help was meager.

That the army was nonetheless supplied during this critical period prior to the French sending larger forces to assist the United States is overlooked by most history books. The heroes were not well-known leaders; they were the dozens and dozens of quartermasters and commissaries who, when government money and credit were exhausted, spent their own money, and then their own credit, and then the credit of their friends and relatives, to obtain supplies: "My Credit is nearly sunk with the people here from my not being able to comply with my promises to them," one such quartermaster wrote. "They now declare they will not part with their property in future to the public without the Money [cash] laid down to them." Estimates of how deeply these government agents went into debt on the country's behalf range from one to five million dollars. Most were never repaid.

Three factors exacerbated the supply problem. Two were beyond Congress's control: the British naval blockade and the Hessian Fly infestation that devastated grain crops. The third was provided by

Congress itself, in an attempt to stem depreciation. In late summer 1779 the members had become frightened upon learning that the amount of the country's debt, the sum total of all those emitted Continentals, had reached $160 million. This should not have been news to them, but they acted as though it was, on September 3 ordering the shutdown of the printing presses once the total reached $200 million.

Would stopping the presses stem depreciation? Franklin, then in Paris, thought there was no need to try. He wrote a friend in Boston that although he understood depreciation's "evil" effects as a "kind of imperceptible Tax, everyone having paid a part of it in the fall of value," he was not unhappy about it: "This Currency as we manage it is a wonderful Machine. It performs its Office when we issue it; it pays & clothes Troops, & provides Victuals & Ammunition; and when we are oblig'd to issue a Quantity excessive, it pays itself off by depreciation."

The September 3, 1779, congressional stop-the-presses decree galled two young outsiders to Congress, James Madison, then twenty-eight, and Alexander Hamilton, then twenty-five. Madison thought the edict was an illusion that Congress was foisting on the public. A Virginian with large landholdings and many slaves, a scholar of Greek and Hebrew and a specialist in religious liberty, before then Madison had interested himself only in Virginia affairs and had refused entreaties to serve in Congress. But once his friend Jefferson had become governor, Madison let his name be put forward, and in the spring of 1780 he would go to Congress, one of a dozen men newly selected by the states in answer to Washington's plea to the governors to "not only choose, but absolutely compel" their ablest men to go to Congress, and once there, to investigate the "causes" of the "disagreeable effects" of congressional poor management and "correct . . . public abuses." Mindful of such concerns, Madison between the September 3 decree and his leaving for Philadelphia penned an essay with a simple title, "Money." He began by observing that when Congress had had the "indefinite power of emitting money on the credit of their constituents they had the whole wealth and resources of the continent within their command." But once they decided to shut the presses, "the power has been entirely given up and they are now as dependent on the states as the King of England is on the Parliament. They can neither pay nor feed a single soldier, nor execute any other purpose but as the means are first put into their hands." He assailed the assumption underpinning the two-hundred-million-dollar cap, that "the value of money will be regulated by its quantity," and blasted the government for trying to justify the cap by claiming that there was a difference between paper money, which was being stopped, and loan certificates, which were still being issued. "No expedient could perhaps have been devised more preposterous and unlucky," he wrote, charging that Congress thought it "a piece of dexterity in finance, by *emitting loan-office certificates*, to elude the necessity of *emitting bills of credit*." The points made in the essay deserved wide consideration, but Madison showed it only to friends.

To Alexander Hamilton the stop-the-presses order and two-hundred-million-dollar cutoff-point edict sent a different signal: of how badly the government's finances needed reform. In a letter whose recipient is believed to have been New Hampshire delegate John Sullivan, Hamilton proposed an alternate way to halt and sink the emissions, by capitalizing a two-hundred-million-dollar bank and having the proceeds from sales of its stock redeem all prior federal debt. "I am aware," he wrote, "how apt the imagination is to be heated in projects of this nature," but "the only plan that can preserve the currency is one that will make it the *immediate interest* of the moneyed men to co-operate with the government in its support." Hamilton would pique that interest by offering to double their money in ten years, and to assert that the proceeds from stock sales would underwrite the war for three years and produce "very beneficial contracts" between the bank and the army, "by which money may be saved to the public, the army better furnished, and the profits of the Bank extended." No one at the time paid attention to Hamilton's ideas either.

Although Hamilton, Madison, and Franklin downplayed the loss in value of the Continentals, commercially active men felt it keenly and it acted as a damper on individual economic patriotism. For example, it forced Derby to cease sending out his vessels as privateers to capture prizes, since he could only sell privateering prizes in American courts and for Continentals. He had done that for several years, but now, instead of sending the ships as privateers he obtained letters of marque-and-reprisal that allowed his ships to transport cargo as well as to capture British commercial vessels and to sell those prizes, along with their own cargo, in foreign ports. In places such as Bilbao they could be exchanged for currency that was more solid than the Continentals—and in sales from which the American government would profit far less. Derby then committed a substantial fraction of his resources to complete the *Grand Turk*. During the remaining years of the war, and even though half of all Derby's other vessels operated at a loss or were taken, the *Grand Turk* captured seventeen prizes, five off Ireland, which were then sold in Bilbao's prize court. He did spend some of his profit to outfit American navy vessels launched from Salem, an activity that brought him little public acknowledgment and no inside track for a government contract.

Privateer owner Stephen Girard responded to depreciation by spreading his bets, a strategy that similarly multiplied his profits and decreased the government's income from his ships. He sometimes sent them out as privateers, sometimes with letters of marque, and at times as straight commercials. He sometimes shipped his cargoes in his own bottoms, and at times in others'. He bought used ships, had them make a few voyages, and resold them before they deteriorated further. He, too, lost half of his ships to the British, but prospered because as the war went on each shipload became even more valuable. The increasing French involvement in America's war energized Girard's connections to Bordeaux, where his father still operated—that year ninety-five ships for America cleared Bordeaux—and to the French Caribbean, where his brother had a firm.

Debtors love depreciation when it enables them to pay creditors and taxes in money whose face value is higher than its current worth.

In Massachusetts, they had done that so frequently that it spooked the constructors of the new state constitution, John Adams, Sam Adams, and merchant James Bowdoin. The latter two ceded the task to John, the country's reigning expert on constitutions, author of the 1776 pamphlet *Thoughts on Government*, a set of letters written when he was helping North Carolina, Virginia, and New Jersey with their constitutions. Since then, Adams had been exposed in Philadelphia to the real-world consequences of Pennsylvania's constitution, which provided the sort of negative lessons from experience that are often more deeply influential than positive ones. While in Adams's draft for Massachusetts he copied Pennsylvania's tenet that the "natural, essential, and unalienable rights" included "acquiring, possessing, and protecting property," he rejected Pennsylvania's debtor-friendly unicameral legislature, powerless chief executive, too-easily-replaced judiciary, and the schemes that gave greater weight to the population of the countryside than to that of the state's largest city. Massachusetts would have a senate to balance a popularly elected assembly. Each town's representation in the assembly would be proportional to its population, but the number of senators would be based on each district's tax burden. He initially wanted for the governor an absolute veto of legislative action, but had to settle for a veto that could only be overridden by a two-thirds vote of the legislature. In a particularly felicitous suggestion, he desired the state to become a "commonwealth," a concept reflecting that much of its true wealth was held in common. How the Massachusetts constitution would operate would depend largely on the character of the first governor: To his and Sam's dismay the leading candidate was Hancock.

In March 1780, as the American and British armies readied to leave winter camps, Congress dropped the second shoe in its plan to halt the rising debt and depreciation. It decreed that henceforth forty dollars of previously issued Continentals would be worth only one dollar, and directed the states to "revise their laws . . . making the continental bills of credit a tender in discharge of debts and contracts." Congress also recommended that these state changes should be the "most conducive to justice, in the present state of the paper currency." While the halting of the presses had done little except make supplying the army more difficult, this devaluation of the currency had a significant effect: At a single stroke, it reduced two hundred million dollars in debt to a more manageable five million. The devaluation produced only shrugs from the merchants, service providers, and farmers who since 1775 had had to accept Continentals in payment, since the currency's value had already sunk quite far. It helped consumers a bit by reducing prices, but helped merchants even more by undercutting the perceived need for price controls. Prior to the announcement, a multistate convention on controls had been called, to adopt "some measure . . . for introducing a stable medium of trade, that will render a limitation of prices unnecessary," as Connecticut delegates wrote home. When the devaluation announcement obviated the convention's need to act, it dissolved.

The devaluation stunned the French. Vergennes told Adams, once again in Paris: "While I admit, Sir, that [Congress] might have recourse to the expedient in order to remove their load of debt, I am far from agreeing that it is just & agreeable . . . to extend the effect to strangers." The norm for a European kingdom was to devalue money to its citizens but to pay its debts to foreigners at the old rate. Adams rejected a two-tier formulation, and French suppliers became more reluctant to send goods. Fortunately the king had already decided to dispatch Jean-Baptiste Donatien de Vimeur, comte de Rochambeau, and thousands of troops to America.

Just then William Bingham was returning home from Martinique. The previous December, when John Jay had landed there en route to Europe, he found Bingham under enormous financial stress, notably from the Cabots' *Pilgrim* suit, and wrote Congress that it needed to pay off debts incurred on its behalf by all American agents. That letter, along with Bingham's eight-page summary of his work, some financial records, and a certificate of appreciation from the French governor helped him with Congress. Rather than forcing Bingham to run the political gauntlet, as it had with Deane, Congress awarded Bingham some money immediately, and within months most of the rest that he was owed, making him overnight one of the country's wealthiest men. Shortly, his marriage to Willing's eldest child, sixteen-year-old Anne, made his personal net worth soar.

Writing to Jay after returning home, Bingham said: "The sentiments of the people in this country I found surprisingly altered since I left it . . . no longer governed by that pure, disinterested patriotism which distinguished the Infancy of the contest; private Interest seemed to predominate over every other Consideration that regarded the public weal." This feeling was shared by many who were far closer to poverty, for instance by soldier-diarist Joseph Plumb Martin of the Connecticut Line—the state's regular troops—which was just then on the verge of a mutiny. Martin wrote: "Here was the army starved and naked, and there the country sitting still and expecting the army to do notable things while fainting from sheer starvation." Martin could do little about his situation, but the newly superwealthy Bingham could, through a plan to aggregate his money and that of his wealthy friends in a bank chartered to help the American army. Three years earlier Laurens's attempt to have private individuals of wealth lend money to alleviate the country's distress had gone nowhere. But now in Philadelphia even Paine was embracing the idea, proposing a subscription to equip the army and pledging his own five hundred dollars. Morris, Willing, and Bingham were more able than Paine to raise the money, and they were spurred by a looming defeat for the American forces in Charleston.

Benjamin Lincoln's army, the country's second largest, was inside that city and was attempting to hold off a much larger British force. Another Continental army had been sent to its rescue but was stuck in transit. And even though Charleston desperately needed more soldiers, the South Carolina legislature had again refused the plan of John Laurens, who had hastened to defend his home city and pleaded for the enlistment of slaves, this time aided by a congressional resolution authorizing South Carolina and Georgia to raise three thousand men each and pledging to compensate owners at one thousand dollars per slave. South Carolina's intransigence was suicidal, for should

Charleston fall, the slave-owning legislators' own crops would be worthless—with Savannah already in British hands, there would be no nearby Atlantic ports from which to send their crops overseas.

It was a moment when the future of the United States of America as an independent, democratic country seemed far less than assured, among many reasons because Charleston, economic center of the South, might soon fall to the British. In late May of 1780, with the fate of Charleston still unknown to Bingham, Morris, and Willing, but much on their minds, they met at the Philadelphia Coffee House and agreed to put up money for recruitment and supplies for the army, and to solicit others to join them in the effort. On June 8 they brought together some of those like-minded friends, and in the following nine days raised £400 in specie and £101,360 in Continentals. Then the news of Charleston's surrender arrived. Benjamin Lincoln, John Laurens, and Louis Duportail, the army's chief engineer, had all been taken prisoner, along with thousands of troops: Charleston was the worst American defeat of the war. Was this loss the "signal misfortune" that would finally spur the populace to action, Bingham wondered in a letter to Jay. It did so for Philadelphia's wealthy: On June 17 Bingham, Morris, Willing, Wilson, and ninety-three others pledged £315,000—an average of £3,250 apiece—to form a bank "to be established for furnishing a supply for provisions for the armies of the United States." Wilson, in a paper presented at this meeting, made the intention explicit: Private support was to be given in exchange for the government's "encouragement of the spirited Aims and Efforts of Individuals."

The establishing of this bank was of a piece with the writing of the new Massachusetts constitution and with the forty-for-one devaluation of the currency: All were acts of a counterrevolution by the wealthy, to take back control from the radicals who had instigated the Revolution but whose governance efforts seemed no longer adequate for a country in serious debt. Paine, always ahead of the curve, summed up this change and emphasized its importance in a letter to Reed:

While the war was carried on by emissions at the pleasure of Congress, any body of men might conduct public business, and the poor were of equal use in government with the rich. But when the means must be drawn from the country the case becomes altered, and unless the wealthier part throw in their aid, public measures must go heavily on.

Reed signaled his agreement by becoming a backer of the bank, in common cause with his opponents who just a year earlier had formed the Republican Society.

Testament to the need for this little bank—and to the clout of its wealthy backers—was Congress's rapid passage of a resolution: "That the faith of the United States be pledged to the subscribers for their effectual reimbursement." Congress also placed fifteen thousand pounds in the bank. On July 17 it opened in Philadelphia and did precisely what it had been established to do—buy and transport supplies to the troops. The Philadelphia bank's pioneering effort was soon replicated in Boston, Salem, and in other coastal towns in Virginia and Maryland. In Connecticut, Wadsworth, now in a private capacity, assured the assembly that he and his partners would sell their goods at deflated prices to keep the state's expenditures for supplies to a reasonable level.

This collective effort, mainly by the wealthy, to sustain the armies in the field was an important factor in America's being able to continue the war. Yet biographies of Washington, his generals, Paine, and important players such as Adams, Jefferson, and even Hamilton do not report it. Hamilton was certainly aware of the little bank, and while he did not participate in it he did mention it in a latterly famous letter to New York congressman James Duane, who had asked him for his thoughts on what was lacking in the government. Too much power remained with the states, Hamilton replied, even though "the public good required, that [Congress] should have considered themselves as vested with full power *to protect the republic from harm*," including raising taxes to fight the war. Hamilton wanted to cease having the states furnish supplies to the army—the central government must do it, through "a foreign loan, heavy pecuniary taxes, a tax in kind, [and] a bank founded on public and private credit." He was dismissive of the Morris bank—"I was in hopes it was only the embryo of a more permanent and extensive establishment"—and argued that its inadequacies made the case for a much larger institution.

Though the "embryo" bank did not impress Hamilton, it did influence the thinking of George III and Louis XVI. The existence of the Philadelphia bank, and of its imitators in other American cities, gave the lie to the British king's prior contention that a combination of America's financial troubles and poor harvests would soon end the American insurgency—the United States had now shown that it would not crumble under financial pressure. As important, the little bank gave the French king ammunition to refute ministerial complaints that France was doing more than the United States to underwrite the war, a necessary assurance obtained at a critical juncture, the July 1780 arrival in Newport, Rhode Island, of Rochambeau, 5,500 soldiers, a small fleet, and many new, long-range cannons.

Rochambeau's was the significant force that Lafayette had cajoled from Louis XVI. It was only a small fraction of France's army of 250,000, but France's resources were spread thin in defending three maritime coasts and its possessions in the Caribbean, Africa, and India. In Newport, Rochambeau, known as a fighting man, demonstrated that he was also a good diplomat who had learned the lessons of the d'Estaing debacle: He charmed Newporters by mounting parades and concerts, and by spending lots of specie.

Washington was eager for Rochambeau's forces to join his and for them together to recapture New York—the only target, he believed, whose fall would end the war. Rochambeau resisted Washington on this, and when they met in person at Wadsworth's home on September 22, 1780, Rochambeau by a series of logical questions led Washington to agree that their joint resources were still too small to attack New York, and to sign a joint letter to Louis XVI asking for more ships, more soldiers, and more money. While Washington was with Rochambeau in Hartford, Benedict Arnold tried to hand over West Point to the British, a calamity only narrowly averted. At about the same time, at sea, the British captured Henry Laurens, en route to the Netherlands to negotiate a large loan, and clapped him into the Tower of London. Congress, learning of Laurens's capture, appointed his son John, recently paroled from Charleston, to complete the mission.

In American mythology, Rochambeau lands with his forces, and soon after, he and Washington obtain the surrender of the British at Yorktown. But fifteen months separate the Rochambeau arrival in July 1780 and the Battle of Yorktown in October 1781. The interim was filled with tension, not the least of it regarding money. While the American forces had to struggle to find enough supplies to survive, the French had plenty of money. American provisioners saw in the French forces a good opportunity to profit. Three American groups actively sought its contracts. One was led by Holker, the former attaché, who by then had been forced out of the legation by the new plenipotentiary, Anne-Cesar, chevalier de La Luzerne, but who was still in a prime position to contract with Rochambeau and had eager partners—Morris, Duer, and Schuyler. A second group was led by Wadsworth, with the enthusiastic backing of Lafayette; and the third, by the lesser-known merchants James Blakely and Gideon Delano, who as Cutterham puts it, "won the bulk of the French business early on by promising speedy delivery of anything General Rochambeau might need. In return they charged extravagant sums in both specie and bills of exchange." Wadsworth, thinking he was a shoo-in, had begun work prior to the expedition's arrival, and was stunned when the cattle that he sent to the Newport camp were rejected as too small. Holker's group was also at work; Duer wrote to his partners of his complicated scheme to make even more money than what they had been advanced: Rather than immediately buy the wheat they promised to deliver, Duer would use the advance to purchase, cheaply, certain dry goods that he knew wheat-growing farmers wanted, and barter these dry goods for the wheat, thereby realizing an extra twenty thousand pounds despite having to set aside money for bribes to the ultimate purchasers, since, as he confided to his partners: "French wheels, as I am informed, require Grease, as well as English."

The Delano scheme was exposed by François-Jean de Bouvoir,

marquis de Chastellux, a literary star and Rochambeau's second in command, who lambasted Delano and his partner as "undertakers without fortune, and without character; who promised everything, performed nothing, and soon threw our affairs into confusion." The epithets also applied to the Duer-Holker group. At Chastellux's insistence Wadsworth was reinstated and, Chastellux wrote, "resumed the affairs with as much nobleness as he had quitted them." Wadsworth did so with a new partner, a French-speaking Newport resident known as John Carter, who was actually British immigrant John Barker Church, who had recently eloped with a Schuyler daughter. Carter was an astute businessman, but what clinched their deal was a well-timed threat by Wadsworth to call in the loan of a man whom Delano had used as a cattle supplier if he did not switch his allegiance. The new firm was also able to accept an arrangement that others refused, a cash advance of only one-third, with two-thirds in bills of exchange payable later in France. But it was no wonder that Rochambeau wrote to the war minister:

> The business of this country hinges on a dozen merchants who are the masters of money and credit. They are not responsible to me or to you, Monsieur, nor even to Congress. They open and close their purses when they will. . . . The [Americans'] naked troops cannot draw an écu from the pocket of the most patriotic merchant, save at an immoderate interest.

Even so, Rochambeau contributed to the increasing dominance of Wadsworth and Carter by agreeing to contract exclusively with them.

Almost before the winter of 1780 had set in, the supplies bought by the small Philadelphia bank had been used up: three million rations, three hundred hogsheads of rum, and other victuals. But the bank's utility during its brief period of operation had highlighted the need for a government-associated bank, as Wilson emphasized in his "Observations on Finance, adapted to the present Conjuncture of Affairs in the United States," issued in the fall. The pamphlet called for rolling over what remained of the little bank's assets into a full-scale national bank that would provide credit to businesses as well as to the government. Steuart had asserted in his 1767 *Political Oeconomy*: "Without credit, there is no borrowing of money, no trade, no industry, no circulation, no bread for the lower classes, not even the convenience of life for the rich." Wilson made that idea more specific in writing that banks were good at "melting down" houses, farms, and other real property into collateral for loans. That was precisely why merchants, traders, and other businessman wanted to have a bank, so they could utilize the underlying value of their assets as a basis for a bank lending them money and credit to expand their enterprises. But there were also cogent objections to banks, based mostly on how the Bank of England had operated: The military veteran and significant western Pennsylvania landholder William Maclay feared a bank would be only an "aristocratic engine . . . operating like a tax in favor of the rich, against the poor, tending to the accumulation in a few hands; and under this view may be regarded as opposed to republicanism." While Maclay granted that the same accusations could be leveled against any accumulations of wealth or property, "the great point is, if possible, to prevent the making of [a bank into] a machine for the mischievous purposes of bad ministers."

By the end of 1780 the little Philadelphia bank's resources were exhausted and so were those of the army at Morristown, New Jersey. According to its general, Anthony Wayne:

> We are reduced to dry bread and beef for our food, and to cold water for our drink. Neither officers nor soldiers have received a single drop of spirituous liquors . . . since the 10th of October last, [and] this, together with the old worn out coats and battered linen overalls, and what was once a poor substitute for a blanket (now divided among three soldiers), is but very wretched living and shelter against the winters piercing cold, drifting snows, and chilling sleets. Our soldiers . . . have now served their country with fidelity for near five years, poorly

clothed, badly fed, and worse paid: of the last article, trifling as it is, they have not seen a paper dollar . . . for near twelve months.

On the evening of January 1, 1781, after carousing to celebrate the New Year, two brigades of privates and noncommissioned officers of the Eleventh Regiment of the Pennsylvania Line, stationed at Monmouth, New Jersey, seized six cannons and announced their intent to march to Philadelphia. There, since their commissioned officers had refused to release them to return home on December 31 as per their contracts, they planned to ask Congress to do so and to pay them. Other units joined the mutineers, some at cannonpoint. Now numbering fifteen hundred, or more than half of the Pennsylvania Line, in their initial clashes they killed a captain and wounded several more officers. Then they marched south.

When Wayne learned what they specifically wanted, he offered to lead them; they declined but did allow him and officers to follow them. Washington, receiving word of the mutiny, did not order other troops to arrest the mutineers, as he had in the past. He advised Wayne to help convey their grievances to Congress, and told Congress himself, in another letter, that while he had repeatedly informed the delegates of the "complicated distresses of the Army," this time "the circumstances [of this mutiny] will now point out more forcefully what ought to be done than anything that can possibly be said by me on the subject."

The British general in New York, Henry Clinton, also learned of the mutineers' march and sent messengers to offer them back pay, full pardons, and their choice of returning home or being absorbed into the British ranks, if they would do what the Americans referred to as "turn Arnold." The mutineers imprisoned the British messengers.

Then Wayne, Reed, John Laurens, and Lafayette, encouraged by Washington from afar, brokered a deal that ended the mutiny. Many soldiers were granted discharges, and most signed up again for new bonuses. Congress appropriated $879,342 to pay the arrears—a cruel joke, as the treasury was empty since the states had not pitched in.

Pennsylvania had refused to, Reed told Washington, after two years of having "borne one-fourth of the entire expence of the war," because while "the sufferings of the army receive at least the sympathy and praise of their Country—we have not even this Consolation."

Washington waited until the mutiny was over to inform Rochambeau about it, not wanting the French to feel that their American partners were in disarray. But two weeks later when a New Jersey Line mutinied, Washington dispatched regiments to surround them and force their surrender, and signed off on having two of the ringleaders executed. He then very quickly reported to Rochambeau: "I believe I may venture to assure Your Excellency that the spirit of Mutiny is now subdued and will not again shew itself."

Washington was keen to demonstrate that because the presence of the French military on American soil held out the most tantalizing prospect in five years for a happy ending to the war. A glimpse into Washington and Hamilton's perception of what might ensue if the long-term inability to adequately mobilize America's wealth for the war effort was not altered emerges from a letter of instruction to John Laurens. It was written by Hamilton for Washington's signature and summarized discussions among the three prior to John's forthcoming mission to France to reinforce the request for more money. It contained a startlingly frank assessment of the reluctance of the wealthy to monetarily support the war even when the prospect of victory was nigh:

> Considering the diffused population of these states . . . the want of a sufficient stock of national wealth . . . and the almost total extinction of commerce—the efforts we have been compelled to make . . . have exceeded the natural abilities of this country. . . . Our finances . . . are principally to be ascribed to an essential defect of means—to the want of a sufficient stock of wealth [which] will make it impossible, by any merely interior exertions, to extricate ourselves. . . . The resource of domestic loans is inconsiderable because there are properly

speaking few monied men, and the few there are can employ their Money more profitably otherwise.

This overstated the case: There was sufficient wealth in America to have funded the war, and some of the wealthy—notably Morris, Bingham, Wadsworth, Derby, Henry Laurens, William Gray, and others—had dug into their pockets to do so. But overall the assessment was correct: mobilization of America's monetary resources had been muted at best. The quickest way to raise the needed money, Hamilton, Washington, and Laurens thought, was to importune Louis XVI for "an immediate, ample and efficacious succour of money—large enough to be a foundation for substantial arrangements of finance . . . and give vigor to future operations." Hamilton privately advised Laurens that if he must choose between additional French forces or French money, to take the money.

Franklin had already been promised a new loan. Some of it, in gold, was at the pier in Brittany with the large French fleet, under Adm. François Joseph Paul de Grasse, being readied for the Caribbean and North America. Laurens upon arrival in Paris deemed the total amount of the proposed loan insufficient, and insisted on direct communication with Louis XVI. In it he was so impertinent that Vergennes complained to Franklin, who apologized for the upstart. Louis XVI too had financial problems: Although the king lived amid great luxury, his country was still in deep debt from the Seven Years' War, the total surging as France beefed up its military and continued to underwrite its profligate nobility. Laurens's bullying included the threat that if America lost the war, it might join with Great Britain to seize France's Caribbean "sugar islands," very large contributors to its treasury. The Laurens-Franklin good-cop-bad-cop approach worked. As Franklin soon apprised Jay: "Mr. Lawrens is worrying the minister for more money, and we shall I believe obtain a farther sum." The final amount was nearly double what Franklin had been promised.

While Laurens and Franklin were bolstering America's money supply, Congress finally began to address the demand. For six years it had mostly failed to curtail government spending. In early 1781, enabled by the final holdout state's (Maryland's) ratification of the Articles of Confederation, it established an executive branch and appointed superintendents of the army, navy, and treasury to perform that onerous task.

"This appointment [as superintendent of the treasury] was unsought, unsolicited, and dangerous to accept, as it was evidently contrary to my private interests," Robert Morris wrote in his diary, explaining: "A vigorous execution of the duties must inevitably expose me to the resentment of disappointed and designing men, and to the calumny and detraction of the envious and malicious." He made his acceptance contingent on being allowed to maintain his private business. After two months Congress agreed, and made him, in effect, the first chief financial officer of the country, able to exercise more power than the chief executive officer, Samuel Huntington, president of the Congress. Washington wrote: "I have great expectations of the appointment of Mr. Morris, but they are not unreasonable ones, for I do not suppose that by art magick, he can do more than recover us, by degrees, from the labyrinth in which our finance is plunged."

What can a successful businessman bring to government service? Along with a new broom, Morris brought his sense of individual economic patriotism, one that obliged him to use his fortune, contacts, and expertise on his country's behalf. He hired as his assistant Gouverneur Morris (no relation), recently defeated for reelection from New York but who had amply demonstrated his abilities despite the recent loss of a leg in a carriage accident. The Morrises then instituted competitive bidding for contracts and strict accounting for government expenditures—measures that Robert had flouted during his own time as a supplier. Opposing on principle a resolution in Congress to permit confiscation for the armies, he fulfilled its objective by persuading two business partners to each send a thousand barrels of flour in exchange for his personal "Morris Notes." Shortly Morris Notes became de facto government securities. Similarly, in an attempt to help Pennsylvania fulfill its obligation to provide supplies to its frontline soldiers, he offered to buy these, explaining that he could use the government's clout to get better prices, and capping his offer with a pledge to personally underwrite the purchases. His not-very-hidden motive was to retire a portion of Pennsylvania's paper money. He informed all the states that they would no longer be permitted to use the dodge employed by individual debtors—paying off install-ment obligations in worthless money—arguing that his office could not use state paper to pay federal invoices. Henceforth only specie would be accepted. The states howled but complied, and the specie they sent in helped to stabilize the currency.

Morris also did what no elected official could have done with im-punity: slash demand by ceasing to pay army salaries, claiming that since the states were not fulfilling their quotas there was not enough "treasure" in the treasury to do so. But while soldiers could be com-pelled to serve, bureaucrats whose salaries had vanished could quit and go home, so Morris found the money to keep the civilian gov-ernment running.

It became even more important for the states to ratify the impost, both for the money that import duties would bring to the govern-ment and to get past the principle in the Articles of Confederation that only the states could levy taxes. However, this prospect of future national taxation firmed the resolve of some smaller states to hold out: The war would have to be won without empowering a national government to levy taxes.

Morris had more success in getting Congress to charter the Bank of North America (BoNA). Before he had become financier he had outlined its scope: larger than the Pennsylvania bank, and with more oversight—the managers would report to him daily.

The bank was an idea whose time had come. Webster had been touting one for years, and Hamilton more recently. The previous fall Hamilton had married a Schuyler daughter whose dowry was con-siderable (and whose wealthy family was also attuned to his ideas), and in March he took the occasion of a spat with Washington to leave the army. He then tried to insert his ideas into the country's new management structure. In a long letter to Morris he described what a superintendent ought to do, how taxes ought to be levied—progressively, so as not to hurt the poor—and the need to create a national debt, which "if it is not excessive will be to us a national blessing . . . a powerful cement to our union." (Webster had earlier said the same about the debt.) Hamilton too recommended a national bank, but only as a necessary evil. Such banks had to be carefully set up, for the one in Spain was "banishing industry and sinking [Spain] in real wealth and importance":

> Great power, commerce and riches, or in other words great national prosperity, may in like manner be denominated evils; for they lead to insolence, an inordinate ambition, a vicious luxury, licentiousness of morals, and all those vices which corrupt government, enslave the people and precipitate the ruin of a nation. But no wise statesman will reject the good from an apprehension of the ill.

Hamilton's letter to Morris, in conjunction with his earlier ones to Sullivan and Duane, laid out a program for national financial stability that was both remarkable and obvious, remarkable because it was insightful, detailed, and workable, and obvious because the solutions offered had long been circulating in the Morris group and in Webster's pamphlets. But any astute reader of Hamilton's letter to Morris would have been impressed, and Morris was: He soon appointed Hamilton a receiver of taxes in New York, and Hamilton worked to rally that state behind the impost. Morris's immediate written reply to Hamilton, though, rejected having the bank's credit "interweaved" with decreasing the country's debt. But then Morris told Jay that his goal was to have the bank replace debased currencies "and thereby to relieve the people from those doubts and anxieties which have weakened our efforts, relaxed our industry, and impaired our wealth." The bank's certificates would unite the states "in one general money connexion, and indissolubly . . . attach many powerful individuals to the cause of our country by the strong principle of self-love and the immediate sense of private interest." Hamilton could not have put it better.

In May 1781 Washington and Rochambeau met at Wethersfield, Connecticut. Both had learned that Admiral de Grasse was en route to the Caribbean and would then bring his fleet to North America, although precisely where along the coast remained uncertain. At the conference Washington and Rochambeau decided to attack New York City once Rochambeau's forces had joined the Americans at the North (Hudson) River, an attack in which Washington expected de Grasse's fleet to participate.

Morris formally asked Congress to charter the Bank of North America, at four hundred thousand dollars in capital, to be raised by the sale of a thousand shares, which were to be purchased only with specie. Morris sent out letters touting the bank. In a typical one, he urged Jefferson, governor of Virginia, to find "other Gentlemen of your Character and Zeal for the service of their country" to become shareholders, because "I dare say few will find the Other parts of their Fortunes to yield them so large or so certain an income. . . . And . . . they will have the Satisfaction to be Consider'd for Ever as promoters of an Institution, which has been found beneficial to other Countries." By midsummer, however, only fifty thousand dollars had been raised.

By then, Rochambeau had moved his forces to the North River. Morris joined Washington at his camp there, to confer about economizing—reducing soldiers' back pay, consolidating posts, and cutting back on hospital expenses. The two friends were deep into the details on August 14 when a letter from de Grasse to Rochambeau arrived, announcing that his fleet was en route from the Caribbean to the Yorktown Peninsula.

The mark of a true leader is a willingness to shift direction when facts demand it. Washington, forced by the de Grasse letter to give up his dream of retaking New York, pivoted brilliantly to the task of moving the combined French and American land forces to Virginia, there to join his smaller armies—led by Lafayette, Wayne, and Friedrich Wilhelm von Steuben—that were already isolating Cornwallis's on the Yorktown Peninsula. With naval superiority provided by the French fleet, Washington and Rochambeau had a tremendous opportunity to capture Cornwallis and end the war.

Morris assisted Washington in seizing the day: Hastening to Philadelphia, he staved off creditors importuning the government and pushing Congress to pass confiscatory authorizations. Learning that John Laurens had arrived in Boston with a cache of French money, Morris made a deal: Rochambeau would lend Morris twenty thousand in coin, which Morris would give to Washington along with ten thousand dollars of his own, borrowed from Morris's regular supplier of specie, financier Haym Salomon, to pay the line troops, who had threatened not to march farther without it. The Laurens stash would soon repay everybody. Diarist-soldier Martin received six French crowns and noted: "This was the first that could be called money, which we had received as wages since the year '76."

As they marched farther south, supply became more difficult, since the area had already suffered from the scorched-earth tactics of Benedict Arnold's British forces. Nonetheless, local officials, apprised of the urgency, persuaded residents to provide such things as oxen teams to haul cannons. That, and the ability of Wadsworth and Carter to deliver food and shoes as the troops marched, kept the armies going, while making them money, as a Wadsworth biographer puts it, at a "dizzying pace."

Even as the armies of Washington and Rochambeau were still on their march south, the fate of Yorktown was decided at sea. In the three-day Battle of the Virginia Capes, de Grasse maintained the upper hand against the large British fleet, and then occupied Chesapeake Bay along with a smaller French naval force that had sailed there from Newport. Those maneuvers forced the Royal Navy's abandonment of Cornwallis's army on a peninsula whose escape routes were blocked.

Two weeks later the Washington and Rochambeau forces began

to besiege Yorktown under the direction of Rochambeau, veteran of fourteen earlier sieges. In three weeks, aided by starvation and rampant disease within British lines, the siege brought about the surrender of Cornwallis and his 7,500 men—and the end of major combat operations in the Revolutionary War.

Part Three

———⦿⦿⦿———

Victory and Aftermath,
1781–1789

8

Triumph, and the Costs of War

*R*obert Morris certainly believed that Yorktown was a triumph for the American cause, and that after it the war was over, writing to Franklin in Paris in November 1781:

> What else could be expected of us? A Revolution, a War, the Dissolution of Government, the creating of it anew, Cruelty Rapine and Devastation in the midst of our very Bowels, these Sir are circumstances by no means favorable to Finance. The Wonder then is that we have done so much, that we have borne so much, and the candid world will add that we have dared so much.

Yet the British remained in control of New York City as well as of Charleston and Savannah, and gave no sign of leaving these bastions voluntarily. So Morris also had to cite to Franklin "the confused State of public Accounts and the deplorable Situation of Credit for want of Funds to secure, or means to redeem the Debts for which the public faith is pledged."

The "deplorable situation of credit" produced problems for Nathanael Greene's army, just then bearing the brunt of the post-Yorktown fighting in the South. Greene's troops lacked supplies because the states had seized on the Yorktown triumph as a new reason for not properly paying in their quotas. He was forced to use his own money and credit to buy the supplies. John Laurens, serving with him, tried once again to persuade the South Carolina legislature to allow slaves to enlist. It again refused. Shortly, in a militarily meaningless battle, John Laurens was killed.

Robert and Gouverneur Morris took as their task putting the government on a sound financial footing before being shorn of what the latter labeled "that great friend to sovereign authority, a foreign war." Their cleanup included paying past contractor bills; however, the historian James E. Ferguson charges, in choosing which of them to honor, Robert followed a "discriminatory policy . . . to benefit his associates both in and out of the government [and] preserve his standing with the mercantile community." Supposedly in response to Wadsworth and Carter's previous too-high charges for supplies, Morris awarded a contract to provision the troops as they returned north to a Duer group. It soon ran into difficulties, and Morris was forced to sign another contract with Wadsworth and Carter, regarding which, a congressman noted, "we pay as much for three months as we did before for four."

The not-yet-settled war gave Morris opportunity to press for the establishment of a new, quasi-national bank, ostensibly for use as a clearinghouse to receive and store the government's income and to loan it money when receivables were slow. Of course such a bank would also fulfill the merchants' longtime wish to aggregate their wealth so it would furnish them with additional credit. Morris was easily able to assemble subscribers from those who had helped him begin the little Philadelphia bank, such as Willing, Bingham, and Wilson, and now including their former opponent Matlack. This group chose for the new bank's president Thomas Willing, known as "Old Square Toes" for his conservative approach to money and life. Chartered by the state of Pennsylvania, the Bank of North America opened for business on January 2, 1782. But since most of its shares had yet to be subscribed and the share price was below par, it was perceived as teetering even though its deposits included most of what John Laurens had brought from France. To save their new institution, the BoNA board engaged in elaborate deceptions.

Would-be subscribers were shown piles of silver brought from the vault to the main floor by a conveyor belt that soon returned it below, to be slightly reconfigured for the next trip up. Messengers publicly departed the bank with silver and gold, ostensibly to redeem certificates, only to return with the coin at day's end. Notes were dispatched to other cities to be bought by pre-arrangement at an undisclosed discount by other agents who then returned the notes to the bank; the buying activity bolstered the notes' value and spurred purchases by those who knew nothing of the machinations.

Within weeks the shares regained par, and within months the bank's solidity became evident as it loaned the government four hundred thousand dollars while paying its shareholders an 8 percent dividend after promising only 6.5. No wonder that Wadsworth and Carter became the largest stockholders, with 202 shares between them, about eighty thousand dollars' worth, followed by Morris with 98 and Bingham with 95. Morris did use the bank to shore up the government: Upon learning that France would issue no further loans, he raised the amount of the government's borrowing from the BoNA.

Foreign Secretary Robert Livingston wrote to John Jay that because of the bank's and Morris's activities, "public credit has again reared its head. Order and economy have taken place in our finances. The troops are regularly clothed and fed . . . the innumerable band of purchasing and issuing commissaries is discharged. . . . Our civil list . . . after many years in arrear, is now regularly paid off." This was wishful thinking and propaganda, sent to Europe to influence peace negotiations. Although the British government had fallen after the report of Yorktown, the king's intransigence had prevented the commencement of meaningful talks between the belligerents.

Had the Bank of North America opened for business prior to Yorktown, it would have mainly serviced the government's needs. But in a post-Yorktown atmosphere that in some cities felt like peacetime even though elsewhere armies were still in the field, the wartime attitude that put country above personal factors faded. And so in 1782 the BoNA's main raison d'être became clear as it issued dozens of loans to directors and their wealthy friends, to buy and develop America's newly opening lands. The most flagrant director-borrower was Wilson, who took one hundred thousand dollars to become more deeply involved in the Illinois-Wabash Company, for which he served as counsel. But many of the country's wealthy caught the land speculation virus, one symptom of which was the irrationally exuberant belief that money could be made rapidly from land sales once the peace treaty had eliminated all obstacles to development. Investors often underestimated the time and money needed to put their acreage in shape to be readily sold at retail. A few of the wealthy avoided this virus: Willing, Wadsworth, Derby, Gray, Girard, and for a while Bingham invested only in assets that they could visit or handle—nearby land, ships, and merchandise.

Those merchants' livelihood was still threatened by the war. King George III's refusal to concede that the Yorktown defeat mandated immediate peace negotiations was accompanied by orders to the British fleet based in New York to commence a new blockade of American ports. It rapidly cut by two-thirds shipments into and out of Philadelphia. And in Charleston, Loyalist John Cruden, the Commissioner for Sequestered Estates under the British, who had already sent boatloads of the city's slaves to New York to toil for the battalion there, wrote that the best way to subdue the remaining rebel wealthy in Charleston was to threaten to free ten thousand of their slaves by inducting them into the British army: "I would not be surprized that those [slaveholders] now most Violent, against us would be foremost in an application for Peace on our Own terms." The idea was quashed, but Cruden confiscated four hundred rebel estates, impoverishing the entire city.

In the late spring of 1782, the British government fell for the second time since Yorktown, and did so because the king had not let it negotiate for peace. George III's grudging acceptance that the successor government might also fall for the same reason finally occasioned the beginning of serious peace parleys. In one set of talks, the United States bargained unilaterally with Great Britain; in the other, the British, French, Spanish, and Dutch horse-traded.

In the American talks, a main subject was bilateral trade, which British merchants missed as much as the Americans did. Even as the negotiators worked on this subject they were undercut in London as John Baker Holroyd, Lord Sheffield, weaponized Adam Smith's

Wealth of Nations and turned it against the United States. He did so in a three-hundred-page pamphlet, *Observations on the Commerce of the American States,* whose theme was "Our impatience to preoccupy the American market, should perhaps be checked rather than encouraged." Using Smith's analysis of mercantilism, Sheffield asserted that the provisions of the Navigation Acts should not now be scrapped but rather employed to recapture America's economy. Americans must ship their goods to the Caribbean only in British-flag vessels; and British merchants must offer increased credit to lure American merchants into buying more and more British-manufactured goods: "The solid power of supplying the wants of America, of receiving her produce, and of waiting her convenience [to repay loans or advances], belongs almost exclusively to our merchants." From statistics on what Americans used, he compiled a list of manufactured items whose production the British could easily dominate: woolens, iron and steel, glass, stockings, shoes, buttons, "tin in plates, lead in pigs, copper in sheets," kitchen implements, drugs, and medicines.

Shortly British Orders in Council, which governed trade and shipping, adopted the Sheffield Rules, and soon France and Spain copied them. France confined its Caribbean colonies' exports to the United States to rum and molasses, insisting that all goods entering those islands be carried in French bottoms; and Spain, which during the war had exempted American vessels from restrictions on trade with its Caribbean and South American colonies, reinstated those restrictions and closed New Orleans to American trade.

The main American peace negotiators were Jay, Adams, and Franklin, all of whom contributed to America obtaining important concessions, on fishing rights off Newfoundland and on various boundaries. The fourth negotiator was Henry Laurens, released from the Tower for this purpose, in exchange for Cornwallis. Laurens's contribution to the peace treaty, seen at the time as trifling, was to insist that the list of property to be returned to Americans be couched so as to include illegally freed slaves. The effect was to embed slavery in the United States for eighty more years.

In France's negotiations it attempted to prevent the growth of a rival by hemming in the United States geographically, asking Great Britain to retain what would eventually become Maine, Michigan, Illinois, Wisconsin, and the upper reaches of the Mississippi River, and Spain to continue control of the lower river, New Orleans, the Gulf Coast, and Florida. The Americans could not prevent Spanish control of the Floridas and the lower Mississippi River, but did get the British to agree to evacuate their forts in the Midwest so as to allow American settlement of areas bordering Canada, from Maine westward.

No information about progress on peace had arrived in Newburgh, New York, by October 2, 1782, when Washington informed Secretary of War Lincoln of unrest among the officers:

> When I see such a number of Men goaded by a thousand stings of reflexion on the past . . . about to be turned into the World, soured by penury & . . . involved in debts . . . after having spent the flower of their days & many of them their patrimonies in establishing the freedom & Independence of their Country. . . . —I cannot avoid apprehending that a train of Evils will follow.

In November, Maj. Gen. Alexander McDougall presented a petition by those officers to Congress: "We have borne all that men can bear—our property is expended—our private resources are at an end, and our friends are wearied out and disgusted with our incessant applications." They asked for back pay and for assurances that Congress would honor the previous commitment to continue to pay them for years after the war's end.

The plea was accompanied by threats. A senior officer warned that if Congress did not accommodate them, "a convulsion of the most dreadful nature and fatal consequences" would ensue. Certain members of Congress saw opportunity in the combination of threat and request. As Hamilton would eventually confess to Washington: "The necessity and discontents of the army presented themselves as a powerful engine" enabling the nationalists to push to have Congress obtain the national taxation power. Hamilton, Morris, Madison, and a few like-minded others coopted the petitioning army officers to agree with the nationalists' plans, which included not only the impost that the nationalists had long championed but an entire new funding system, ostensibly so that the troops could be paid. Lincoln saw through this facade and railed to Knox about it and about the "mushroom gentry" who had profited from the war. To further pressure the delegates, Morris tendered his resignation. The delegates voted to keep it secret. He published it anyway, and Congress caved, agreeing in exchange for his staying on to pay the officers a lump sum equivalent to five years' wages.

Washington, although by inclination a nationalist, had no idea that the Congressional nationalists had interwoven the officers' grievances with their political plans because he had been deliberately kept in the dark about them. He remained in ignorance until a Hamilton letter dated February 13, 1783, urged him to "take the direction" of the army's anger, as it would "enable you . . . to guide the torrent, and bring order, perhaps even good, out of confusion." From this letter, Washington figured out that the army's discontent was being used for a political purpose, but he felt unable to do anything about it until an excuse for action arrived in Newburgh in the form of an unsigned letter demanding that the officers send Congress an ultimatum. The officers called a meeting to discuss that idea, and Washington insisted on attending and on speaking to them. In his March 15 address, Washington asked the officers whether it was possible that they could do "something so shocking [as] plotting the ruin of both [Congress and the army], by sowing the seeds of discord and separation?" They must oppose anyone who "wickedly attempts to open the floodgates of civil discord and deluge our rising empire in blood." Fumbling in his pocket for help in reading a supportive letter, he said "Gentlemen, you will permit me to put on my spectacles, for I have not only grown gray but almost blind in the service of my country." The officers, shamed, gave in to his entreaties.

A month later, after the officers agreed to full pay for five years and not to press for more, demobilization began. Morris in a final patriotic action advanced eight hundred thousand dollars in his notes so that each soldier, regardless of rank, could immediately have three months' pay. However, the notes did not arrive in the camps before most of the troops left, and so while the commissioned officer gentry were able to finance their returns to their hearths, the soldiery had to trade away their notes even before they arrived, for fractions of the notes' value, to purchase shoes, clothes, and food to travel home.

In September 1783, Congress ratified the peace accords. Shortly the British evacuated their last bastion, New York City, and the United States of America entered upon a new existence as an independent nation to which Great Britain no longer laid claim and whose independence was also certified by France, Spain, and the Netherlands. Its survival as an independent nation, however, was not at all certain.

During the two years between Yorktown and the final British evacuation of New York, the difficulties encountered by the United States of America made it clear that the country had won only political independence. Some Revolutionaries believed that economic independence had also been earned, since, as editor Noah Webster was writing: "A general and tolerably equal distribution of landed property is the whole basis of national freedom," and 50 percent of the country's white males now owned enough property to be listed on the tax rolls—a higher percentage than was the case throughout Great Britain and much of Europe. But property ownership was an inadequate indicator of broad prosperity in America. What of the propertyless white males? Females? Blacks? Native Americans? What of the sinking of the average American's income to 20 percent below the 1774 level? A quarter million Americans unmoored by war were roaming the country. They included tens of thousands of former slaves, freed by the British and unwilling to return to bondage. An equal number were white farmhands, day laborers, sailors, warehousemen, dockworkers, and former indentured servants, unable to find work. Many roamers, black as well as white, were veterans and still suffering from years of starvation and privation.

Also on the move, toward Canada and Florida, was a much wealthier group: seventy thousand Loyalists. They constituted only

20 percent of all Loyalists—80 percent chose to remain within the United States. American mythology has the Loyalists' angry neighbors shaming them and confiscating their assets. This is mistaken. Most loyalists successfully reintegrated into their communities. South Carolina confiscated the property of only 277 out of its several thousand Loyalists, and in the northern states the percentages were similar. That was because most people understood that the money the ex-Loyalists would spend in the community was of greater value to the populace than their former political stance—and because America prided itself on being the country of second chances. Christopher Gadsden, who as one of the earliest advocates for independence and as a man who had spent years as a prisoner of war under execrable conditions might have been vindictive toward Loyalists, wrote to the frontline hero Frances Marion: "He that forgets and forgives most . . . is the best citizen." Gadsden's rival Laurens, too, forgave the Loyalists, in particular one nephew, extracting an apology and giving him a job to restore his fortune as well as his reputation. Adams, Franklin, and Jay all wrote letters chastising the town councils of Norwalk and Fairfield for adopting harsh measures against former Loyalists.

Laurens, who had returned to America after the deaths of two of his three sons and in poor health from his incarceration, found his Charleston home burned and his plantations a shambles, losses he estimated at forty thousand pounds. The plantations of Jefferson and Dickinson had been looted; Butler's had been specifically targeted because he had led troops against the British; Knox and Greene's prewar businesses were in tatters. But the wealthy could recover. Governor Hancock of Massachusetts, dunned for back payment of taxes in New Hampshire, would sue his prewar debtors and win enough to restore his fortunes. The returning veterans did not have the wherewithal for such legal maneuvers, and no one in the American government structure did very much to alleviate their lot. They were considered to be the states' problems now.

Veterans found their farms' and workshops' productivity diminished by years of bad winters and confiscatory sweeps, and fettered by taxes in arrears. Seven states printed money, in part so that the veterans could use it to pay their back taxes and other debts; relief-by-depreciated-currency was touted as akin to doling out veterans' benefits, and as effective as direct subsidies. It wasn't. And such small-bore relief helped widen the gap separating rich and poor.

Some of the wealthy were able to pyramid their fortunes because their state governments were under pressure. Massachusetts, for instance, had to use most of its tax income to pay down debts, which left very little left for needed public works. So it turned for the underwriting of public works to entrepreneurs who had accumulated cash, the privateer owners George Cabot and Thomas Russell. They contracted to erect and operate bridges, turnpikes, canals, and docks near Boston in exchange for exclusive franchises and most of the toll receipts. Soon Cabot and Russell had enough income to eclipse Hancock in wealth and to ensure their families' fortunes for generations to come. A Salem Loyalist neighbor of the Cabots, upon his return from England, was astonished at how far up the wealth ladder they had ascended.

In each state, such opportunities further enriched a few dozen men. Many more of the already wealthy added to their fortunes by taking advantage of an entirely new factor: access to bank credit. While today our banks are eager—sometimes too eager—to lend to anyone whom they judge to have sufficient collateral, in the 1780s the few American banks lent almost solely to their directors and to those in the directors' social circles, routinely rejecting the loan applications of all farmers, artisans, small merchants, and small manufacturers. That business model was adopted by Hamilton as he planned to open a Bank of New York with one of his brothers-in-law, to cater strictly to businessmen. He wrote that his bank would not accept, as security for loans, either mortgages or rent rolls, a policy that would exclude small fry. To clear the path for his bank, Hamilton had to block a proposed rival bank backed by the Livingstons. That older family touted their proposed bank, in purposeful contrast to Hamilton's, as a new iteration of a land bank. The New York State Assembly liked neither group's bank plan and would not charter them, but Hamilton opened his bank anyway. Carter and Wadsworth soon owned 20 percent of the Bank of New York to go with their 20 percent of the BoNA.

At war's end, on paper Wadsworth and Carter had been owed £300,000—roughly the same amount that ninety-seven Philadelphians had pledged in 1780 to support the troops. Only £75,000 of it was due from Congress; the remainder was due from the French. But Louis XVI's government issued an *arrêt*, a halt to payment, to last a year, after which the rest would be paid, plus 5 percent. In July 1783, even before the peace treaties had been signed by the government, Wadsworth and Carter hastened to France, and through intense trading there with other merchants on bills of credit, by the end of 1783 they obtained most of what they were owed. Wadsworth then invested the proceeds in French luxury goods to send to America, while Carter took most of his to Great Britain, from which he had fled in 1775 to escape considerable debts. Carter's new wealth and American expertise became sought after by Britons looking for American opportunities, and he prospered. But Wadsworth's cargoes of French luxury goods reached Philadelphia just when America was glutted with similar merchandise, and he lost money. After several more failed ventures he decided to invest in better utilizing his acreage near Hartford. As Washington did, he imported gardeners and farm managers and built greenhouses to nurture crops such as wheat that was resistant to Hessian Fly, and apple orchards that within two years turned a few pennies' worth of seeds into a cash crop. As Robert Morris did, Wadsworth imported sheep, pigs, and black bulls, and soon made money. But nearly every penny he had was tied up in nonperforming loans, and he came to depend heavily on dividends from the Bank of North America.

At least Wadsworth had something. Greene, his business partner in the Barnabas Deane firm, was broke from having advanced his own money to his army's suppliers and not having been adequately repaid. Awarded by the state of Georgia two confiscated properties, Greene sold one to Wadsworth to wipe out some debt, and settled his family on the other, but in June 1786 he died. The Greene estate's financial problems became Wadsworth's, since he was an executor; that estate owed the most to Morris, whose own fortune had become stressed to the point that he was no longer able to be tolerant with friends' debts. Wadsworth knew that problem well. Among the letters he had recently received was one from a longtime friend and supplier:

> To be the informer of my own misfortune, is . . . a task almost too grating to my feelings, for me to encounter, but much more so when I am to become the unwelcome messenger of ill-tidings to a friend. . . . In short, Sir, the Peace, and the failure of two or three gentlemen who were indebted to me in large sums, has completely ruined me. . . . I have been driven by the most remorseless creditors . . . to seek shelter under an Act of Insolvency.

Washington, Jefferson, Laurens, and others took losses on similar loans. They cut back on personal lending, not only to avoid further risk but because they now had other investment possibilities, such as dividend-paying bank stocks.

The decline in personal lending by the wealthy to those on lower rungs of the economic ladder had social as well as financial consequences, breaking down former habits of fealty from the poor to the wealthy. The absence of personal loans from rich neighbors, coupled with bank refusals of credit, pushed small- and midsize merchants to combine assets. Tench Coxe, surviving an inquest into his Loyalist activities, became an ardent Whig and found a partner in Nalbro Frazier of Boston and New York. Coxe & Frazier had enough cash to send cargoes to cities on the Atlantic coast, the Caribbean, and in Europe, developing a near-monopoly on very-high-priced imports. The BoNA helped, not by loans but by quickly paying out on Coxe & Frazier's invoices for clients who were BoNA depositors, which allowed the firm to undertake new projects.

Many other merchants did not fare as well, because instead of inventing new businesses they went back to relying on Americans' taste for imported British manufactured goods, and to reliance on British credit. The combination soon produced sixty-eight merchant bankruptcies in Philadelphia alone. The Browns of Providence, far from inept merchants, also fell into the trap. Prior to ratification of the peace treaty,

Nicholas Brown received solicitations from a half-dozen British firms. He accepted some and for a while did very well, even though he had to pay his London providers 5 percent interest, twice the prewar tab. Then the Sheffield-inspired levy on American whale products took effect and wiped out Brown's profit. Then his London provider refused to advance him credit for the next season's shipments. Brown wrote a confessional to his prewar London factor, to whom he still owed money:

> It is painful to us to reflect on the magnitude of our debt and on the variety of impediments which crowd to obstruct our most vigorous exertions to abate the sum. The alient duty on oil, the impossibility of securing hard money, the great scarcity and advanced rate of bills [of exchange], the exorbitant price of Southern production [of rice and cotton to resell to Great Britain], and superadded to all, the present and deranged state of political affairs in this government all conspire to defeat our best exertions.

One hoped-for economic trend also solidified in the postwar period: the growth of small entrepreneurship. The story emerges from the major cities' tax rolls and property transfer records, as examined by Allan Kulikoff and other scholars of the postwar period. In Philadelphia, prior to the war, the Quaker elite had owned most of the real estate, but once that elite had been banished for refusing to profess loyalty to the rebel cause, some 50 percent of the city's property came into the possession of the bottom 90 percent of the populace. Later in the war a different sort of shift occurred, due to the actions of many artisans, mechanics, and former indentured servants. Unable to find enough work from employers, they opened their own workshops, and when they needed more hands they hired some rather than take indentured apprentices, as had routinely been done in the colonial era. The results were startling: By 1790, the lower 90 percent owned only 33 percent of Philadelphia's property, and the remainder of the 50 percent that the top men once owned, and more, had come into the hands of those who in 1780 had not even been on the property tax rolls—artisans and mechanics who had pulled themselves up the ladder. In New York and Boston the change in property ownership was similar. According to Kulikoff, among the reasons was that these new business operators were "more national, practiced more innovative financing, searched for more efficient production techniques, and employed more wage labor."

Some of that labor came from a particular set of immigrants to America, Britons who had illegally fled their homeland. Although British law forbade skilled artisans and mechanics from leaving, five to ten thousand annually managed to cross to America, many of them knowledgeable about the manufacturing of textiles, leather, clocks, glass, and paper. They willingly risked arrest and imprisonment to come to America, where they knew they had the chance of one day opening their own workshops, emporiums, and factories—something far less possible for them in the British Isles. American manufacturers were ready for them: During the war several states had passed laws forbidding export of "foundation" crops, such as hides, to encourage the manufacturing of the hides into shoes, coats, leather aprons, and furniture seats. Immigrant expertise enabled Americans to manufacture products similar to British ones but less expensive to American buyers. The availability of skilled immigrants encouraged such astute businessmen as the Browns to shift some of their capital from importing to textile manufacture, and to pay premiums to immigrants who had memorized plans for the critical machinery that Great Britain was desperate to keep from leaving the country.

The rise of an American middle class began to fulfill the Revolution's promise that property would not be solely reserved for those who already owned a lot of it.

In Boston the old guard and the nouveau riche flaunted their finery at the Sans Souci nightclub, where two wealthy women proprietors offered costly foods, wines, and entertainments. The high level of ostentation brought condemnation from Samuel Adams as insufficiently republican, and from Mercy Otis Warren in a satirical play, *Sans Souci, Alias Free and Easy, or An Evening's Peep into a Polite Circle.* "Damn the old musty rules of decency and decorum . . . Spartan virtues—republican principles," a proprietress says. "They are all calculated for rigid manners . . . they are as disgusting as old orthodoxy; Fashion and etiquette are more agreeable to my ideas of life—this is the independence I aim at." The Sans Souci was not an outlier: In this period the pursuit and flaunting of wealth was first acknowledged to be as thoroughly American as waving the flag.

Benjamin Lincoln, prior to the war a middle-class farmer in rural Massachusetts, had since then rubbed shoulders with the elite enough to develop a taste for high living. After the war, to acquire wealth he made use of the emotional capital that he had earned—the trust of that elite—to obtain loans to open a flour mill and, when that did well, to commission ships to transport the flour. British naval restrictions put a crimp in that trade, so in association with the Lowells and with credit from a bank in Boston he acquired fifty thousand acres in Maine. His thoughtful stewardship there contrasted with his friend Knox's absentee development of the Maine acres inherited by Knox's wife. But both ex-generals were soon overextended financially, and the strain started to show.

George Washington, too, was a "projector," the name then given to entrepreneurs. The commander agreed to participate mostly in projects that he believed were of benefit to the country's growth, especially those facilitating the transport to the Atlantic coast of products from the interior. He became involved in canals, steamboats, and turnpikes, not only in the hope of eventual profit from thousands of western acres that he had been acquiring for thirty years, but to tie East and West together so that western areas would not be tempted to declare independence or ally themselves with Great Britain, France, or Spain. He traveled to western Pennsylvania and Virginia to determine the best route from there across the Alleghenies to the Susquehanna River, whence goods could be carried the rest of the way to the Atlantic. Startled to find more than a dozen families squatting on his land, he sued them. At a meeting he convened in western Pennsylvania on routes from East to West, he met young Albert Gallatin, a well-educated Swiss from a prosperous family who had emigrated in 1780, taught at Harvard, become a surveyor, and had bought a quarter-interest in 120,000 acres nearby. Gallatin's suggestion for the cross-mountain route was the best Washington heard. He offered the young man a job as his land agent, but Gallatin declined, wanting to develop his own acreage. Afterward Gallatin took his first interest in local political affairs.

The increasing white populations in the western portions of the Atlantic-bordering states and in those states' "reserves" in the Midwest changed the states' economies, the makeup of their legislatures, and those legislatures' concerns. Jackson Turner Main, who studied their makeup and decisions, found that the "proportion of the wealthy in these legislatures [went] from 46 percent [before the war] to 22 percent; members from prominent old families declined from 40 percent to 16 percent." The *American Herald* of Boston sniffed that Massachusetts was now "worse governed," men of property having been pushed out and "blustering, ignorant men, who started into notice during the troubles and confusion of that critical period [the war] have been attempting to push themselves into office." The westerners sought military aid for staving off Native Americans and to send farm products down the Mississippi River system, while the easterners continued to focus on state activities that would assist them in exporting their products overseas.

British pressures were turning one state against another. New York levied duties on all goods imported through its largest city, even if destined for neighboring states. Pennsylvania did the same for goods coming through Philadelphia. To avoid the New York surcharge, Connecticut expanded harbors and docks at Hartford, New Haven, and New London to accommodate transoceanic cargoes. Since New York's import duties accounted for more than half its revenue, it rescinded its former yea vote on the national impost.

The national war debt was a drag on the economy. At $27 million at war's end, and growing at the 6 percent a year owed in interest, it was composed of nearly equal thirds of loan certificates, unpaid quartermaster and commissary bills, and soldiers' notes. Morris "settled" many individual claims, in the sense of having them evaluated and the creditors issued certificates for redemption, but thousands remained unresolved, including very large ones. Massachusetts had mounted a failed expedition to Penobscot—could it charge the cost to the United States? And what of Virginia's expeditions in the West? When the states cut down on sending money to keep the central government running, Morris as financier felt forced to cease paying interest to France and on Loan Office certificates.

The French could do little about it. But the Pennsylvania Assembly, still a radical group, threatened to directly pay the bond interest to their resident bondholders. Since doing so would undermine what little remained of Congress's authority, Madison and Hamilton paid a call on an assembly committee. If all other states would be as good in "doing their duty," they said, Congress would have no problems meeting the interest payments. Alas, all other states were not of equal integrity, so a remedy was needed to encompass them all. "The [Pennsylvania] Committee appeared to be considerably impressed by these remarks," said Madison's report, and a solution was worked out: States could directly pay the interest to resident creditors on behalf of the national government. A few months later the Pennsylvania radicals went further, giving buyers of state paper an interest-paying certificate tied to receipt of taxes, a more reliable debt instrument.

Critical to the understanding of the postwar crisis regarding the debt is that the debt was not evenly distributed: Pennsylvania, New York, and New Jersey owed 83 percent of it. The southern states' shares were much lower, and their legislatures had all but eliminated their share in the postwar years by setting high tax rates. The much larger northern states' shares of the national debt were more burdensome to those states. Some New England states exacerbated the problem by not only setting tax rates high but also by sending nearly all of their incoming tax receipts right out again to federal and state bondholders. This brought immediate taxpayer reaction: Voters rapidly unseated whole assemblies that made such "pro-bondholder" decisions.

Our mythology about the national debt holds that after Yorktown the debt just continued to grow and grow until 1789, when Hamilton as secretary of the treasury cut it down. That scenario is overly simplistic, and avoids acknowledging that many states did tackle the debt earlier, with some success. One method differentiated between repayment to original bondholders at par, and to speculators at current market prices. A second refigured the amount of interest by pegging it to a bond's current value; this saved taxpayers hundreds of thousands of dollars. The third had the most ramifications: A state would print money and allow obligations to be paid with it even as the paper rapidly lost value. Seven states did that.

But Congress refused to adopt either of two megaways put forward to retire the debt: national direct taxation of one to two dollars a year per person, and the rapid sale of western lands. Direct taxation was still anathema. The sale of western lands was a real possibility, since the federal government held title to some western lands and the states were obligated by the Articles of Confederation to sell to the central government the remainder of their "western reserves." They did not, because the national and state legislators realized that if too much land was offered for sale at once, the price per acre would drop and ruin everyone. However, Congress did minutely debate plans to develop those reserves. In the 1780s, Jefferson submitted an ambitious plan with Latinate state names and remarkably democratic practices: that only small parcels could be sold; that primogeniture, entail, and slave ownership were forbidden; and that the territories must use some of their tax income to establish free schools. These principles were incorporated into the Northwest Land Act. That act was a blueprint for extending the small-farms pattern, and its concomitant small-town democracy, throughout the West, to create a culture that favored the average-income family.

Standing in the way of such an outcome was the unbridled nature of postwar capitalism. It had several enablers, first among them that the government lacked enforcement mechanisms, and second the inability of the legislators to resist the lobbying of the wealthy. In what Jeffrey L. Pasley, a scholar of early Congresses, labels the greatest feat of lobbying in American history, a group led by Massachusetts preacher Manasseh Cutler, ostensibly representing New England war veterans but really a set of moneyed interests, persuaded Congress to sell it several million acres in Ohio for a half-million-dollars' worth of old federal debt certificates. This, writes Pasley, "required abandoning, without even a single trial, the land policy Congress had just established in the very slowly and painfully created Land Ordinance of 1785." In even shadier self-dealing, New Jersey representative John Cleves Symmes, with the participation of fellow New Jersey representative Jonathan Dayton and the investment of Pennsylvania representative Elias Boudinot, persuaded their colleagues to sell Symmes a million acres along the Great Miami River for sixty-six cents an acre. The coalition lured the then-president of Congress, Gen. Arthur St. Clair, into becoming governor of the new territory and head of a federally financed army to combat the Native Americans. Pasley traces the success of these lobbying efforts not to the legislators' greed, but rather to Congress's general susceptibility to petitioners who, like them, exhibited the qualities they associated with gentlemen.

Congress's ineptness also shone through in its weak response to Spain's aggression in closing New Orleans to American goods, a calamity for the commerce of the Mississippi River system. Some states talked of mustering an American army to seize the area, but there was no national appetite for war so soon after the close of the Revolution. All that Congress did was designate John Jay to negotiate with Spanish attaché Diego de Gardoqui. On the Paris peace treaty, Jay had been an excellent bargainer, but in a year's worth of secret meetings with Gardoqui, Jay agreed to a treaty that would cede to Spain for twenty-five years the use of the Mississippi River and adjoining territories, in exchange only for expanded American trading rights in Spain and Spanish territories. This was such a terrible deal that Congress refused to honor it. Congress then sent Jefferson to Europe, where he joined Franklin and Adams, and they successfully negotiated commercial treaties with the Netherlands, Sweden, Prussia, Morocco, and France. However, these produced very little trade: 90 percent of American exports continued to go to

Great Britain and its colonies, and 85 percent of American imports to come from them.

To get beyond such limitations Morris and other high-net-worth "projectors" tried to sell American exports elsewhere in the world. The Philadelphian would later assert that, on balance, he came out of the war without notable gain in his private fortune. After the war, he tried to make up for lost time. He converted a former privateer into the *Empress of China,* the first American cargo ship to attempt to break Great Britain's total control of the China trade. To get the *Empress* under weigh, though, entailed laying out a good deal of money, and his finances were also adversely impacted when coinvestor Daniel Parker, who had been put in charge of outfitting the ship, absconded just prior to its departure with a reported three hundred thousand dollars in cash, leaving behind Morris to pay the bills for the collecting of its cargo of Virginia ginseng—the root so prized in Asia grew naturally and in abundance in the Piedmont area.

Derby, learning of the *Empress of China,* decided to send his *Grand Turk* to buy Chinese tea, but he did so mainly without partners. His wealth was such that he was then paying eleven thousand pounds annually in taxes, yet his neighbors complained that he ought to pay more. The *Grand Turk* sailed first for India, since Chinese tea was also available there. This was a lucky guess, because en route the *Grand Turk*'s captain met a British master who helped arrange an exchange of the *Grand Turk*'s rum for the desired tea. Thorndike, Peabody, Gray, and other privateer owners began to send their ships to India and China and thereby to increase their fortunes. Derby and Gray also sent some to Russia, which in terms of trade became as profitable as China: Iron from Russia proved important to the United States, as it enabled the forging of new kinds of nails that better stabilized buildings. Shortly Gray was challenging Derby for the title of wealthiest Salemite.

9

Targets of Ire

*I*n the mid-1780s, with the economy only slowly recovering but with some wealthy people prospering, people of modest means looked to assign blame, and an easy target was the Order of the Cincinnati, composed of five thousand former commissioned military officers who had been lobbying for their interests. Formed on May 10, 1783, by Knox, Steuben, and Hamilton, the Cincinnati was named after the Roman general and farmer who left his plow to take up the sword on his country's behalf, and after victory returned home. They elected Washington as "president general," Steuben as operating officer, and issued to members ceremonial badges and sashes to distinguish them from the two hundred thousand other men who had served in the armed forces. Membership was reserved only for commissioned officers who had served at least three years, and for the sons of fallen ones.

Anger at the Cincinnati was a proxy for anger at the wealthy, although the Cincinnati and the wealthy had only a partial overlap because with a few notable exceptions the latter had avoided military service. The most active generals had come mainly from the middle class: farmers William Heath and Benjamin Lincoln, former tanner and surveyor Anthony Wayne, and Nathanael Greene, owner of an ironworks. Opposition to the Cincinnati combined resentment at the wealthy for avoiding service yet benefiting from the war, with the fear Laurens had identified in his warning to Washington that a pensioned officer corps would be perceived as an aristocracy.

A widely distributed pamphlet, written by Aedanus Burke of South Carolina, painted the society as "a deep laid contrivance to beget, and perpetuate . . . an aristocratic Nobility, to terminate at last in monarchial tyranny." Such conspiratorial worries could have been easily dismissible, but to Washington's dismay, opposition to the Cincinnati also arose from Jefferson, Adams, Jay, and Franklin. Jefferson objected to the hereditary aspects as presaging the resurgence of primogeniture and entail. Washington, having absolutely rejected wartime suggestions that he crown himself king, was perturbed that such critics would consider the Cincinnati a stalking horse for ending democracy, so at the Cincinnati's first national meeting he threatened to quit should it not tone down its ostentation and attempts to accentuate the distance between its members and other Americans. The ex-officers were not very chastened, but did agree to wear their regalia only during military parades, funerals, and conventions.

A much more realistic target of lower- and middle-class ire at the wealthy was the Morris-Willing Bank of North America, accused in a 1785 article of having "sucked all the available specie in the state into its vaults and then shipped it overseas to pay for European luxuries imported by rich merchants." The Constitutionalists who still controlled Pennsylvania's legislature aimed its power at the BoNA, after they kicked out of their midst Matlack, who had become a bank director. Their push to decharter the bank was cheered on by John Witherspoon, a signer of the Declaration and president of the College of New Jersey, who chastised the BoNA for giving credit only to merchants and not "to husbandmen, or those who improve the soil." The historian of the radicals Terry Bouton calls such attacks warranted because the BoNA had "drained the countryside" by substituting its paper for government currency, even as farmers were being dunned to pay new taxes in specie: "Stripped of purchasing power ordinary citizens stopped ordering new goods, which caused trade to stagnate. . . . People had trouble acquiring funds to pay outstanding debts and taxes, leaving creditors dissatisfied, treasuries empty, and courts filled with bereft debtors and taxpayers."

Conversely, the Republican Society men charged that the assembly's laws were the true cause of Pennsylvania's economic difficulties, warning that if the bank were dechartered, "The merchant of *moderate* capital, the *farmer* and the *mechanic* will be the first class of citizens that will complain of this impolitic measure." Thomas Willing then undercut this argument by declaring a second dividend, bringing the year's total to 14.5 percent—a very high return, almost twice that of 1782—and by announcing an issue of new shares at five hundred dollars apiece.

The real sin of the BoNA, writes a historian of early banking in the U.S., Howard Bodenhorn, lay in its attempts to maintain a monopoly through "opposition to [Pennsylvania's] emission of £100,000 in bills of credit, its refusal to accept notes issued by a £50,000 loan office or loan bank, and above all, its adoption of high-pressure lobbying practices against any measure to limit its voracity." It targeted a potential rival bank being put together by Coxe and Edward Shippen IV, mostly from Loyalists, plus Philadelphians who had cooperated during the British occupation, and Quaker businessmen. Coxe was no rebel: He owned BoNA stock and was a Willing son-in-law. But like the proposers of the Livingstons' bank in New York, he and his investors announced their intention to loan money to the sort of people routinely spurned by the BoNA—smaller merchants, artisans, and farmers—a stance that greatly appealed to the radicals of the Pennsylvania Assembly. To coopt Coxe, Shippen, and the other principals, Willing offered them BoNA shares at below market price. They bought in and withdrew their application for a new bank.

That roused the assembly, which fought back by legislatively advancing decharter. Willing then commissioned Wilson to write a pamphlet giving the many reasons for continuing the BoNA, and as payment to Wilson arranged to have the director's friends cosign his notes—Wilson had spent too much money to improve the very large western tracts that he controlled, which were still not ready for retail sale. His pamphlet smartly answered questions about the bank's legality, but the Pennsylvania legislators were concerned with the bank's fairness in lending, which Wilson did not address. In arguments in an oral session, he contended that it was not the bank that was drawing off America's specie, it was the British, so that "control of commerce in the name of the common good of all the states is the only effective answer," and therefore the bank should be rechartered. Whitehill countered by labeling the bank "an engine of destruction . . . inconsistent with the [state constitution's] bill of rights, which says that the government is not instituted for the emolument of any man, family, or set of men." He believed that "enormous wealth, possessed by individuals has always had its influence and dangers in free states," and that if special privilege were given to that wealth in the form of the bank, "Democracy must fall before it."

Paine and Pelatiah Webster jumped into the fray, each with his own pamphlet. Webster's addressed the opponents' underlying accusation, that the bank was only enhancing the wealth of the merchants:

> The parson lives on the sins of the people, the doctor on their diseases, and the lawyer on their disputes and quarrels. But the merchant lives on the wealth of the people. He never wishes for a poor customer or a poor country. . . . The richer the merchants are, and the greater their trade, the better market they afford for the produce of the country[side]. . . . Indeed, the husbandman and the merchant ever mutually support and benefit one another.

Coxe inserted himself into the controversy in a series of articles that lauded the bank while chastising the legislature for not having properly regulated it. Recharter must put the BoNA under public supervision, and he specified just how: By limiting its capital, its holdings (not too much land), the duration of its charter, and by requiring it to maintain a sinking fund to assure that it would meet payments.

The assembly dechartered the bank anyway. Its stock began to fall, its cash reserves dwindled from $59 to $37 million, and foreign investment dried up. The Dutch minister—Dutch banks held a considerable amount of stock in the bank, and many U.S. bonds—appealed to Congress, with the implied threat of no longer buying American bonds. Wadsworth, the largest BoNA shareholder, had previously complained about the issuance of new stock, feeling that it had been a Morris attempt to lessen the value of Wadsworth's shares. But at the same time Wadsworth instructed his deputy to buy up "as great an amount [of new shares] as you can," in his own name as well as in those of his sisters. He now let it be known that he might sell those shares and further invest in Hamilton's Bank of New York, for which Wadsworth now served as a director. Hamilton then rounded up proxies from five other significant shareholders of the BoNA, including the Dutch and French attachés, for Wadsworth to wield at the next shareholders' meeting.

Morris headed off that threat by receiving Wadsworth privately ahead of that next shareholders' meeting. When Wadsworth suggested he might force the share representation issue into the Pennsylvania courts, Morris claimed that might shutter the bank. But when Wadsworth also objected to being blocked from a more active role in the leadership, Morris sweetened Wadsworth's pot enough to induce him thereafter to remain at home and cash his dividend checks. A substitute charter for the BoNA was soon obtained from Delaware. And, as Wadsworth had prophesied to Morris, the bank benefited from the backlash over its Pennsylvania dechartering, which spurred the election to the state's assembly of enough Republican Society men to finally achieve a majority. Franklin then agreed with that majority that the bank should be rechartered; the enacting legislation included many of Coxe's recommended changes.

The poor had not actively taken part in the tussle over the bank. But they were direct participants in the battle over the third of the targets of ire in this chapter. A crisis was triggered when the states rejected the last of the schemes Congress had put forth for repaying the national debt. Congress then sent "final" bills to each state for its share of the total, and in reaction states raised taxes to pay these bills—in some states to beyond what most citizens could tolerate.

Massachusetts historian George Richards Minot had been keeping notes on the increasing split between the lives and fortunes of those he referred to as the "traders" in Boston, Salem, and Gloucester, who could sell inventory to pay their share of taxes, and of the "agriculturalists" of central and western Massachusetts, who could not partially sell their farms to pay taxes. Underlying the agrarians' belief that they were being unduly penalized was a moral stance articulated by Hector St. John de Crèvecoeur in his *Letters from an American Farmer*: "This formerly rude soil has been converted . . . into a pleasant farm, and in return it has established all our [family's] rights; on it is founded our rank, our freedom, our power as citizens." That rationale was understood by the legislatures of Maryland, New Jersey, Pennsylvania, and Connecticut, which had similar urban–rural ratios and numbers of debtors, and their understandings produced various attempts to alleviate their farmers' debt loads. Not in Massachusetts, though.

John Hancock had resigned as governor in January 1785, citing his declining health, although critics charged that the resignation was due to his realization that his hands-off governance had done too little to ameliorate the state's burgeoning problems, which would soon reverse his popularity. James Bowdoin, having lost to Hancock in three previous elections, then ran against Thomas Cushing, Hancock's lieutenant governor, and against retired general Benjamin Lincoln. Bowdoin ally Sam Adams tried to tarnish Cushing by tying him to the Sans Souci club, while Cushing's partisans accused Bowdoin of cowardice during the war. A split vote threw the election into the courts; Bowdoin won. Then, in what Perkins labels "an ill-considered fiscal policy that drained excessive monies out of the pockets of ordinary tax-payers," Bowdoin raised taxes, twice, so that the state could pay all of what it owed in five years. Judge and congressman Rufus King estimated to John Adams that one-third of the incomes in Massachusetts were being spent to pay taxes, which "considering the prostrate situation of our commerce, [was] beyond what prudence would authorize." The taxes rankled the farmer-veterans,

Minot wrote: They could not fathom "that they had shed their blood in the field, to be worn out with burdensome taxes at home; or that they had contended [in the war], to secure to their creditors, a right to drag them into courts and prisons." Shortly whole towns refused to pay taxes. Bowdoin bristled, but as a friendly biographer points out, during the war when he had suffered losses, he "had lodged a formal plea for tax abatement with the town of Boston; but as governor he showed little sympathy for the harassed farmers whose tax payments were in arrears." Massachusetts's actions seemed all the more insensitive because other states with arrearage problems were addressing them in ways that dissipated incipient tax revolts. Minirebellions in Pennsylvania and South Carolina were calmed by sympathetic courts suspending action so that few people were jailed, and by local sheriffs refusing to make undue collections from neighbors. When Virginia realized that three-quarters of its counties were behind in taxes, it agreed to payment in crops, which eased the burden on a specie-deprived economy. Hancock had not actively pursued debtors unable to pay tax arrears, but Bowdoin reversed that policy and used the state's enforcement apparatus to dun and jail debtors. That spurred into existence, in early summer 1786, county conventions that encompassed most of the nonurban population of Massachusetts. These demanded the closing of the state senate, a revision of the statutes to make the assembly more democratic, and the abolition of various courts—in short, to make the state's governance more like Pennsylvania's, so it could enact more debtor-friendly laws.

Since the legislature was on hiatus, some county-convention delegates and friends decided to shutter the courts that had so uniformly ruled against them. They numbered in the single thousands, and a large percentage were veterans, providing a startling contrast to that other veterans' organization, the Cincinnati. They took the name of one of their leaders, Daniel Shays. An army captain at Saratoga, Shays had received a ceremonial sword from the hand of Lafayette. Since then he had become so indebted that he had sold the sword. On August 29, 1786, several hundred Shaysites, many armed, tried to block a Worcester court session. Bowdoin ordered the Worcester militia to disperse them, but the militia refused and some members joined the crowd. The court was closed.

The governor's reaction was immediate. He declared:

> This high-handed offence is fraught with the most fatal and pernicious consequences, must tend to subvert all law and government [and] introduce universal riots, anarchy and confusion, which would probably terminate in absolute despotism, and consequently destroy the fairest prospects of political happiness, that any people was ever favoured with.

The Shaysites ignored him. A large group precluded Springfield's court from sitting, and at Great Barrington eight hundred of the one thousand militia who had been ordered to prevent a similar closing voted not to do so, and it closed.

Washington's former aide David Humphreys wrote that the rebels were "levellers" looking to "annihilate all debts private and public," and a Virginia congressman advised Madison that the protesters' "ostensible object is the revision of the constitution but they certainly mean the abolition of debts public & private, a division of property & a new government founded on principles of fraud & inequity." What they meant by leveling was that a group aimed to seize the property of the wealthy and redistribute it to the poor. No such leveling had occurred in the United States of America; the radical Pennsylvania Assemblies had not seized or redistributed property, and during the war and after it when Tory property had been confiscated, it had not been generally redistributed but had been sold intact, and the proceeds used for community purposes.

While Washington downplayed the exaggerated claims about the implications of Shays's Rebellion, he did tell Humphreys that "commotions of this sort, like snow-balls, gather strength as they roll, if there is no opposition . . . to divide and crumble them," and he warned Knox: "There are combustibles in every state, which a spark might set fire to." Jefferson, in Paris, receiving reports of the uprising, wrote Madison that the Shaysites' exposure of the "incroachments on the rights of the people" was a positive, since for democracies "a little rebellion now and then is a good thing."

In September 1786, Madison, Hamilton, Coxe, and a few other nationalists traipsed to Annapolis for "A Meeting of Commissioners to Remedy Defects of the Federal Government." Lacking representatives from more states, the Annapolis participants petitioned Congress to convene a larger gathering. Through the remainder of 1786, Madison lobbied Washington to come to Philadelphia with Virginia's delegation, to no avail. In Massachusetts, Shays and other leaders hid from Lincoln, who, with the financial backing of Bowdoin, the cooperation of Congress, and support from the likes of Gerry and King, was raising a force of four thousand militia. When Shays learned that Lincoln was on the march, on January 25, 1787, he and two thousand men attempted to storm the Springfield Armory and seize its cache of arms. Shays expected the arsenal guards to join the cause, as had happened in other assaults, but the guards fired on the Shaysites: Four died, and twenty were wounded. Shays withdrew. Two days later Lincoln's army effectively ended the rebellion. Washington, on learning of the attempt on the armory, decided to join the Virginia delegation to the Convention. As he wrote Lafayette:

The pressure of the public voice was so loud, I could not resist the call to a convention . . . which is to determine whether we are to have a Government of respectability under which life—liberty, and property [are] secured to us, or whether we are to submit to one which may be the result of chance or the moment, springing perhaps from anarch(ie) Confusion, and dictated perhaps by some aspiring demagogue who will not consult the interest of his Country so much as his own ambitious views.

10

Curing the Defects

*N*othing would ever more directly affect the affairs of wealthy Americans, from 1789 to the present, or the prospects of other Americans joining their ranks, than the Constitution of the United States of America. By transforming a confederation of former vassal colonies into a sovereign democratic union of states, and by providing basic rules for commerce and trade, it enabled an economic structure conducive to citizens' bettering their lot in life.

Its wealthy framers had such ends in mind prior to the Constitutional Convention, but in the spring of 1787 they envisioned their foremost task as limiting the actions of certain state governments that they believed had been overly subservient to debtor pressure. As Madison would later explain to Jefferson: "The evils issuing from these sources contributed more to that uneasiness which produced the Convention . . . than those which accrued . . . from the inadequacy of the [Articles of] Confederation."

One of those "evils," Shays's Rebellion, was mostly over by the spring of 1787, but two elements of its aftermath contributed to the thoughts of Washington, Madison, Wilson, Hamilton, and Dickinson, who almost alone among the future convention delegates were becoming specific as to how to revise or replace the Articles of Confederation.

Massachusetts's governor Bowdoin had tried a carrot-and-stick approach with the state's debtors, delaying collection of taxes in arrears and scaling back enforcement, and at the same time attempting to institute a Disqualification Act to take from those debtors their right to vote him out of office. It didn't work. In the spring election, Hancock easily defeated Bowdoin, and the newly elected legislature was more debtor-friendly than the previous one. That switch, Madison commented to Monroe in a letter, put legislative power "into the hands of the discontented party, and it is much feared that a grievous abuse of it will characterize the new administration," by which Madison meant that Massachusetts would soon issue an emission to allow debtors to get out of debt easily. According to another Madison letter, the problem was as much Hancock as the legislators, since the governor's "acknowledged merits [were] not a little tainted by a dishonorable obsequiousness to popular follies." At the end of Hancock's political career as at the beginning, he was called a traitor to his class.

The framers feared a Massachusetts emission because six other states had already issued them to ease their debtor-farmers' burdens. Rhode Island was the glaring bad example in the framers' minds, having issued three times as much in notes as New York had done and having accompanied the notes by an edict that allowed them to be used for private debts as well as for paying taxes. Even states that had not issued emissions had taken some actions that worried the framers: Connecticut, when faced with a potential rebellion over taxes, had elected a new assembly that reduced taxes enough to cool tempers; by 1787 that same assembly, alarmed that the rebellious spirit from Massachusetts might engulf them, to avoid having to raise taxes, refused to pay the state's latest installment on the federal debt.

Shays's Rebellion and the catering to debtors of Massachusetts, Connecticut, Rhode Island, and other states solidified the framers' beliefs as to what needed to be changed in the nation's governance. Washington identified it in a letter to Madison: since the coming reform of the country's governmental system was "indispensable," any reconfiguration must enable the national government to "exercise the powers with a firm and steady hand, instead of frittering them back to the individual states." The convention must "adopt no temporising expedient, but probe the defects . . . to the bottom, and provide radical cures."

The Constitution of the United States of America was conceived, refined, and championed through to ratification by a very small subset of the country's wealthy. If we add to the fifty-five men who attended the Constitutional Convention at one time or another, twice or three times that number of nondelegates who later joined the delegates in taking the lead in urging ratification of the Constitution in their respective states, the total is at best a few hundred men—mostly the same men who during the war had been intimately connected with the central government and its armed forces, augmented by younger men who since the war had involved themselves in national affairs. This small subset of the wealthy did not seek change for the sake of change or as an opportunity to try out untested ideas; rather as seasoned leaders they recommended only those specific changes that experience had taught them were necessary.

That is to say that not only did the vast majority of the American public not participate in framing the Constitution, but also, nearly all of the wealthy had no say in making it or in getting it accepted by the populace. Some who did not participate in the creation of the Constitution did support it when presented to the public, including the shipping magnates Derby, Cabot, Peabody, Gray, and Brown of the Northeast and many former merchant trader colleagues of Laurens in Charleston and of Morris in Philadelphia (Morris himself was a key player at the convention). The activist subset at the convention also did not include many of the acknowledged best minds in America. To name just a few: academics Ezra Stiles and John Witherspoon; newspaper editors James Breckenridge and Mary Katherine Goddard; astronomer David Rittenhouse; historians David Ramsay, George Minot, and Mercy Otis Warren; entrepreneurs Bingham and Wadsworth; poet Joel Barlow, and politicians who were then abroad, Jefferson, Adams, and Jay.

According to Robert A. McGuire's statistical analysis of the delegates' backgrounds, their median age was forty-three. Nearly all had served as delegates to Congress or to state legislatures. Thirty had seen active service during the war. Seven had signed the Declaration of Independence. The delegates were five to ten times wealthier than most Americans, although not as wealthy in relation to their fellow citizens as the delegates to the first Continental Congresses had been. Half of the delegates to this convention, mostly the younger ones, had made their own fortunes, not inherited them. The inheritors were mostly the slaveholders: nineteen delegates owned an average of more than a hundred slaves apiece. Only three delegates were in serious debt—James Wilson; Gouverneur Morris, who had recently tripled his debt to purchase his ancestral home; and Roger Sherman of Connecticut, a former shoemaker.

The framers of the Constitution arrived in Philadelphia with four already formed, firmly held, shared beliefs, none of which had to do with extending democracy. First: The country's future economic greatness was inextricably tied to improving its governance. Second: The central government must have the power to prevent any one element of the governing mix—a reactionary or overly liberal state official, a runaway legislative chamber, a tyrannical executive—from compromising that future. Third: The central government must have a taxation power independent of that of the states. Fourth: The central government must possess the tools and the authority to enforce its decrees and to deal with such national problems as the debt, development of the western lands, interstate commerce, and international trade. The core contingent of activist wealthy at the convention had also reached consensus on the basic structural elements of the "radical cures." The central government must consist of a bicameral legislature with one chamber of popularly elected representatives and a second chamber of senators who would serve longer terms and balance the impetuosity of the more popularly elected house; the central government's chief executive must have enough power to curb excess legislative actions;

and the central government's judiciary must be independent of its other branches.

These beliefs were not then universally shared by Americans. Many citizens, for instance, did not agree that their central government needed a power of taxation, since some of the states were doing well in paying down their shares of the war debt. Many also had the sense, articulated by a former Connecticut congressman, that "those indomitable spirits, who have stood forth in the foremost ranks of this revolution, will never give up so much of their natural or acquired liberty as is absolutely necessary to form a strong and effective national government." Moreover, potential delegates who understood what the framers' "cures" were likely to be and disagreed with them refused to attend the convention. Patrick Henry and Richard Henry Lee of Virginia, Sam Adams of Massachusetts, and Samuel Chase of Maryland, to name just a few, all believed the outcome of the convention foregone, and even before a new Constitution was written they began to prepare to urge their constituencies to reject it.

The framers' consensus received a boost from a publication that became available just as the delegates were gathering, John Adams's *A Defence of the Constitutions of Government of the United States*. Still in London, Adams had rushed the book into print so the conventioneers could read it. His research had taught him, he wrote, that a pure democracy was not the best solution for the United States, as that configuration worked best with a small geographic area and a homogeneous population. He agreed with the generalizations of Charles-Louis de Secondat, Baron de Montesquieu, that "the natural property of small states is to be governed as a republic; of middling ones, to be subject to a monarch; and of large empires, to be swayed by a despotic prince," and had recommended a "confederate republic [as having] all the internal advantages of a republican, together with the external force of a monarchical government." Adams championed such a confederate republic, a "representative democracy."

In his opus Adams addressed head-on a subject to which the framers only alluded, Adams insisting that it was inherent in a democracy and had to be guarded against: "A free people are the most addicted to luxury of any." It was part and parcel of the promise of America, where people who had very little always had the possibility of gaining more:

> In a country like America, where the means and opportunities for luxury are so easy and so plenty, it would be madness not to expect [luxury], be prepared for it, and provide against the dangers of it in the constitution. . . . Luxury, to certain degrees of excess, is an evil; but it is not at all times, and in all circumstances, an absolute evil. . . . The evil lies in human nature; and that must be restrained by a mixed form of government, which is the best in the world to manage luxury.

The prevention of luxury's overinfluence was a prime reason for what Adams called the "tripleheaded balance," the apportioning of governing powers among legislative, executive, and judicial branches in such a manner that each branch acted as a check on the worst urges of the others, and in the legislature, the balancing of a house that drew its members from the poorer ranks of society with a senate that drew its members from those who possessed much more property and education. "If we will not adopt that," Adams warned, "we must suffer the punishment of our temerity."

Madison, in an April memo prior to the convention, agreed with the need to balance the government to prevent any single aspect of it from promulgating evils, but he identified an even more basic problem with a democracy:

> If the multiplicity and mutability of [state] laws prove a want of wisdom, their injustice betrays a defect still more alarming: more alarming not merely because it is a greater evil in itself, but because it brings more into question the fundamental principle of republican Government, that the majority who rule in such Governments, are the safest Guardians both of public Good and of private rights.

Society would always be composed of groups holding opposite views, "creditors or debtors—Rich or poor—husbandmen, merchants or manufacturers—members of different religious sects—followers of different political leaders—inhabitants of different districts—owners of different kinds of property." In a democracy the only way to prevent domination by one group was to configure a government to encompass them all.

This was quite reasonable, but the minority about which Madison had complained the most, in the previous year, and whose rights he believed had been egregiously abridged by state governments, were creditors. Wilson and Hamilton agreed. The rationale for giving the creditor minority enough weight had also been provided by Montesquieu, in his contention that in a modern republic "the spirit of commerce [was] naturally attended . . . with frugality, economy, moderation, labor, prudence, tranquility, order, and rule" and could therefore stand as a proxy for the civic virtue of the ancients, the restraining element in the admired Greek and Roman governments.

The Virginia delegation arrived in Philadelphia weeks prior to the convention. A formidable group including Madison, Washington, Mason, and Edmund Randolph, they took the opportunity to produce the Virginia Plan, fifteen resolutions to be offered as a basis of debate. When enough other delegates arrived to make a quorum, the delegates voted to keep deliberations secret, to have no official notes, and for delegates not to write home about the proceedings. To further ensure frankness of debate, they had the windows papered over.

On May 31, in the Assembly Room of the Pennsylvania State House, the delegates took up the Virginia Plan's resolution to establish two legislative branches. The delegates, having had a dozen years' experience with the disastrous legislative products of unicameral bodies—the Pennsylvania Assembly's and the Continental Congress's were mentioned—and with the better legislative results of bicameral state legislatures, readily agreed to the concept of two houses of Congress. Pennsylvania abstained in deference to Franklin, who had never gotten beyond his distrust of bicameralism, which he likened to a cart with horses front and back, pulling in two directions at once.

But the Virginia Plan's next resolution, that the House of Representatives be popularly elected, brought surprising opposition. Sherman, a signer of the Declaration, objected to this bedrock democratic notion, declaring (according to the notes that Madison took and intended not to have published until after the participants' deaths): "The people . . . should have as little to do as they may be about the Government. They want information and are constantly liable to be misled." Massachusetts's Gerry, also a signer—and reputedly, the convention's most significant holder of government-issued paper—agreed: "The evils we experience flow from the excess of democracy. . . . He said he had been too republican heretofore; he was still however republican, but had been taught by experience the danger of the levelling spirit." These negative views spurred Mason and Wilson, both known as aristocrats, to defend direct elections. To Wilson the government was a pyramid that must rest on the broadest base possible: "No government could long subsist without the confidence of the people. In a republican Government this confidence was peculiarly essential. He also thought it wrong to increase the weight of the State Legislatures by making them the electors of the national Legislature." Mason, as Madison wrote,

admitted that we had been too democratic but was afraid we sd. Incautiously run into the opposite extreme. He had often wondered at the indifference of the superior classes of society to this dictate of humanity & policy; considering that however affluent their circumstances . . . might be, the course of a few years, not only might but certainly would, distribute their posterity throughout the lowest classes of Society. Every selfish motive therefore . . . ought to recommend such a system of policy as would provide no less carefully for the rights and happiness of the lowest than of the highest orders.

A vote was taken. Of the ten states present, Connecticut and Delaware were divided on the issue, and only six states assented to popular election of the House. That was a narrow majority, but enough for the measure to become part of the Constitution.

The narrowness of the victory did reflect an antidemocratic bent, but it was more reflective of a belief that popular voting for representatives would undercut state power. Those holding such beliefs were dubbed localists, and they also tended to decry the potentially increased clout of the wealthy as a result of centralization of power. Woody Holton, a historian of the radicals, writes that the localists, states righters, and champions of individual rights who emerged at the Convention would mesh their ideas with the out-of-doors rural farmers and urban mechanics who shared the belief that recent national and state rulings had "enriched some free Americans while impoverishing others, endangering the very existence of republican government. Their great fear was not that excess democracy would scare off capital but that the methods being used to foster capitalism posed a threat to democracy." Evidence for this view was that delegates to this convention had not been democratically chosen but selected by state legislatures. Some delegates were even obligated by contract to vote as their legislatures demanded. However, most delegates considered themselves independent and not even obliged to vote as their home constituents might want them to. As a result, within delegations most questions were carried by majorities, not by unanimous votes.

The power of state legislators to shape the national government became the bone of contention when Dickinson introduced a motion to have senators chosen by them. His former law student, Wilson, opposed this and emerged as the convention's most inveterate champion of the democratic principle. But the view that swayed the majority was that of Gouverneur Morris, who expressed what he saw as a hard truth. In the national legislature, he insisted:

One interest must be opposed to another interest. . . . Vices . . . must be turned against each other. The aristocratic body [senate] should be as independent and as firm as the democratic [assembly]. . . . The Rich will strive to establish their dominion and enslave the rest. They always did. They always will. They will have the same effect here as elsewhere if we do not, by the power of government, keep them in their proper spheres. The proper security against them is to form them into a separate interest. These two forces will then contend with each other. Let the rich mix with the poor in a Commercial Country, they will establish an Oligarchy. Take away commerce, and democracy will triumph.

Hamilton was even more explicit, saying, as recorded by Robert Yates, a fellow delegate from New York:

All communities divide themselves into the few and the many. The first are the rich and well born, the other the mass of the people. . . . The people are turbulent and changing; they seldom judge or determine right. Give therefore to the first class a distinct, permanent share of the government. They will check the unsteadiness of the second. . . . Nothing but a permanent body can check the imprudence of democracy.

Dickinson wanted senators to be "distinguished for their rank in life and their weight of property," like members of the House of Lords, "and he thought such characters more likely to be selected by the State Legislatures." Franklin chimed in that senators should not be paid, to ensure that they came only from the independently wealthy. That aspect was rejected, but the Dickinson petition passed. Wilson tried again with a new resolution "That the right of suffrage in the second branch ought to be according to the same rule as in the first branch," proportional to the population. Should this pass the larger states would have more senators than the smaller ones.

With five states saying yea and five nay, the convention deadlocked and referred the matter to a committee of one delegate per state. To Wilson's distress, the Pennsylvania member was Franklin, not him. Then and later, critics charged that in rejecting equality of suffrage for the Senate, the delegates disregarded the basic democratic principle that government should exist only by consent of the governed. Further undercutting came from Madison's proposal to enlarge the geographical areas of voting districts to elect members of the House; he was explicit that larger districts would make voters more likely to choose significant property owners to represent them, contending that in smaller districts the impulse would be to vote for local characters. Critics saw further diminutions of democracy in the decisions to allow the chief executive to veto a majority vote of the legislature, to have a long-serving judiciary able to overturn state laws, and to deny state legislatures the power to recall senators or even to determine the level of senatorial salaries. According to critics, these perceived abridgements of democracy constituted a "framers' coup," which seized from those who fought the Revolution what they believed they had won: the basic right to govern themselves in a fully democratic manner. To critics, it seemed that every time, at the convention, that the framers were faced with a choice between democracy and capitalism, they chose capitalism and limited democracy.

That critique presumes there was a choice to be made and that alternative, democratic, experience-tested solutions for large-scale limiting of capitalism were available. But the workability of any alternative democratic system—say, of the communist or socialist sort (although these had not yet been well articulated)—had not been proven with a sizable, dispersed, diverse population. Moreover, a decade's worth of evidence had accumulated on the ill effects of unbridled democracy in the powerful unicameral assemblies of Pennsylvania, Rhode Island, New Hampshire, and New York. All these could be legitimately faulted for producing neither stability of governance nor economic health. At the convention, the only alternative offered to the "framers' coup" was a New Jersey plan that would leave the individual states in charge by retaining the Articles of Confederation, amended to enhance a congressional power of taxation. The New Jersey plan would only allow Congress to tax imports, and would not alter the unicameral nature of the national legislature nor any state's ability to negate congressional decisions.

Hamilton liked neither the Virginia nor the New Jersey plan, and the people out-of-doors would also not like them, he told the delegates in a daylong speech. Yates noted that Hamilton "sees the Union dissolving or already dissolved—he sees evils operating in the States which must soon cure the people of their fondness for democracies—he sees that a great progress has been already made & is still going on in the public mind." Therefore Hamilton proposed a structure akin to that of the British constitutional monarchy, with the equivalents of the Houses of Lords and Commons, and a chief executive, not crowned but chosen for life. In Hamilton's plan the executive and the senators would serve until "death, resignation or removal," the last only by "impeachment for mal- and corrupt conduct."

Hamilton's plan was so reactionary and monarchical that it made the other plans seem even more republican. He was soon explaining that he advocated a strong central government and the weakening of state power. Yates and the third New York delegate, as well as some from Maryland and Virginia, sensing this to be the mood of the convention, chose to return home. Hamilton did too, to take care of private business, and upon his later return he played less of a part in the convention.

Some convention decisions deliberately avoided thorny issues. The most important involved a proposal for the new national government to "assume" all the individual states' indebtedness and pay it off at face value. South Carolina planter and war veteran Pierce Butler expressed anger at the possibility of the government compelling payment on such notes to "bloodsuckers" who had purchased them from those who had bled for the country. As there was no consensus, the decision was left to the future; the new government's ability to deal with the national debt was considered covered by an all-purpose "general welfare" clause giving power to the central government to "lay and collect taxes, duties, imposts and excises; to pay the debts and provide for the common defence and general welfare."

During a lull, when the convention's activities were being carried on in small committees, the delegates were entertained and importuned by economic opportunists. On the Schuylkill, two competing models of steamboats chugged their way upstream to the delight of the delegates, whom the entrepreneurs hoped would license or fund one of their contraptions. A few delegates attended the convocation of the Pennsylvania Society for the Encouragement of Manufactures and the Useful Arts, and were harangued by its president, Tench Coxe, not to continue their resistance to manufacturing in the United States and instead to direct the country to reject all imported manufactured goods and "employ [our] own people as much as possible in making those [things] that are necessary." He urged that the new government provide premiums to help native manufacturers.

That convention committee consisting of one delegate from each state became the locus of the action, its behind-the-scenes nature allowing the eighty-one-year-old Franklin to shine. "The diversity of opinion turns on two points," he advised in regard to the big-state-vs.-small-state problem. "If a proportional representation takes place, the small states contend that their liberties will be in danger. If an equality of votes [among the states] is to be put in place, the large states say their money will be in danger." By such a formulation Franklin made a trade inevitable. Sherman then offered a "Connecticut Compromise": that representation in the House should be proportional and in the Senate should be equal among the states. It was accepted along with two more-republican compromises. The first rejected the notion of Congress choosing the president in favor of semidirect elections in which voters would choose electors to select the president; and the second added to the clout of the House by having all funding bills originate there.

As discussions on these and other issues became more granular, each delegate's votes increasingly reflected his economic interests. McGuire's analysis shows an inverse relationship between how far a delegate lived from navigable water and his vote—those living close to water invariably favored nationalist positions. The second most significant factor affecting voting was slaveholding. On a crucial issue, of whether a national legislature should have veto power over state laws, a delegate who owned no slaves was eleven times more likely to vote yea—and the proposal was defeated because there were plenty of slaveholders in Delaware and Maryland as well as in Virginia.

The most emphatic limiting of state economic prerogatives was the wording of Section 10 of Article I of the Constitution: "No State shall enter into any Treaty, Alliance, or Confederation; grant Letters of Marque and Reprisal; coin money; emit Bills of Credit; make any Thing but gold and silver Coin a tender in Payment of Debts; pass any Bill of Attainder; ex post facto Law, or Law impairing the Obligation of Contracts, or grant any Title of Nobility." With the exception of granting titles of nobility, the states had previously passed legislation on all those things.

Madison believed, as did the others who had studied the history of governments, Hamilton and Adams, that the failure of several ancient confederacies and the enfeebling of the current Netherlands Stadtholderate stemmed from the lack of a national veto over local edicts. But at the Convention, Madison's plea for Congress to have an absolute veto over state laws was rejected as taking too much power from the states; instead, there was a compromise: federal laws were declared "supreme" and power was given to judges to reject state laws that infringed on this supremacy.

The most noxious convention compromise was the three-fifths rule, which counted a slave as 60 percent of a white male for determining a state's number of representatives, presidential electors, and tax assessments. It is worth underscoring that at the convention this was not contentious: A two-slaves-to-one-freeman rule had been suggested in the 1776 debate over the Articles of Confederation, and had been put into law several times since then. At the convention it was proposed by a committed abolitionist, Wilson, so as to induce slave states to agree to the Constitution. The three-fifths rule was decidedly antidemocratic, not only because it disenfranchised slaves but because it diminished the power of northern voters and augmented that of southerners. After it passed, there was no meaningful opposition to another slaveholder proposal, to allow importing of slaves until 1808, or to one that fugitive slaves must be returned to owners even from nonslave states.

After a summer recess the delegates returned in September to address how the Constitution would be ratified and how it could be amended. Hamilton made the naive proposal to have the extant Congress ratify the Constitution and then send it to the states. Other delegates pointed out that this could easily run into Rhode Island–type blocking, and that things would go better if the Congress simply directed the states to conduct special elections for ratification conventions. Hamilton's notion was buried. As for amending the Constitution, most delegates did not want to re-create conditions that had allowed a single state to overturn the will of the other twelve, or allow easy passage of amendments that would leach power from the central government. The bar for proposed amendments was set high: They could become law only if approved by three-quarters of all state legislatures.

A Committee on Style, led by Gouverneur Morris and including Hamilton and Madison, boiled twenty-three articles into seven, so that opponents would have fewer points to seize on. The document proposed a limited but workable democracy, and was very much protrade and pro–wealth holder in its eliminating of tariff barriers between states, provision for a stable currency, and for the federal government to negotiate future overseas commercial agreements.

It was remarkable that the United States, only four years after the Peace of Paris, had managed to identify its structural problems and find very reasonable ways to fix them. This notion energized Franklin in his response to a request to speak at the conclusion of the convention. He and Gouverneur Morris wrote a speech, but Franklin was too ill to give it, so Wilson did. After confessing that he (Franklin) did not approve of everything in the Constitution, which was to be expected when so many competing interests had a hand in it and made so many compromises, "It therefore astonishes me . . . to find this system approaching so near to perfection as it does. . . . The opinions I have had of its errors I sacrifice to the public good," and he asked each delegate to do the same, to "doubt a little of his own infallibility," and unanimously approve the Constitution and then actively stump for its ratification.

This Constitution was as much about capitalism as about democracy, and as helpful to wealth holders, entrepreneurs, and creditors as they could have hoped. It also reaffirmed basic principles of fairness and of economic opportunity that would aid those on the lower rungs of the economic ladder in climbing it toward greater wealth.

Stephen Girard, that relatively new citizen of the United States, and then on the verge of great wealth, on the day after the Constitution's passage read the entire document in the *Pennsylvania Packet*. He celebrated it, among other reasons, for the sanctity of contracts article, behind which he discerned the hand of Hamilton. He worried that the Constitution was a document more for tomorrow than for today, and that those who did not understand that might well vote against it. His visits to the Coffee House, City Tavern, and Black Horse Tavern confirmed his fears: Ratification was far from assured.

Three delegates had already refused to sign it: Mason, Randolph, and Gerry. They had advocated permitting individual states to offer amendments to the Constitution during the ratification process; a majority of the convention delegates, fearing that amendments would eviscerate the Constitution, decreed that the ratification vote would be only a yea or a nay by state conventions. Once nine states had ratified, it would come into effect.

On the back of a committee report Mason wrote out his criticisms. He charged that the Constitution did not contain a bill of rights, that the House was not powerful enough, that the Senate was too powerful and too entwined with the executive branch through its fiat to accept or reject treaties and cabinet officers, that Congress had too much power vis-à-vis the states, and that the Constitution would permit the arrogation of even more power to the central government. His points were copied by others at the convention and elsewhere, and became a template for opposing adoption of the Constitution. He became a leader of that opposition in Virginia, along with Patrick Henry; in Massachusetts, Gerry was a similar leader against ratification; and in New York, the opposition featured Yates, who had left the convention so that he would not have to sign, and who was joined in his leadership by Governor George Clinton.

The battle over ratification of the Constitution engaged the largest fraction of the nation's populace ever in a debate that was salutary because it so thoroughly hashed over every word. In each state the most active proponents, eventually known as Federalists, had been delegates to the convention: Wilson, Franklin, Dickinson, Sherman, Madison, and Hamilton. Washington did not take an active part in promoting a document that, if ratified, would likely make him president, but a visitor to him wrote to Jefferson: "I never saw him so keen for any thing in my life, as he is for the adoption of the new form of government," although, the visitor added, Washington was reluctant to "appear once more on the Publick Stage."

Dividing the pros and cons were splits that had been growing for decades, those separating cities and countryside, the eastern and western areas, the creditors and the debtors. Those differences had a greater impact on potential ratification than Mason's structural concerns about the overconcentration of power.

The proadoption Pennsylvania contingent wanted the state to act quickly so as to put it in prime position to host the new national government. That plan ran into immediate objections from Whitehill and other old state Constitutionalists. During a dragged-out process, on October 7 Wilson made an important speech, soon reprinted in newspapers throughout the country, in which he promised that the new national government would exercise and pursue only the powers that the Constitution explicitly granted to that government. It was on this understanding that many states agreed to ratify.

Despite the drawn-out nature of Pennsylvania's debate, the state was considered highly likely to ratify. New York, not so much, at the time when its newspapers took up the matter. The most significant early pro-Federalist essay, in terms of its eventual impact on the New York ratifying convention, was by John Jay. The anti-Federalist cause had fewer such big names, although Governor Clinton changed the eligibility rules for voting for New York's convention delegates to include all adult white males, in the hope that increased rural voter participation would ensure rejection.

Clinton made two mistakes thereby—the first in not understanding that mechanics and artisans would be for ratification because they believed the new government would be good for their employers' businesses and thus for them, and the second in lumping all farmers together and presuming they were all anti-Federalists, when the ones who lived nearer the cities and whose main trade was in providing fare for city dwellers were part of the market economy and voted in ways similar to the urban artisans and mechanics. A statistical analysis of state delegates throughout the country showed that automatic yea votes were more likely to come from those with "merchant interests and private securities holdings," and less likely from those in "deep personal debt," but that the balance of power lay in the hands of rural market-economy farmers and the urban mechanics and artisans.

Ratification of the Constitution is often credited in our mythology to the Publius essays in *The Federalist*, written by Hamilton and Madison, with an occasional one by Jay. But as the historian of ratification Pauline Meier points out, these essays did not begin to appear in the *New York Packet* until quite near the time of the New York convention, and were only sporadically republished elsewhere. Not until the spring, when some states' voting had already been completed (but not New York's), were they issued as *The Federalist Papers,* achieving wider distribution and influence. They remain as a sterling guide to the framers' thoughts, and to their unremittingly elitist nature, most blatantly exhibited in "Federalist 35," in Hamilton scoffing at having each class represent itself:

Mechanics and manufacturers will always be inclined . . . to give their votes to merchants, in preference to persons of

their own professions. . . . They are aware, that . . . their interests can be more effectually promoted by the merchant than
by themselves. They are sensible that their habits in life have
not been such as to give them those acquired endowments,
without which, in a deliberative assembly, the greatest natural
abilities are for the most part useless; and that the influence
and weight, and superior acquirements of the merchants render them more equal to a contest with any spirit which might
happen to infuse itself into the public councils, unfriendly to
the manufacturing and trading interests.

In "Federalist 12" Hamilton was quite specific as to the aim of
a new government under the new Constitution: "the prosperity of
commerce." He believed that was "the most productive source of national wealth," since it served to "vivify and invigorate all the channels
of industry and to make them flow with greater activity and copious-
ness." As evidence he observed that Europe's lands, although as fertile
and as productive as any on earth, were constrained in producing
wealth that could be shared with large segments of the population
because Europe's monarchs refused to allow enough commerce to
take place; the new American plan of governance would encourage
commerce so that it would benefit a much larger fraction of the
population than in Europe.

The Publius arguments were not aimed at the swing voters, and
the Federalists also overestimated the popularity of their cause in rural areas not directly touched by the war or the market economy,
areas whose pride was their independence, in the sense of their ability
to sustain themselves without reference to the world beyond their
borders. Such a resistance resulted in an early vote in New Hampshire
that was an unexpected no to the Constitution.

There were also positive state surprises. Delaware, usually quite
divided on big issues, on this one was united, its convention deciding
unanimously to ratify. Another surprise was New Jersey, also known
as deeply divided, and which had submitted the small-state plan at
the convention that had caused so much difficulty. New Jersey ratified

because it needed a protection that only a national government could bring, from the excess taxation on incoming goods by both Pennsylvania and New York. Georgia had been counted on by its southern brethren to raise objections to perceived northern control, but it ratified for a reason similar to that of New Jersey: to obtain the benefit of federal armed forces to put down Native American uprisings and slave revolts.

After a handful of states had ratified and more seemed on the verge of doing so, the value of state monetary paper declined and the value of federal paper climbed. Pelatiah Webster rejoiced in print: At last true redemption was nigh.

The rural-urban divide still troubled Massachusetts. Governor Hancock, quite ill, tried to let others carry the fight over ratification. Sam Adams also attempted to remain aloof, but as he was still known for listening to the voice of the people, the Federalists organized a meeting in Boston so he could hear that voice. Paul Revere's speech for ratification and a vote convinced Adams. His agreeing to ratification changed others' minds. Only after that did Hancock rise from his sickbed and, carried into the hall, throw his political weight behind ratification. He argued—in a position later noted approvingly by Jefferson—that those seeking amendments to the Constitution, as he did, needed first to ratify it and have it become law before offering amendments.

Virginians' general disagreement with one another about ratification was epitomized by the permanent rupture that it caused between Washington and Mason. The former commander in chief believed his neighbor's opinions on the subject to be in bad faith. Patrick Henry took up them up, though, and by commingling Mason's with southerners' worries about northern domination and fear of creeping abolitionism, created the likelihood that Virginia would not ratify. (Henry's effectiveness was attested to by Jefferson's wish that he die.) Madison had not yet been able to corral enough votes in Virginia for ratification when news arrived that the number of yea states had risen to nine, because New Hampshire, pressured heavily by the Federalists and by its downstate citizens, had reversed its earlier decision. For

Virginians the worry that the federal government would come into effect without them and then pass bills deleterious to them finally yielded a yea. New York also feared the loss of considerable business should it not ratify and the new Congress locate the capital elsewhere than in Manhattan; these matters persuaded a majority of the state's convention to ratify.

By June enough states had ratified so that there could be celebrations throughout the country on July 4, 1788, that the United States of America would henceforth be governed under a better and fairer set of laws. Ratification also occurred in enough time to schedule the elections of the first president, vice president, and Congress for the fall, and after the results became known, for the newly elected officials to take office in the spring of 1789.

Part Four

———∞∞∞———

The Federalist Ascendancy,
1789–1796

11

Washington:
Creating the Establishment

The adulation of the crowds in every town along Washington's route from Mount Vernon to New York City in the spring of 1789 made him wonder whether a president ought to appear in public with the trappings of a monarch. Bingham, whose elegantly decked-out Second Troop of Philadelphia Light Horse accompanied him across Pennsylvania, thought so. Vice President elect John Adams wrote him: "Neither Dignity, nor Authority, can be Supported in human Minds collected into nations or any great numbers without a Splendor and Majisty, in Some degree, proportioned to them," but did admit: "My long Residence abroad may have impressed me with Views of Things, incompatible with the present Temper . . . of our Fellow Citizens." Hamilton thought Washington should only interact with elected officials, important people, and foreign dignitaries. Washington, wary of republican familiarity, soon embraced monarchical distance. As he explained to a friend:

> Gentlemen, consulting their own convenience rather than mine, were calling from the time I rose from breakfast—often before—until I sat down to dinner—This, as I resolved not to neglect my public duties, reduced me to the choice of . . . either to refuse them *altogether,* or to appropriate a time for the reception of them—The first would, I well knew, be disgusting to many—The latter, *I expected,* would undergo animadversion,

and blazoning from those who would find fault, *with,* or *without* cause. To please every body was impossible.

Washington agreed to a weekly levee as the only time when he would meet ordinary citizens, an arrangement that irked those who believed that a democracy's leaders should be more regularly accessible to the people.

Senator William Maclay of Pennsylvania, an anti-Federalist who had known Washington since they were colleagues in the French and Indian War, was flabbergasted at the Senate devoting so much time to whether to call the president "His Mightiness" or "His Excellency." Madison regaled Jefferson with the tale of Virginia's R. H. Lee, "tho elected as a republican enemy to an aristocratic constitution," seconding Adams's motion for "His Highness the President of the United States and the Protector of Their Liberties." Fortunately, Madison added, the House refused to agree to a title that would have "subjected the president to a severe dilemma and given a deep wound to our infant government."

Adams, who had opted to preside over the Senate in a powdered wig and ceremonial sword, soon realized that the expenses attendant on his position, from habiliments to entertaining, were catapulting him into debt from which he would "not easily get out." Secretary of War Knox fretted because his expenses for a year in New York, which he tabulated at £1,314, exceeded his salary of £980. The senators voted themselves six dollars a day for expenses; most of them were wealthy and could afford to dig into their own pockets to maintain themselves in appropriate style, but the small per diem troubled some House members. Speaker Frederick Muhlenberg—a pastor, not a wealthy man—told a correspondent it was impossible to exist in New York on that, as "it is in vain at this place to talk of frugality, Oeconomy, & a Republican Stile of Living."

Adding to Knox's concern was that he was also supporting Benjamin Lincoln, recently thrown out of his office of lieutenant governor of Massachusetts. Lincoln joined a long list of people importuning Washington for a federal post. After a delay Washington appointed

Lincoln port collector for Boston. Thereafter his income grew steadily, as did the office, to more than fifty people directly and hundreds more in private enterprises that served it. He was able to award lucrative contracts to his sons to build lighthouses.

Morris declined Washington's invitation to be secretary of the treasury. His business affairs had taken a disastrous turn, and he had to deal with a report by the final pre-Constitution Congress holding him responsible for two million dollars unaccounted for by the Secret Committee. He recommended as secretary "a far cleverer fellow," Hamilton. Washington professed not to have thought of his former aide for the senior position, but Morris assured him of Hamilton's knowledge of finance and his innate abilities.

How should the individual economic patriot now act, as the new nation was taking shape under the Constitution? Some answers emerged from the deliberations of the first sessions of the new Congress. The Federalists' floor leaders in the House were two of the wealthiest members, Madison and Wadsworth. Madison was a representative because Virginia's governor, Patrick Henry, had denied him a Senate seat. Wadsworth had been an easy choice for Connecticut. The two had much to do with shaping legislation, usually in concert with Hamilton, and even before Hamilton had officially taken office. Since there was still an aversion to direct taxation, at Hamilton's behest Madison introduced what everyone had expected the new government to rely on—an impost on "imported goods, wares, and merchandise."

With the sort of deep common sense that seems to have vanished from today's discussions of tariffs and taxes, Pelatiah Webster had long advocated placing the heaviest import duties on goods "the consumption of which are least necessary to the community" and the lightest on those "the use and consumption of which are most necessary to the community." Congress, then composed of fairly well-to-do merchants and lawyers, seemed to agree with him: Taxation, even indirect taxation, should not fall too heavily upon the majority of the country's populace that was relatively poor. But they also knew that taxing the truly wealthy's new chaises and coaches at 15 percent could not fund a national government since only a thousand families could afford such luxuries. There must be tariffs on the two dozen items bought regularly by hundreds of thousands of households. Anti-Federalist House members such as Aedanus Burke, that enemy of the Cincinnati, argued that salt, as a necessity of life for the poor, must carry no tax. The leadership and members accommodated that reasonable position, as they did others that shielded the incomes of the poor. To these wealthy legislators, patriotism still meant honoring their obligation to protect the incomes of the vast majority of their constituents who were considerably less wealthy.

But some of the legislators were also quite protective of their own business interests and those of their neighbors. According to historian of lobbying Pasley, demands for exceptions to the tariffs, and for greatly reduced tariffs, came mostly from legislators with "personal connections to the industries they were speaking for, [and whose] ability to defend local interests was greatly enhanced by Congress's incestuous tendency to appoint the members most interested in a particular measure to the committee charged with considering it." The duty that provoked the most pyrotechnic rhetoric was on molasses, a basic raw material for distillers, and for the fishing industry as a component of grog for sailors, and for the poor who could not afford sugar. Northeastern distillers complained that duties on molasses would allow competitors to undercut them in price, and western producers contended the opposite. Maclay confided to his diary the underlying story:

> I fear that the impost will be rendered in a great measure unproductive. . . . The New England men . . . want molasses quite struck out, or at least greatly reduced; therefore they will strike at everything, or, to place it in a different point of view, almost every part will be proscribed either by one or the other . . . for every conspirator must be indulged in the sacrifice of his particular enemy.

But even Maclay had an ax to grind, rising to defend tariffs on imported cordage to protect his constituents, western Pennsylvania's rope makers.

Madison reported to Jefferson that this initial debate was a "favorable symptom" of democracy. He also saw it as an opportunity to advance his own agenda: to slap the toughest levies on British products, to punish Great Britain for having "bound us in commercial manacles, and very nearly defeated the object of our independence." Hamilton objected, because the funding of the government relied on the very large portion of the tariff income that derived from British imports; he was able to persuade enough congressmen of that need to defeat "discrimination." That debate too was a sign of democracy, since despite twenty-three of the twenty-six senators being Federalists, enough of them disagreed with Hamilton to force an Adams vote to break a tie and pass the bill.

Madison tacked to the wind and next introduced tonnage charges on foreign-owned ships that were higher than those on American-owned ones. This was a more blatant attempt to punish the British. His idea was met by a hail of quotes from Adam Smith asserting the free-market notion that commerce would regulate itself. Madison retorted that if the United States did not regulate its own trade, other countries—meaning Great Britain—would dictate the parameters. Hamilton again intervened, and the majority accepted his plea to lessen the burden on British ships but not on French ones. Hamilton sought to punish the French and favor the British, but his other agenda regarding the tariff and tonnage charges was to keep them low overall, so as to cap the American government's income, lest an excess spur calls to use it to pay down the principal of the national debt. Carrying that debt intact was central to Hamilton's program.

Salem merchant Derby had problems with the tariff and tonnage bills. One was that the latter's definition of what was an American ship excluded the sort of foreign vessels that his had captured during the war and that he had since repurposed as American carriers. The second was that the new tariff on tea, instituted since he had sent several ships to India to buy that commodity, had him immediately owing the government $35,000. To pay it now would mean selling his inventory at a huge loss. He sent to both houses of Congress a "memorandum," in which he referred to himself in the third person:

> His situation is peculiarly distressing, requiring him to sell his property at so low a price as to make him, in fact, pay the duty out of his own pocket . . . or to suffer his bonds to be put in suit, and thereby to have his credit impaired, and lose his reputation of punctuality. . . . Whichever step he takes, it will be a painful, really painful one to him. Under this melancholy expression, he flies to your honors for relief.

Derby offered to pay the tax over time, a bit whenever he sold some of the tea. Congress yielded to this reasonable request, and Derby became an even-stauncher Federalist.

After the tariff bill Madison honored another promise of ratification by introducing the amendments that would become the Bill of Rights. In the past he had believed such a bill unnecessary because the rights were inherent in the Constitution. Jefferson had thought so too, but his experience in Paris—where the Bastille had just been stormed and he was assisting Lafayette in writing France's Declaration of the Rights of Man and Citizen—taught him that there was a need in America for the overt expression of such rights. Another two years would elapse before all the states ratified the Bill of Rights.

Next, Congress established three executive departments: Treasury, War, and Foreign Affairs. It was generally understood that Washington would nominate for these, respectively, Hamilton, Knox, and Jefferson.

The most unexpected appointment was Jefferson's. For while he and Washington had both lost fathers when young, operated Virginia plantations with hundreds of slaves, and had always been solicitous of each other—after the war Washington had repeatedly asked Jefferson for advice and included him as a partner in several development schemes, and Jefferson always expressed his deep admiration for what Washington accomplished—they were not close nor did they think alike. Washington wanted Jefferson in the cabinet because he respected Jefferson's intellect and desired contrarian views, and Jefferson accepted the position because he believed the president needed to have such views.

While Jefferson took months to return and begin work, Hamilton started immediately. Confirmed on a Friday in September, by Monday he had already borrowed $150,000 from banks to tide over the government until the tariff revenues began to flow, and met with the French minister to discuss rescheduling America's debt to France. Congress directed him to produce several reports. Having sought the assignment, Hamilton had his First Report on the Public Credit ready on January 9, 1790. It was the culmination of thoughts begun in his *The Farmer Refuted* of 1775 and developed in 1779–1781 letters to Sullivan, Duane, and Morris. His notions were influenced by the analyses of Smith and philosopher David Hume, and by Jacques Necker's attempts to rescue France's finances.

The United States prospered in the early Federalist era, and Hamilton's program has been deemed the reason for that prosperity. There were other reasons: During the postwar years the country's economy had healed and resumed its growth, spurred by the increasing settlement of new lands and their productivity. When Washington took office, America was poised for strong growth. What the Hamilton program did accomplish was the generation of "capital in mobilizable form, accessible credit both foreign and domestic, a stable currency for the transaction of business, and government encouragement for the kinds of enterprises that would be of greatest benefit to the entire community," according to the historians of the Federalist era Stanley Elkins and Eric McKittrick. Those were considerable engines for growth. But Elkins and McKittrick also point out that the Hamilton program's engine for growth was aimed almost solely at unleashing the creative activities of the merchant class— none of it directly uplifted the vastly larger working-class segment of the populace. Hamilton's was the original American trickle-down economic plan, as paternalistic as any in a monarchy. More: It created a new, capitalistic aristocracy whose hold on power was seated in the differential in liquid capital and credit between it and the working classes. Had the working classes been encouraged in equal proportion—say, by more progressive taxation, or by using national income for infrastructure enhancement—would the result have been any more salutary? Madison, Jefferson, and others thought so. But the objections they raised did not directly address such issues. Rather, they focused on Hamilton's presumption that the public would be best served by paying off the debt very slowly. Hamilton's contention was that paying only the interest on the debt and a bit of the principal each year would not only allow the debt to continue to serve as a binding common obligation that united the states, but would enable the use of tariff income to establish the federal departments and thereby add to the power of the central government. That debt had grown considerably larger. No longer at $27 million, it stood at $40 million, plus an additional $12 million owed to foreign creditors and $25 million owed by the states to their citizens—for a total of $77 million owed, at a moment when the GNP was less than $200 million a year. The critics argued for speedy repayment so that government income could be used for enhancing the country's economic capabilities.

Three ways to get rid of this debt had been bruited about: repudiation, discrimination, and redemption. Full repudiation was the equivalent of a declaration of bankruptcy, which no one wanted, and partial repudiation would create a nightmare in determining which obligations to spurn. Discrimination—paying off some paper at face value and some at market value—was being championed, notably by Madison, to make whole the soldiers, farmers, and merchants who had fought the war and supplied the troops. Hamilton said no: He was only for full face-value redemption and for full federal assumption of the states' debt. Face-value redemption, Hamilton insisted, was a moral obligation, necessary to assure foreign lenders that the United States stood behind its pledge of "full faith and credit." As for assumption, in his eyes that too was a moral imperative, and it would also lower citizens' overall tax bills once the states no longer had to obtain money for debt service and could impose smaller rates of taxation on their inhabitants. Washington agreed with Hamilton on those points.

Practical objections to the Hamilton plan arose. Assumption would be good for northern states that owed a lot but not for southern states that owed very little and would not be able to lower their state taxes even as their national taxes rose. Face-value redemption would be unfair because three-quarters of the certificates were no longer in the hands of the veterans, farmers, and small merchants to whom they had originally been issued as payment for services rendered. For instance, 42 percent of the Massachusetts debt's owners held just 3 percent of the total, while 62 percent of the debt was in the hands of just 7 percent of the owners, who also controlled virtually all of the higher-denominated certificates. Nathan Prime of Boston, the original owner of only $79 worth, had acquired $196,000, likely on behalf of the wealthy broker who had first employed him as a coachman. In Maryland and Pennsylvania these ratios were similar, although in other states they were less lopsided. Derby had been accumulating certificates for decades, and had several hundred thousand dollars' worth, as did Bingham.

"It would be hard to aggravate the misfortune of the first owner, who, probably through necessity, parted with his property at so great a loss, by obliging him to contribute to the profit of the person, who had speculated on his distresses," Hamilton admitted, arguing nonetheless that early sellers had gotten their value through transactions at then-current market prices, and now ought not to kick. Hamilton also had an ulterior motive, according to Elkins and McKittrick, a paternalistic one: He "did not want holdings in the public debt widely dispersed. He wanted the resources which they represented concentrated as much as possible in the hands of a particular class of men [to be] maximally available for productive economic uses."

No specie would be paid out, in Hamilton's plan, even though that broke the existing certificates' promises of being redeemable in gold or silver. For every $100.00 in old certificates that holders turned in they would receive $66.67 in new government currency, plus new certificates paying 6 percent for ten years, and then the remaining

$33.33. This would mean an effective interest rate of 5 percent on the new certificates—less than the 6 percent they had been paying. For the assumed state paper, the federal government would pay only 3 percent.

Attesting to how good a deal that was for certificate owners, as the date for redemption approached, and although its details had deliberately not been made public, speculators bought up the old debt certificates. They did so mainly based on insider information, some directly from Duer, who was then Hamilton's assistant and, despite Treasury rules, a foremost speculator in the paper. Jefferson received reports from home on speculators and soon charged that they bought certificates cheaply by telling holders the bald-faced lie that the new government planned not to redeem the certificates at all. Pelatiah Webster raged: "A Crisis of public distress is the proper time for this vermin [speculators] to swarm, like flies about a sore, or crows around a carcase," adding that America was wealthy enough to pay market price to original holders and current ones, as the government could simply raise tariffs on silks, jewelry, and fine wines to underwrite the extra. This polemic was Webster's last: After it, he fell ill and wrote no more.

Madison, citing this flurry of last-minute speculation, decided to stand in the way of assumption and face value. This surprised Hamilton, who prided himself on seldom being surprised. Madison's real dismay was at Hamilton's breaking of the covenant of ratification, the assurance given to the states that the national government would not seek additional powers beyond those explicitly granted by the Constitution. Madison found allies in southern congressmen who believed that assumption would shortchange their states' taxpayers, in anti-Federalists who disliked it on states' rights grounds, and in others who agreed with him that it would put off the retirement of the debt and unduly burden the next generation. Just then a particularly large cohort of children was in evidence in the United States, a higher percentage of the populace than ever before. Madison's argument on their behalf was influenced by Jefferson's latterly famous "usufruct" letter:

The question Whether one generation of men has a right to bind another, seems never to have been started either on this or our side of the water. . . . I suppose to be self-evident, *that the earth belongs in usufruct to the living.* . . . I say the earth belongs to each of these generations, during it's course, fully, and in their own right. The 2d. generation receives it clear of the debts & incumbrances of the 1st. the 3d of the 2d. & so on. For if the 1st. could charge it with a debt, then the earth would belong to the dead & not the living generation.

For that reason also, Jefferson wrote, constitutions should be tossed out every nineteen years and new ones fashioned. Madison was not so sure about recycling constitutions, believing that first generations did pass on helpful advantages as well as debts, but was upset that Hamilton's plan would overly burden later generations.

On April 12, 1790, Madison called a vote on the Hamiltonian assumption plan, and it failed to pass, 31 to 29. Hamilton was chagrined but not yet ready to admit defeat. He made a pact with Morris: to site the country's capital permanently in Philadelphia in exchange for Morris obtaining enough votes for assumption. Two months later, when neither man could produce enough votes, the debt bill stalled.

The next morning, June 20, 1790, Jefferson met Hamilton by chance near the door of Washington's official residence in New York. Hamilton appeared "somber, haggard, and dejected beyond description. Even his dress [was] uncouth and neglected." He told Jefferson that if assumption did not pass he might have to resign, and New England might leave the union. Jefferson asked that Hamilton dine with him and Madison the next evening, "to find some temperament for the present fever." In American mythology, at that dinner Madison agreed to corral the few additional votes needed to pass assumption in exchange for Hamilton persuading enough northerners to locate the new capital, after an interim decade in Philadelphia, in a new city to be built on the banks of Potomac. But Congress had already decided to move the capital to the Potomac—Morris was buying up property there and predicting that building lots "will continue rising in price for one hundred years to come!"—and Madison had said publicly that he could agree to assumption provided certain adjustments were made. At the dinner he demanded only that Hamilton lower the overall amount of state debt to be assumed, and give Virginia better terms. The total of those changes being under three million dollars, Hamilton readily agreed.

For a while the deal was kept secret from Congress, but Maclay figured it out and dubbed it inherently corrupt; in his view assumption was unnecessary since western lands could be sold to pay off the debt, therefore, "to bind down the public by an irredeemable debt . . . is equally absurd as shackling the hands and feet with fetters rather than walking at liberty." He blamed Washington for becoming, "in the hands of Hamilton, the dish-clout of every dirty speculation, as his name goes to wipe away blame and silence all murmuring. . . . [He is] the constant cover to every unconstitutional and irrepublican act." In letters home, Maclay began to refer to New York as Hamiltonia. Dickinson agreed with Maclay that Maclay's enemies were conspiring to defeat his reelection.

The passing of time mooted objections to the debt program. Within a few years there were twenty thousand new bondholders, most of them owners of the smaller bonds—the median holding was $571.19. Early in the war Laurens had not been able to enlist five hundred Americans to bail out the debt, but now twenty thousand people around the world—there were many foreign buyers—believed enough in the stability of the government of the United States of America, and in its future, to buy that debt.

It was concerns about the country's economic stability that swayed the discussion when slavery was thrust onto the agenda of Congress by Franklin and a contingent of Quakers, who presented petitions calling, respectively, for restrictions on the slave trade and for outright abolition. Michael J. Stone of Maryland, an anti-Federalist representative and scion of a tobacco family, warned "that if Congress took any measures indicative of an intention to interfere with the kind of property alluded to, it would sink it in value very considerably, and might be injurious to a great number of the citizens." This economic argument was accepted as truth without significant opposition, and then the matter was sent to a committee that the members knew was likely to be less aggressive on restraining slavery than any individual congressman might be. As expected, the committee cited the Constitution's limiting of Congress's ability to forbid the importation of slaves prior to 1808 as reason for Congress to now do nothing about slavery.

The state governments of New England were currently considering and would shortly enact emancipation and abolition laws; even so, too many of those states' national representatives accepted the argument that, as Matthew Mason, a scholar of slavery legislation, puts it: "Slavery was a necessity in the Deep South . . . indispensable . . . to agricultural labor in the Southern climate," and so to halt it "would be fruitless or even dangerous." Then too, the New England representatives were quite aware of the northern economy's partial dependence on slaving, reaping profits from transporting the products of slave-labor plantations, as well as slaves for sale. Their refusal to address slavery in the earliest Congresses after the adoption of the Constitution was a missed opportunity, one that set the pattern of slavery for the remainder of the century. Throughout the presidencies of Washington and Adams, who both professed to desire abolition, the practice of slavery increased, extending without national governmental opposition into what would become Kentucky, Tennessee, Alabama, and Mississippi.

This was an American failure, but it should be noted that just then most of the slave-importing trade was British and French: in the decade after the Peace of Paris they made, respectively, 1,073 and 727 slaving voyages to the United States. The expansion of slavery into the new territories also increased as an unexpected result of the awarding of one early national patent, for the cotton gin. B. Zorina Khan, who studied early patent systems in Great Britain and in those

American states that prior to 1789 had patent-awarding powers, writes that these systems favored the elite and manufacturers while shortchanging inventors. The Constitution, however, "consciously created patent and copyright institutions that were intended to function as the keystone of a democratic society." Washington formed a three-cabinet-member committee to review applications for national patents, under the chairmanship of Jefferson, that inveterate tinkerer and sometime inventor. As did Franklin, a more notable inventor, Jefferson had once believed that inventors should simply gift their creations for the public good, but by 1790 he had recognized that not all inventors were wealthy enough to give up the potential income. The committee awarded noncontroversial patents for potash, fire retardants, the distilling of liquor, and the placement of piles for bridges, but also an important one—to Eli Whitney, for the cotton gin, which mechanically removed the burrs that made cotton harvesting so labor-intensive. Jefferson worked assiduously with the young Yale graduate, helping refine his drawings and submission papers.

Whitney had had two hopes for his invention: One was to make his fortune; that did not happen because the cotton gin became so necessary that it was widely reproduced without paying him royalties. His second hope was that since the cotton gin enabled one man to do the work of fifty, it would end slavery. In this he similarly misjudged human greed: In response to the cotton gin planters bought fifty to a hundred times more acreage and purchased more slaves to work them with the new machines.

The second important patent awarded by the three-secretaries committee was for the steamboat. The trio were initially unable to decide among four competing inventors' designs. Two, by James Rumsey and John Fitch, had been demonstrated in nearly full-size model form at the Constitutional Convention. Currently Fitch's *Perseverance II* was making daily runs from Philadelphia to Trenton faster than a stagecoach could, and Rumsey's prototype was due for a trial in Great Britain. Unable to choose among the applicants, Jefferson decided to award patents to all four at the same hour on the same day,

so that none had precedence. Intended to help, this decision scut-
tled the commercial chances of all four, which delayed the large-scale
commercial introduction of the steamboat for more than a decade.
Shortly the cabinet-secretary system of review of patent applications
was replaced by having the task done by governmental experts in the
law and in mechanics.

Hamilton knew better than to introduce all the elements of his grand
plan at once, although he considered them interdependent. Only after
Congress relocated to Philadelphia in December 1790 did he ask it
to charter the Bank of the United States, of a size and with a fiat that
would put more power in his hands than the Bank of North America
had in Morris's. The BUS's capital would be ten million dollars, far
less than the two hundred million he had once envisioned but still
making it the country's largest enterprise. The government would buy
two million dollars in shares. The remaining eight million would be
sold, two million for gold or silver, the rest for certificates.

Philadelphia, home to the largest cluster of the country's wealthy,
was the ideal place to introduce such a bank. In addition to the BoNA,
a two-million-dollar Pennsylvania Bank had recently been chartered,
with the state buying half of its shares. The city's high society was led
by Bingham, his wife Anne, and her sisters, the daughters of Thomas
Willing. The Binghams had built the country's most expensive in-
town home, and entertained there in a style that visitors thought mar-
velous, although John and Abigail Adams dubbed Mrs. Bingham's as
perhaps too French. The Washingtons took up residence in Robert
Morris's home, next door to Willing's, while the Morrises moved to
another. Mrs. Morris's hurt at her eclipse as social arbiter was apparent; Morris responded by going deeper into land speculation, to
become rich enough to seize back the lead from Bingham.

There was backlash at the flaunting of opulence by wealthy Philadelphians to welcome the new government, and some of the anger
was directed at the planned Bank of the United States, castigated as
intended only to augment the wealth of the wealthy. To emphasize

the bank's public benefit, Hamilton proposed that the dividends paid on the government's shares go into a sinking fund to retire the debt principal. He also had the charter forbid the BUS to buy government bonds, or to issue more in notes than its capital, or to remain in existence indefinitely—restrictions echoing those proposed by Coxe for reining in the BoNA.

Was a national bank a good idea? Didn't the BoNA already fulfill that function? Would a national bank be as vulnerable to manipulation by stock trading and consequent corruption as the Bank of England was, or as similar ones in the Netherlands were? Hamilton did nothing to avert such possibilities, nor did he try to avoid concentrating the new bank's stock ownership in the hands of the capitalist aristocracy; instead he assured their ownership by pricing the stock beyond the means of ordinary citizens and by structuring the BUS governance so that it had no real governmental—public—oversight.

These issues were never seriously debated because Hamilton assured the easy congressional passage of the bank bill by inserting a provision that the bank would accept, as payment for share purchases, government bonds at par. When news of this leaked out, the price of all such old bonds zoomed, and the bill passed the Senate by voice vote. In the House all that slowed its progress was Madison's argument that nothing in the Constitution allowed for such a bank, and that the framers had deliberately omitted the process of chartering corporations from the Constitution for fear it would result in government-sanctioned monopolies—which the BUS would surely be. This time Madison did not have the votes. "An Act to incorporate the Subscribers to the Bank of the United States" passed the House by a 2-to-1 margin and landed on the president's desk on February 16, 1791. Washington could have let it become law without his signature, but that was not his style. He sought opinions on its constitutionality from Jefferson and Randolph. They agreed with Madison: The proposed bank was unconstitutional. Washington sent the opinions to Hamilton. He refuted them, supposedly pulling an all-nighter to write a defense of the need for executive power. In any definition of government, Hamilton asserted:

Every power vested in a Government is in its nature *sovereign*, and includes by *force* of the *term*, a right to employ all the *means* requisite, and fairly *applicable* to the attainment of the *ends* of such power; and which are not precluded by restrictions & exceptions specified in the constitution; or not immoral, or not contrary to the essential ends of political society.

Washington agreed. He signed the enabling legislation on February 25, 1791, for a staged rollout that would culminate in the opening of the Bank of the United States at the end of the year.

12

Progress, Panic, and Paternalism

*I*n mid-May 1791, as Washington set out on a presidential meet-and-greet tour of Virginia, the Carolinas, and Georgia, Jefferson and Madison commenced their own tour to New York State and New England. The expressed intent of the Jefferson and Madison trip was botanizing, and while Jefferson did research on the Hessian Fly infestation and whether additional maple-tree cultivation could replace imported sugar, the real agenda was politics. Stunned by the ramming through of the charter for the Bank of the United States and the breaking of the agreement with the states on ratification, Jefferson and Madison sought to learn if enough other people were upset to warrant mounting meaningful opposition to future Hamilton initiatives.

Washington found that his time on his trip was taken up by local dignitaries, and so he hardly ever exchanged more than a few words with ordinary people. Jefferson and Madison, too, met with high officials, such as New York's chancellor Robert Livingston, Governor George Clinton, and Aaron Burr, who to Hamilton's dismay had recently defeated Schuyler to become New York's new senator; but their most important meetings were with ordinary citizens in small towns who sought to voice to high government officials their concerns, grievances, and future hopes. They also met with Philip Freneau, an American-born editor, former Madison college classmate, and noted poet, and agreed to help him move to Philadelphia to start a rival newspaper to the *Gazette of the United States*, which was being edited by Hamilton's friend John Fenno. Jefferson further arranged to provide Freneau with a State Department translator's fee.

After their return to Virginia, Madison received a boost to their antiadministration group in the form of a reconciliation overture from George Mason, one of the most vocal critics of the Constitution and still quite influential among anti-Federalists.

Antiadministration efforts have the most success when they have a specific target to oppose. The Washington administration provided an egregious one that summer—the frenzied activity attendant on the buying of "rights" to acquire shares of the not-yet-opened Bank of the United States. Although the initial sale of rights was held on July 4, 1791, in Philadelphia, New York, Boston, and Baltimore, it was far from an occasion for patriotism. "If a golden mountain had been kindled, emitting from its crater a lava of the purest gold," a Boston buyer commented, "the crowd would not have . . . exhibited more intense eagerness to share in the plunder." The reason became apparent in the ensuing weeks as the price for a right was bid up to $300 before plunging to $110. Then Hamilton, acting like a central banker, pushed the Bank of New York to buy rights on the open market, which it did, stabilizing the price at $150, meaning that any would-be shareholder in America's quasi-national bank had to pay around $150 for the right to own a share, plus the listed share price of $400, which put the tab far beyond what the average worker earned in several years. Moreover, the handling of the sale echoed what Americans, particularly wealthy Americans, had detested about the British during the colonial era—the restriction of a desired good to those who had liquid capital, and the shutting out of those who could not afford the price of entry for an expected good investment.

Success breeds selective memory: Because the Bank of the United States became such a necessary part of the financial structure, Hamilton's favor-the-wealthy configuration of the bank's ownership has been judged as the only one possible for it. Yet there were alternatives to the four-hundred-dollar share price for a bank, and also alternatives to the bank's objectives and how it chose its leadership. At the time of the establishing of the BUS, the Union Bank of Boston was being opened. Its one hundred thousand shares were snapped up at eight dollars apiece. As a banking historian notes, the Union Bank was "a legislative attempt to balance the growing demand for commercial banking with democratic principles." A fifth of its funds were reserved for loans to the "agricultural interest"; some of its directors were appointed by the state rather than by private share owners, and none of the new bank's directors were permitted to serve also as directors of any other banking institution. The BUS inculcated no such democratic operating principles. Its twenty-five board members, were elected, by Hamilton's design, on the basis of share ownership, adjusted slightly so that additional states would be represented. Pennsylvania's nine directors were enough to control the BUS board and to install Willing as president. George Cabot, who also had banking experience, withdrew his candidacy for president since he knew that Pennsylvania's nine directors would prevent his selection. New York City got seven board memberships, Boston four, and the remaining five were allotted one to a state. Wadsworth was Connecticut's, and he soon felt almost as powerless to affect the BUS as he had the BoNA, for which he had owned the largest block of shares.

There was no prohibition on government officials buying in, so BUS shares were bought by sitting cabinet secretaries, thirty current members of Congress, and a dozen former members. The potentially dangerous interweaving of the bank's interests and those of elected governmental officials irked the Virginia senator known as John Taylor of Caroline, a wealthy plantation-owner friend of Jefferson's. In a book-length letter to Washington, Taylor chided both the people's representatives who bought BUS stock, warning that "a *monetary impulse*, and not the *public good*, is operating on Congress," and Washington as president for permitting it, because "[His] general assent to laws ought to be ascribed to republican principles." Taylor charged that Washington should have vetoed the enabling legislation, although he acknowledged that "assaults on the virtue of men in power" by corrupters were "hard to withstand." Nonetheless "The wheat can only be separated from the chaff by sifting," and at that task, Washington had failed.

On October 31, 1791, Freneau's *National Gazette* began to appear. He predicted that the bank stock mania would continue, to the detriment of the poor, until the actual transfer of the shares. The problem was not simply the existence of the bank, according to Freneau and others; it was that the government seemed in thrall to the merchant-investor class to the detriment of the vast majority of the country's citizens who could not participate in those activities. Thus when Freneau reported that the main investors in the bank were also the projectors of the new factory that Hamilton and Coxe were attempting to open under the auspices of the Society for the Encouragement of Useful Manufactures (SEUM), he warned of ill effects from more than the SEUM investment structure: He railed that labor itself was threatened by the new venture's plans to provide only low-paying jobs that could be taken by the unskilled, as that would throw out of work the better-paid textile-making artisans who had been producing most of America's textiles.

That point was made more acutely by a mid-Connecticut newspaper in a series of articles by "a mechanic" that further connected the dots by revealing the relationship between factory wages and government favoritism. The articles' theme was "The uniform and universal tendency [of governments] is to assist those who have property and power against those who have none." The writer, a cobbler, soon joined forces with the largest employer in Norwich, a factory owner who resented the edge given by the state to a rival factory in the form of tax relief for that factory's employees. The cobbler and his fellow artisans had to pay three kinds of local taxes, but those rival factory employees paid only two. Twenty years ahead of the time when Luddites would assault and trash factories for using unskilled laborers, the Connecticut "mechanic" charged that Great Britain's Manchester and Birmingham factories' practices in hiring low-skilled workers for low-paying jobs were decimating the artisan textile-making communities there.

But the BUS and other aspects of the Hamilton program also had cheerleaders beyond John Fenno. Prior to the actual opening of the BUS, Noah Webster, now the author of a bestselling speller, wrote to the wealthy investor James Greenleaf that the Hamilton programs were having "an amazing effect upon the face of business and the country. Money circulates freely and every one almost appears to [be] contented and easy. Commerce revives . . . manufactures are increasing . . . and in the large towns vast improvements are making in pavements and buildings." In just a few months an "astonishing increase in capital" had taken place, Webster asserted. Hamilton soon loaned Webster fifteen hundred dollars to move to New York and start the pro-Federalist *American Minerva.*

Congress had continued to worry about Great Britain's attempts to undermine the American economy, and asked Jefferson for a report on those matters, particularly in reference to the cod fisheries that were vital to the New England economy. Jefferson documented the nasty British practices and also identified, as a contributor to the problems, the recently enacted American tariff structure, not only because it was not very tough on Great Britain but also because in operation it had the effect of benefiting only the American merchandisers of the fish while forcing the actual fishermen to pay too much for the imported salt they had to buy to preserve their catch. Jefferson recommended paying a tonnage bounty directly to the fishermen. Congress debated this. Madison was against it until he was for it: He initially objected to the payment because it was a bounty, but after Elbridge Gerry and Massachusetts delegate Fisher Ames explained that it would really be a "rebate" on what the fishermen had already paid for the salt, Madison changed his mind. The language of the bill was accordingly altered. An additional change recommended by Jefferson went almost unremarked because at the time it raised few hackles, but it was quite radical—profit sharing. Rejecting pressure from fleet owners to allow them to keep all of the rebate, Jefferson recommended splitting it among owners, captains, and crews. Coxe supported this idea by giving to Jefferson a letter from a merchant in the industry who asserted that crews were "generally found the most attentive, when their Dependence was on a Share of what they Caught."

Derby had already embraced that principle, to the degree that rival Salem fleet owners Thorndike and Peabody objected: "Although often urged by other merchants to reduce the liberal compensation [Derby] gave to his officers, no persuasion could induce him to change his policy," a Derby grandson concluded from a reading of his papers. And as one of Derby's captains later recalled: "In the transaction of affairs abroad, he was liberal—greatly beyond the practice in modern times—always desirous that every one, even the foremost hand, should share in the good fortune to which he pointed the way." Derby's practices also resulted in his fleet's having the best safety record and the healthiest crews, both of which enabled more voyages per year per ship. Derby became so wealthy that he was seen around Salem in garb imported from London and with a gold-tipped cane that Hancock might have envied. At the urging of his wife, Derby finally began construction on a grand mansion. It progressed very slowly.

Girard's income from shipping soared because he shared with Derby an investment strategy: While other owners, to assure not losing much should a ship sink or be captured, laid off on other investors considerable shares in a prospective voyage, Derby and Girard took nearly all the financial risk themselves, so when their ships returned they reaped a larger share of the rewards. Shortly Derby would become the wealthiest man in the United States, with Girard not far behind.

The Bank of the United States opened officially on December 12, 1791, and immediately began "accommodation lending"—loans to the wealthy and well connected—and also blackballing certain loan applicants, both of which were common practices among American banks at that time. Years later Oliver Wolcott, Jr., who worked closely with the BUS in this period, would comment:

> I can assure you that this great power [of approving and disapproving loans] has been placed in the hands of men, not possessing the requisite prudence ability or impartiality. [Potential

loan applicants] will suffer much, and for a long time before they will speak out what they think, respecting an Institution which can advance or depress their interests at pleasure.

It soon became clear that such practices also added more risk to the bank's operations, because loans to directors were less likely to be repaid than others. The chief cashier of the Baltimore BUS soon wrote to Willing that the majority of the branch's loan failures were from loans to board members.

Shortly after the bank officially opened, it had a crisis now known to history as the Panic of 1792, which has been attributed almost solely to the actions of Hamilton's former assistant at the Treasury, William Duer. It was far more complicated, an almost inevitable sequel to the frenzy over the sale of rights in 1791. Duer was quite culpable, though. As his biographer Robert F. Jones writes, Duer had "used his offices under both the old and new governments to move himself up from a New York figure to an internationally known financier, land speculator, and promoter." A charmer, he was a frequent host to members of Congress and to petitioners who came to New York to importune Congress and government officials. One such petitioner, the preacher Manasseh Cutler, after a Duer dinner at which fifteen different wines were served, wrote home that Duer "lives in the style of a nobleman." In 1791 Hamilton had fired Duer for cause, including his prior leaking of information about face-value redemption and his speculations while under investigation for nonfulfillment of old provision contracts. But the two had remained friends, and Duer had also continued his friendship with Secretary of War Knox. In a deal that could not have been made without the indulgence of Hamilton and other insiders, Duer had since obtained a one-hundred-thousand-dollar government contract to supply St. Clair's troops, which were then readying a major offensive against the Miami. Duer used the advance not to buy supplies but to purchase, with Knox, an enormous tract in Maine. The absence of supply fatally compromised the St. Clair expedition. And Knox let it happen by only mildly reproaching Duer: "I have written you twice . . . relative to the supply of rations upon the frontier to which you have not particularly replied. . . . I am really concerned on your account as well as the public that the supplies should be adequate to the demand." But then, Knox himself was in too deep in Maine to reproach his partner there, and Duer was under additional pressure from the failure of an Ohio land company in which Hamilton and Knox were also involved, and he was about to lose a malfeasance suit to Holker.

As the BUS launch date neared, Duer and fellow New York land speculator Alexander Macomb (during the war, a British supplier and paymaster) tried to corner the market in shares of the BUS and also of the Bank of New York, with backing from a member of the Livingston clan. The BUS share price did rise rapidly until the end of January. Then some astute investors, notably Bingham, having expected that rise, decided to sell and take a reasonable profit rather than wait to reap a larger gain.

Hamilton was tracking the BUS stock price daily, because a speculation-fueled price rise was a threat not only to the bank but also to the entire financial superstructure, and even to the ability of a democratic government to rein in the excesses of capitalism. As he warned the Bank of New York in January, the "extravagant sallies of speculation [are harming] the entire system of public Credit, by disgusting all sober citizens and giving a wild air to everything." The Bank of New York in response curtailed lending to Duer and his associates by refusing to roll over their one-month loans. This bank demand for immediate repayment forced Duer to find cash. To do so he went beyond his usual circle of wealthy investors, enticing the less wealthy with the promise that for a five-hundred-dollar investment he would pay 5 percent a month. "Shopkeepers, widows, orphans, butchers, cartmen, Gardeners, market women & even the noted Bawd Mrs. McCarty" quickly agreed, according to a later account by a Duer partner. This cash enabled Duer to repay his loans to the Bank of New York and keep on buying BUS stock.

The BUS tightened the noose further by then refusing to renew many other investors' loans, which in just one week removed $625,000 from a loan pool of $2.6 million. Bank stock prices plummeted as fearful depositors withdrew cash. The BUS's reserves dropped by half; on February 10 an alarmed Hamilton asked the Bank of New York to loan the BUS $100,000 to bolster those cash reserves, and advised: "Every existing bank ought within prudent limits to abrige its opera- tions. The superstructure of Credit is now too vast for the foundation. It must be gradually brought within more reasonable dimensions or it will tumble."

It was not until three weeks further on that Hamilton penned his latterly famous note of warning to Duer: "'Tis time, there must be a line of separation between Honest men & knaves, between Respect- able stockholders and dealers in the funds, and mere unprincipled Gamblers." Duer had long since crossed that line and could not now sell because prices were tumbling so quickly. Moreover, other mem- bers of the Livingston clan had started betting against him, bears to his bull. Wolcott had predicted that the "mania" would only be "cured by a few bankruptcies which daily may be expected, I had almost said desired." On March 19 Hamilton made sure that those bank- ruptcies occurred: By using the government's sinking fund to make strategic buys, he stabilized the stock prices. He used the sinking fund for this purpose over the objections of Jefferson, who as a cabinet member had a say in its usage, and who saw in this Hamilton action precisely the sort of government overreaching that he and Madison had feared. At nearly the same moment Wolcott notified Duer that he would be arrested if he did not immediately pay back the one- hundred-thousand-dollar St. Clair contract.

The sinking fund's purchases did turn around the stock prices of the BUS, the Bank of New York, and other banks. Their upturn was boosted by the timely arrival of the news that the Dutch were extend- ing to the United States a new loan of three million florins, which, as Hamilton was quick to point out, was a vote of confidence in America's economy.

Duer was arrested and imprisoned. A mob attempted to storm the New Gaol to lynch him, but was deflected. More than a few well- to-do men in New York, Philadelphia, and cities farther south were shorn of about three million dollars by the Panic of 1792. Rush noted the now-empty bespoke carriages of paper brokers, and was relieved that the only known suicide was that of a French immigrant. Duer offered to sell his stake in the Maine venture to satisfy his creditors; Bingham bought it for a low price that did not enable Duer to buy his release, so he remained in prison. Macomb had not defrauded the federal government as Duer had, and so was able to get out of jail by selling assets. The third principal, Livingston, fled to his country home and concealed his assets to prevent their being taken by creditors. The small fry lost all of what they had invested.

The BUS was not harmed. Shortly Hamilton had Wolcott supervise its expansion to four branches, and that in turn spurred private groups to start banks in Providence, Wilmington, and Baltimore. The market for stocks and bonds was also not badly impacted, but the scare impelled twenty-seven regular traders to organize a structured exchange. In a document signed under a buttonwood tree on Wall Street, they restricted their trade to one another and pledged not to sell to or buy from outsiders. This "exchange" became a further positive for the economy as it established the value of the securities no matter who owned them, which made it possible for banks to accept them as collateral for loans.

Bingham's purchase of Maine lands occasioned a countermove by the Cabots. Since George Cabot was now a senator, with clout that could balance Bingham's, the Cabots resuscitated the *Pilgrim-Hope* privateer case of 1779. Their motive was to force Bingham to sell them his portion of the Maine holdings at a very low rate, one set by state officials beholden to the Cabots. Bingham, then leader of the Pennsylvania Senate, asked for help, and Hamilton persuaded Washington to assign the attorney general to defend Bingham. The case eventually ended up in the Supreme Court, then led by Washington's appointee as chief justice, John Jay. It ruled against Bingham and the United States. Short of cash and having become overly entangled in various land speculations, Bingham still managed to avoid paying the Cabots or selling the Maine lands. The Cabots brought the case again, with "new" documentary evidence that the *Hope* had actually been a British ship masquerading as Danish. Bingham learned that they had known about this for years, and had concealed the information so as to get him to sell the Maine lands. Once more the case went to the Supreme Court. Bingham lost. But he still did not pay up, and there was no attempt by the federal government to make him do so.

Just then, through his position in Pennsylvania's Senate, Bingham was busy expanding the country's economic base—and, he hoped, his own fortune—through new transportation projects such as canals, bridges, and the Lancaster Turnpike. In the legislature Bingham relied heavily on Albert Gallatin, appointing him to some forty-five different committees. Gallatin soon became a floor leader for passage of various measures. They teamed up for the Lancaster Turnpike, Bingham providing money and Gallatin obtaining approval for the use of eminent domain to acquire right-of-way. Shares were so popular that at three hundred dollars each they were oversubscribed.

The resulting road was a marvel and a model. It was twenty-one feet wide, which allowed two wagons to pass each other in opposite directions without stopping. It spawned sixty inns and trebled the value of acreage along its sixty miles. The Lancaster Turnpike conveyed in Conestoga wagons tens of thousands of new immigrants and generations of younger American-born on the first leg of their journeys westward. Helping along the growth of new settlements and businesses countrywide was the proliferation of post offices and post roads, from 75 post offices in 1789 to 903 by 1800, and from 2,000 miles of roads to 21,000. But as an investment the Lancaster Turnpike was a bust, paying less than 2 percent per year.

Gallatin accompanied his close friend Alexander Dallas on a trip to New York City. Also an immigrant, born in Jamaica and educated in the law in London, Dallas was then secretary of the Commonwealth of Pennsylvania. He knew that Gallatin was lonely, still in mourning for his adored wife who had died only five months after their elopement, and succeeded in introducing Gallatin to Hannah Nicholson, daughter of their New York host, Cmdre. James Nicholson, a war hero and financier whose wife and Dallas had known each other in the islands. The Nicholsons' other three daughters were married to influential men. To induce Hannah to marry Gallatin, since he lived in the Far West, remote from the big-city social whirl, he revealed that he had been selected as senator from Pennsylvania, and thus would be spending part of the year in cosmopolitan Philadelphia.

As the 1790s wore on, banking and securities furnished credit to modestly larger fractions of the American populace. Coupled with the Constitution's provisions about the sanctity of contracts and forbidding the states to make new laws that undercut the rights of creditors, these bank loans and securities with recognizable values spurred the chartering of several hundred corporations by 3,884 "incorporators." But now the character of the corporations changed: To obtain a state charter it was no longer necessary to show that the new entity would be of some public benefit in addition to providing a way to earn profits. Purely commercial corporations provided the wealthy with a new way to make money while being legally shielded from lawsuits and financial recriminations should a venture fail. But in embracing the new corporations the wealthy also—and increasingly—distanced themselves from the prior understanding that private profit in a corporate activity was, and ought to be, allied with civic responsibility.

Such corporations were lauded in Hamilton's third major opus, the *Report on the Subject of Manufactures,* delivered to Congress just before the BUS opened. It owed much to the research and formulations of Coxe, then the most knowledgeable person in America on manufacturing, and cited as positive examples the SEUM corporation's facilities in Passaic, New Jersey, and in Philadelphia, and those of the Slater Mill in Pawtucket, a Brown family–backed textile manufactory. Hamilton expanded Coxe's paragraphs into an entire program of support for manufacturing, ostensibly to prevent the United States from ever again being dependent on imported war matériel. He recommended eliminating duties on the raw materials used to manufacture arms, ammunition, and powder, while doubling import duties on finished products such as clothing, which, he argued, could as readily be made in the United States as in Great Britain. He also asked for federal money to lure skilled immigrants and subsidize nascent manufactories.

Hamilton's touting of manufacturing as the future was on target. But its accuracy in prediction has been overrelied on to denigrate those who at the time still thought of America as agricultural. It remained a 90 percent rural country, and so most Americans agreed with Jefferson's contention, in his 1785 *Notes on the State of Virginia*, that agriculture was the preeminent mover of the economy and the best employment for its people: "While we have land to labour," Jefferson had written, "let us never wish to see our citizens occupied at a workbench. . . . The mobs of great cities [in Europe and Great Britain] add just so much to the support of pure government, as sores do to the strength of the human body." This view tracked with that of the French economic philosophers known as the physiocrats, who contended that all wealth derived from the soil and therefore from agriculture. America had more than enough land to support tens of thousands of new farms and an expanding populace, and even more land seemed likely to become available in the foreseeable future.

Hamilton, while conceding that agriculture was then America's mainstay, disagreed with the principle that wealth came directly from the land: In Hamilton's view it derived from the labor involved in farming—labor, he asserted, that would be more productive if engaged in manufacturing. Ten years earlier Sheffield had touted the capacity of British factories to overwhelm the American market, and they had done so; Hamilton sought to multiply America's factories to reverse that situation. He argued: "The spirit of enterprise must be less in a nation of mere cultivators [of the soil], than in a nation of cultivators and merchants; less in a nation of cultivators and merchants, than in a nation of cultivators, artificers [manufacturers] and merchants." Adam Smith, who had made the same argument, had used it as a reason for laissez-faire—letting the market set prices without government interference. Hamilton—later touted as the champion of laissez-faire—was not in favor of it in the early 1790s, recognizing that "the incitement and patronage of government" was still needed to grow American manufacturing, which meant protective tariffs as well as subsidies. Since other countries were subsidizing their manufactures, the United States must do so too; Hamilton asserted that the main task set by the Constitution—providing for the general welfare—encompassed making such subsidies.

The reception of this *Report* in Congress was negatively affected by the aftermath of the Panic of 1792, and by an investigation that tied Hamilton to the failure of supply of the St. Clair western expedition, both of which raised questions about his entire financial program. Freneau would soon encapsulate the objections in a single paragraph in his newspaper, asserting the "deplorable truth":

> A system of finances has issued from the Treasury . . . and has given rise to scenes of speculation calculated to aggrandize the few and the wealthy by oppressing the great body of the people, to transfer the best resources of the country forever into the hands of the speculators, and to fix a burthen on the people of the United States and their posterity, which time, instead of diminishing will serve to strengthen and encrease.

American mythology holds that Hamilton's manufacturing program was too ahead of its time to be appreciated by Congress and was therefore rejected. Not so. Congress actually adopted most of his tariff revisions; and it is important to note that congressional revisions of Hamilton's recommendations targeted the wealthy through raised duties on silks, wines, china, and glass. Hamilton had once rejected raised levies on luxuries but now agreed to them in exchange for keeping tariffs low on goods that could be manufactured here into war matériel. Boudinot even proposed a new tax on the wealthy, on certain financial transactions including property transfers, even though he himself was heavily involved in land speculation and would have to pay up. Congress approved them all. But Congress did balk at paying proposed subsidies to manufacturing, in part because of Hamilton's attempt to justify the subsidies as being covered by the Constitution's general welfare clause. That contention, Madison wrote, "broaches a new constitutional doctrine of vast consequence. If Congress can do whatever in their *discretion* can be *done by money*, and will promote the *general welfare*, the Government is no longer a limited one possessing enumerated powers, but an indefinite one subject to particular exceptions."

Jefferson voiced this same constitutional objection in person to Washington and, not getting much of a response, decided to explain further in a letter. In this remarkable missive Jefferson accompanied his "disquietude" about governmental aggrandizements of power with a plea to Washington not to retire. The president had indicated his inclination to step down at the end of his term, and had even asked Madison to prepare a retirement address; Madison had done so, but had also begged him to reconsider. Jefferson linked the two matters by asserting to Washington that the general public's confidence in trying to "walk alone," without the great man to guide them, had been shaken by the assumption of the states' debt, the establishing of the BUS, and the recent financial panic. Had the war debt been addressed without sleight of hand, Jefferson charged, it would not have raised hackles. The "strain" on the impost was already provoking attempts to get around it, and there were fears that even more adamant resistance would arise to the new excise tax on whiskey as it was already doing to sales of BUS stock to foreigners. To Jefferson the worst thing about the financial program was that it had given influencers—such as those foreign owners of the BUS—tools for corrupting the legislature. Jefferson was also on solid ground in contending that "the Antifederal champions are now strengthened in argument by the fulfilment of their predictions" that the federal government would aggrandize itself, which state of affairs "has been brought about by the Monarchical federalists themselves, who, having been for the new government merely as a stepping stone to monarchy, have themselves adopted the very constructions of the constitution, of which, when advocating it's acceptance . . . they declared it insusceptible."

Since we know that the United States never became a monarchy, we judge Jefferson's fears as overblown, but at the time they were realistic—there was talk of secession in the Deep South and in New England—and shared by many people because the American mix of democracy and capitalism was not yet so firmly established as to inspire total confidence that it would continue. Moreover, as Washington would shortly write, the country was still "encompassed on all sides with avowed enemies and insidious friends," namely Great Britain, France, and Spain. Jefferson made clear that he did not fear Washington as a monarch; rather, what frightened him were the sort of activities that accompanied current monarchies in Great Britain and in Europe, and had been widely remarked on. These were the elements that in the twentieth century were succinctly identified by the economic philosopher Karl Polanyi: an extending of governmental power, allied to and enabling aggressive capitalist endeavor that concentrates wealth and power in an antidemocratic elite. Polanyi saw these as not just leading to fascism but as enabling it. In the eighteenth century Jefferson's objections were to the sort of one-aristocratic-party rule that he and others associated with corrupt monarchies. In his peroration Jefferson underlined the need to have a leader committed to democratic principles yet capable of restraining any untoward elements: "The confidence of the whole union is centered in you. Your being at the helm, will be more than an answer to every argument which can be used to alarm & lead the people in any quarter into violence or secession. North & South will hang together, if they have you to hang on."

Shortly after reading Jefferson's letter, and similar ones from Madison, Hamilton, and others whom Washington respected, all counseling him to run once more for president for the good of the country, he decided to do so, although he understood that henceforth the Washington administration would meet much more opposition to its programs.

13

New Resistance to Authority

*T*he subject of political parties had been taboo during the Revolution and since then, mostly because parties were too closely associated with the ills of the British governmental system. The belief was that true democracy had to be a cooperative enterprise in which parties had no place. Washington, for instance, found it necessary to maintain that he governed without reference to party. But Madison, in an important article in Freneau's *National Gazette* for January 12, 1792, broke that taboo by discussing political parties directly. He did not come right out and scoff at Washington's assertion of being above party; he also resisted asserting that Washington was the de facto leader of a Federalist party, or that another party was coalescing around opposition to the administration's programs. Rather he observed that it was reasonable in a democracy to expect political parties to form and foolish to pretend they would not. However, he cautioned, certain "evils" usually attendant on their establishment must be countered in advance of their official formation, by "withholding unnecessary opportunities from a few to increase the inequality of property" and "by abstaining from measures which operate differently on different interests, and particularly such as favor one interest at the expence of another."

Later that year Freneau made this charge more specific: The new Federalist excise tax on whiskey favored the wealthy eastern interests and undermined poor western farmer-distillers. Washington took offense at Freneau's articles, asserting to Jefferson that he would "be a fool indeed to swallow the little sugar plumbs here & there," and "that in condemning the admn of the govmt they condemned him for if they thought there were measures pursued contrary to his sentiment, they must conceive him too careless to attend to them or too stupid to understand them." Hamilton struck back at Freneau and Jefferson in a pseudonymous letter to the Fenno paper, asking whether it was "possible that Mr. Jefferson, the head of a Principal department of the Government, can be the Patron of a Paper, the evident object of which is to decry the Government?" He accused Jefferson of being "too little scrupled" in this regard—but avoided mentioning his own, similar relationship to Fenno's paper and his giving out of hundreds of patronage jobs. Hamilton continued this attack under pseudonyms, and in these latter "ravings," Elkins and McKittrick argue, he made charges against Jefferson that could not "be taken seriously."

Pained by the secretaries' ad hominem attacks, Washington pleaded in letters to them that because the country was still faced with enemies, they must find ways of working together. Jefferson's response refuted some Hamilton charges and pointed out that in regard to the public debt: "This exactly marks the difference between Colo. Hamilton's views and mine, that I would wish the debt paid tomorrow; he wishes it never to be paid, but always to be a thing wherewith to corrupt and manage the legislature." Washington again wrote them that since "both of you are pure, and well meant . . . [and] have no sinister views to promote," he wondered why "should either of you be so tenacious of your opinions as to make no allowances for those of the other?" They praised his efforts but did not back down.

Jefferson had frequently warned Washington that his above-parties stance would be fatally compromised should the president use military force to do what one party advocated and the other objected to. That possibility arose when resistance in western Pennsylvania to paying the "whiskey tax" went beyond refusals into more active measures. A distillers' petition to Congress had resulted in a slight reduction in the tax, but by August 1792 they still had not paid in a penny of it, and the report to Hamilton of that nonpayment was accompanied by stories of harassment of tax officials, such as that of a federal official who accused a Pittsburgh landlord of refusing to rent an office to him. Hamilton wrote to Washington: "Such persevering and violent opposition to the Law gives the business a still more serious aspect than it has hitherto worn, and seems to call for vigorous & decisive measures." He drafted a proclamation that sounded apocalyptic notes of warning similar to those in Bowdoin's proclamation during Shays's Rebellion:

> Whereas certain violent and unwarrantable proceedings have lately taken place, tending to obstruct the operation of the laws . . . which proceedings are subversive of good order, contrary to the duty that every Citizen owes to his Country and . . . of a nature dangerous to the very being of Government. . . . Now therefore I, George Washington . . . admonish and exhort all persons . . . to desist from all unlawful combinations and proceedings whatsoever . . . tending to obstruct the operation of the laws aforesaid; inasmuch as all lawful ways and means will be strictly put in execution, for bringing to justice the infractors thereof and securing obedience thereto.

Madison responded in an essay castigating "anti-republicans" who said by such proclamations that "the people are stupid, suspicious, licentious. They cannot strictly trust themselves. When they have established government they should think of nothing but obedience, leaving the care of their liberties to their wiser rulers." He made manifest what he had earlier only hinted at, that the Washingtonian Federalists were anti-democratic:

> Those, who from particular interest, from natural temper, or from the habits of life, are more partial to the opulent . . . and having debauched themselves into a persuasion that mankind are incapable of governing themselves, it follows with them, of course, that government can be carried on only by the pageantry of rank, the influence of money and emoluments, and the terror of military force.

This was a summons to voters: In the coming election the citizenry must choose "republicanism" or risk losing the very freedoms they had fought the Revolution to achieve. His conception of individual economic patriotism included the need to assure fully democratic governance that allowed to the less wealthy as much of an influence on the country's laws as that enjoyed by the wealthy.

The 1792 election did see the first appearance of distinct parties, although the opposition to the administration did not yet have a name; but even more evident from the election results were the shifts occasioned by the adjustments to voting patterns mandated by the results of the 1790 census—the addition of the states of Kentucky and Vermont, and the increasing population of the western portions of all the eastern states.

The Federalists had tried to prevent these alterations from upsetting their political control of the country. Washington's attempts to delay the enfranchisement of certain sectors of the electorate, and the augmented empowerment of certain areas of the country, evoke comparisons with the worst excesses of what later became known as gerrymandering, and that have at present once again become burning issues. When Madison's coalition in Congress insisted that the new states have, in addition to two senators apiece, the number of representatives that were commensurate with the size of their populations, Washington vetoed the bill. Madison managed to get a slightly amended one passed and signed by brandishing the argument that the Constitution mandated that each aggregation of thirty thousand people was entitled to its own representative. The Federalists also tried to object to readjustments of the size and composition of the delegations from Virginia, Maryland, and Pennsylvania, that would give proper weight to the newly populated western sections: Such added representatives, the Federalists knew, would dilute the clout of the eastern, Federalist-voting sections that had previously dominated the state delegations, since new delegates were very likely to be antiadministration. Other census data revealed that the Federalists had previously skewed districts so that anti-Federalist districts were 30 percent more densely populated than the Federalist ones, which meant that the citizens of the more densely populated areas had been denied their correct political weight. In 1792 that imbalance too was adjusted. These steps toward regional fairness had the effect of reducing the clout of wealthy coastal-city dwellers.

The Federalists' election difficulties were exacerbated by Hamilton's sub-rosa attempts to replace Adams on the ticket with George Clinton. New England Federalists such as Cabot were aghast at the idea of a switch: "The ruin of Mr. Adams would be a triumph of the Jacobins, and would be an important step toward that general overthrow of our establishment which is evidently intended." Cabot blamed Jefferson for the attempt to replace Adams, having no clue that Hamilton, whom he admired, was behind the plot.

Washington was reelected by unanimous vote of the presidential electors, and Adams turned back Clinton's challenge and would again be vice president, but the Federalists' Senate majority was thinned and in the House it was reversed. The new House majority was a loose coalition of anti-Federalists, plus former Federalists who now agreed with the ideas of Madison and Jefferson, and new representatives from the west. Because the House was now in their hands, the second Washington administration would not have as easy a time legislatively as the first.

In December 1792 Hamilton survived a scandal that could have curtailed his career and economic programs. Frederick Muhlenberg, Speaker of the House, and James Monroe, a Virginia senator, visited Hamilton, but not on Treasury business: They had been given materials documenting the married Hamilton's affair with the married Maria Reynolds. Confronted with the evidence, Hamilton conceded the affair and that he had made blackmail payments, but insisted that these had had nothing to do with his public duties. His visitors agreed with his rationale, and did not then pursue the matter.

Thus reprieved, Hamilton shortly had a bill introduced in the

House authorizing the Treasury to divert two million dollars in funds, already borrowed abroad for paying off French loans, to re-pay the Bank of the United States for its loans to the government to purchase its 20 percent stake. The potential switch raised questions. If servicing the BUS debt cost only two hundred thousand dollars per year, why use two million to pay it off now? And why stiff France? Congressman William Branch Giles of Virginia introduced a reso-lution requiring Hamilton's answers. Hamilton replied that he was exchanging a loan at 6 percent for one at 5 percent, and was delaying payment to France because of its revolution. Giles pressed on, intro-ducing resolutions demanding that Hamilton account for Treasury discrepancies, including use of the sinking fund to shore up stock prices. Hamilton again justified his actions. Jefferson then wrote a set of ten resolutions that included a recommendation to Washing-ton to fire Hamilton. Giles excised that one, and the other nine were resoundingly rejected.

Hamilton's anti-French stance seemed retroactively justified when Americans learned that Louis XVI had been guillotined in January, and that on February 1 France had declared war on Great Britain and the Netherlands, two nations with which the United States was then on peaceful terms.

News of France's war declaration reached Washington at Mount Vernon. The breakout of declared war in Europe threatened the big boost to the American economy that had come from purchases of American war supplies by many European countries and Great Britain. Returning quickly to Philadelphia, Washington queried his cabinet: Should the United States still officially receive the emissary from France, Edmond-Charles Genêt? The young diplomat was in Charleston, where he had been recruiting American ships to become privateers for the French cause and enticing volunteers to fight on the Gulf Coast against Great Britain's Spanish allies. Such activities violated American neutrality, which was being observed even though it had not been declared.

Jefferson argued that the United States was obligated by the 1778 treaty to assist France, and that a declaration of neutrality would gut that treaty and would also be an unconstitutional encroachment on the powers of the Senate. Washington issued the neutrality proclamation anyway, reasoning that the still-young United States of America could not afford to go to war, and also that neutrality might allow the continuance of the profitable trade in military supplies. Hamilton, writing as Pacificus, penned seven articles for the *Gazette of the United States* arguing that the matter necessitated a major extension of executive power, contending that the executive branch, as the "organ of discourse" to foreign countries, could unilaterally interpret treaties and act on the country's behalf even if doing so constrained legislative prerogative. In August, Madison made lengthy responses. As Helvidius he highlighted the proclamation's eroding of the intent and letter of the Constitution, citing also Hamilton's "Federalist 75," which said the treaty-making power was shared between executive and legislative. The dueling Pacificus-Helvidius articles refined the Constitution's separation of powers.

"Citizen" Genêt presented a startling list of demands to the Washington administration: immediate payment of the full amount owed to France; a new commercial treaty granting France most-favored-nation status; and permission for French-backed American privateers to take British vessels. The French cause was then popular in America—news of the full extent of the Reign of Terror had not yet arrived—and for several months a battle for public opinion raged between the administration and those in new "democratic societies" throughout the country who cheered Genêt's activities. Washington rejected Hamilton's call to declare void the 1778 treaties with France, but he was willing to consider paying off America's debt if France would accept payment in the form of military supplies and would allow American ships to trade freely in French ports. Then Genêt's brashness became so egregious—dispatching a privateer from Philadelphia after being denied permission—that even Jefferson agreed to demand his recall. By the time the recall notice reached Paris, the Terror was at its height. Genêt feared execution, and was granted asylum in the United States. In New York he continued to make trouble for a while but then married a daughter of Governor Clinton and settled down.

Throughout 1793 the fighting in Europe escalated, with large armies clashing in the German-speaking areas as well as in France, the Iberian Peninsula, and the Low Countries. American income from the belligerents sank. Once Great Britain realized that France was allowing U.S. ships to carry on no-tariff trade, the Royal Navy seized hundreds of American commercials, including five of Girard's and several of Derby's and Gray's.

Jefferson, ostensibly upset about Hamilton's poaching on his territory, informed Washington that he would resign at the end of 1793. The president did not dissuade him, having Randolph available to fill the position. The attorney general had just won the first important case decided by the Supreme Court, then led by Chief Justice John Jay, and with Associate Justices James Wilson and former war profiteer Samuel Chase. In *Chisholm v. the State of Georgia*, a provisioner sued the state for not repaying him for supplies he furnished during the war. Georgia said it did not have to pay him because the federal government had assumed all state debts. Randolph argued that Georgia could not shirk its private obligations or pass them on to the federal government—and won.

On September 18, in the federal district, Washington laid the cornerstone of the new Capitol Building. Among the spectators was James Greenleaf, a Philadelphia businessman just returned from Amsterdam, where for years he had successfully sold American bonds and BUS stock. Already a speculator in western lands, on this trip Greenleaf bought up many federal district lots. In Philadelphia he joined forces with Morris and James Nicholson, the former state treasurer; by year's end the trio owned 40 percent of the federal district's building lots, and millions of western acres in a half-dozen states. The escalating war in Europe threatened their enterprise because they had planned to sell most of their acres to European buyers.

Their problems were echoed in a *Report on Commerce* that Jefferson submitted to Congress just prior to his resignation taking effect. He had been preparing it since 1791, but had withheld it in deference to Hamilton's plea that issuing it would upset attempts to ameliorate European ship seizures. Echoing his earlier list of British bad behavior in the Declaration of Independence, Jefferson's 1793 report contained a new list, and recommended action: "If particular nations grasp at undue shares [of ocean commerce], and, more especially, if they seize on the means of the United States, to convert them into their own aliment for their own strength, and withdraw them entirely from the support of those to whom they belong, defensive and protecting measures become necessary." The "defensive and protecting measures" that Jefferson recommended were the punishing tariffs on Great Britain long advocated by Madison. Congress again refused to impose them, but then Great Britain proved Jefferson's point, informing the ambassador in London it would continue naval operations against American shipping and never give up its Midwest forts, which were holding back America's westward expansion.

In reaction, Congress passed an embargo against trade with Great Britain. The abbreviated version of American history has forgotten this embargo, remembering only the one that preceded the War of 1812. This earlier embargo was the product of the Federalists, and it had a positive effect. London, faced with a decrease in the transatlantic commerce that was still of major importance to the British economy, soon relented a bit on returning seized American vessels. Washington took that as an opening to send an emissary to London to negotiate a new commercial treaty and to settle issues left over from the Revolutionary War. Hamilton wanted the negotiating job, but Washington told him his public image was too negative, and appointed Jay. Hamilton then laid out Jay's task: "To obtain reparation for the wrongs we suffer and a demarkation of a line of conduct to govern in future—to avoid . . . all measures of a nature to occasion a conflict between the motives which might dispose the British Government to do us the justice to which we are intitled and the sense of its own dignity."

John Hancock (left) of Boston was an early leader of the resistance. His merchant counterpart in Charleston, Henry Laurens (right), came more reluctantly to rebellion. Both would be presidents of the Continental Congress. Although Great Britain rescinded the Townshend Acts in 1770, it left in place another form of "taxation without representation"—on tea, resulting in the economic protest of the Boston Tea Party.

194

After Lexington and Concord, Robert Morris (left) led Congress's overseas acquisition of supplies, and for that purpose had it send his firm's junior partner, William Bingham (right) to Martinique. Bingham made a fortune thereby. Congress also issued "Continentals," shown below, to pay for troops and local supplies.

By upending the colonies' economic system, the Revolution created opportunities for new fortunes. Elias Hasket Derby of Salem became a leading privateer owner, and Jeremiah Wadsworth of Hartford (portrayed with his son in later years) a reliable commissary for and provisioner of the army.

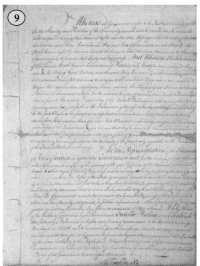

Reflecting the uneasy alliance of democracy and capitalism Pennsylvania's Constitution of 1776 was the most radically democratic, anti-wealth-holder document produced in the new United States of America.

When a Congressional committee visited the encampment at Valley Forge in early 1778, General George Washington made sure its members understood that the troops there were starving even though adequate supplies were available elsewhere in the country.

It was not until October of 1781 that French financial backing, as well as French troops and ships, made possible the victory at Yorktown.

Daniel Shays and Job Shattuck were leaders of the 1786 Massachusetts anti-tax revolt known as Shays's Rebellion. It spurred the 1787 Constitutional Convention to limit the thirteen states' ability to print money, pass pro-debtor legislation, and regulate interstate commerce. The new Constitution helped the wealthy become more so, while also better enabling the not so wealthy to join their ranks.

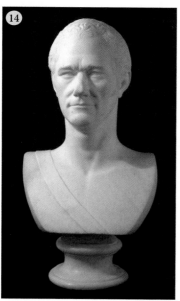

Alexander Hamilton, as secretary of the treasury under President Washington, established the Bank of the United States—the largest enterprise in the country—the National Mint, and other pillars of the American financial system.

Between 1801 and 1813, Presidents Thomas Jefferson (top) and James Madison (center), working with Secretary of the Treasury Albert Gallatin (below), cut the federal debt in half, substantially decreased the size of the federal government, and eliminated all internal taxes. Yet even as war loomed, Gallatin could not prevent the demise of the first Bank of the United States.

As the War of 1812 began, a "syndicate" of wealthy immigrant investors, led by Stephen Girard (left) and John Jacob Astor (right), bought government bonds when most American banks refused to do so, enabling the United States to struggle through what was known as "the second war of independence."

While awaiting the results of the Jay negotiations, the administration began again to build naval vessels and to amass military supplies, which raised expenditures just when tariff income was declining. To fill the Treasury it seemed necessary to more aggressively collect the excise tax on whiskey. At the Constitutional Convention Hamilton had been against excises, since "the genius of the people will ill brook the inquisitive and preemptory spirit of excise laws." In 1790 he had changed his mind and obtained congressional approval for an excise on whiskey distilling. Few distillers had paid it in 1792, and by 1793 resistance to it had hardened even as the government's need for its revenues grew.

Western Pennsylvania was home to a fourth of all the country's distillers. Farmers there found it more profitable to distill their crops rather than sell them as grains because liquor was easier to transport and in that still-remote region was also used as a medium of exchange. Critics of the excise charged that Hamilton, envisioning a new American industry of large-scale distilling, sought by means of this tax to force the consolidation of smaller distillers. His forcing mechanism derived from the way the tax could be paid, either as a flat fee or as a fee per distilled gallon; the flat fee amounted to much less per gallon but could only be afforded by large distillers. The design of the tax, writes a historian of the Whiskey Rebellion, William Hogeland, "didn't merely redistribute wealth from the many to the few, subdue rival economies, and pound the restless, defiant west. It also served as one of the heavier cogs in a machine for restructuring all of American life."

That resistance had not yet erupted into violence in October 1793, when an epidemic of yellow fever ground the activity in Philadelphia to a halt. It killed five thousand people and caused Washington and twenty thousand of the city's fifty thousand inhabitants to flee. The cause of the fever was then unknown. Among the heroes of the epidemic was Stephen Girard, who gave money, opened his home to assist those in need, and personally carried many ill people to noninfected areas; for this he was celebrated and began to take a larger role in the city's social and political life.

After the epidemic the Pennsylvania legislature selected a new senator, choosing Gallatin over candidates that included Bingham. Gallatin became a leading senatorial critic of Hamilton, a telling one because of his thorough knowledge of economic theory, which he had studied and seen in operation in Europe. He cosponsored a resolution to force the government to sell its stake in the BUS. Ending interest payments to the BUS would decrease the government's need for money and ease the pressure to collect the whiskey excise. The measure passed on a first vote but on a second was defeated. By then the Federalists had already ousted Gallatin from the Senate for not having been an American citizen long enough to qualify him for his post. Actually, he had been in the U.S. since 1780, had taken an oath of citizenship in 1785, and owned considerable property. Kicked out anyway, he found that the controversy had heightened his fame, and on returning to western Pennsylvania he was able to cultivate the constituency that would send him once again to Congress, after first embroiling him in the resistance to the whiskey tax.

A clause in the enabling excise legislation obligated anyone charged with evasion of the tax to travel to Philadelphia to have the case heard. In May 1794, more than sixty such western Pennsylvania tax refusers were summoned, but chose to stay home and protest. The protesters were "the toughest and hardest of westerners: farmers, laborers, hunters, and Indian fighters; most were disillusioned war veterans," Hogeland found. The harassed tax collector enlisted aid from the army. In the ensuing standoff between a dozen soldiers protecting the collector and a larger number of tax protesters, the collector killed one protester and fatally wounded their leader, a veteran, after which the protesters burned the collector's home to the ground. The slain veteran's funeral occasioned larger protests and led to a gathering near Pittsburgh of six to seven thousand people, a substantial fraction of the surrounding regions' population. They threatened local officials and burned down the mayor's home.

Hamilton next prepared a memo for Washington to issue as a proclamation. It painted the participants and the area as being on the cusp of insurrection:

By formal public meetings of influential individuals, whose resolutions and proceedings had for undisguised objects, to render the laws odious, to discountenance a compliance with them, and . . . by a general Spirit of Opposition (thus fomented) among the Inhabitants—by repeated instances of armed parties going in disguise to the houses of the Officers of the Revenue and inflicting upon them personal violence and outrage—by general combinations to forbear a compliance with the requisitions of the laws . . . their execution within the Counties in question has been completely frustrated.

Hamilton persuaded Justice Wilson to deem the western counties of Pennsylvania in a state of rebellion, which permitted the president to summon militias. Washington did not want to use regular troops, fearing that would negatively impact his concurrent attempts to create a permanent army. Three days later his proclamation ordered tax resisters to cease and desist by September 1, or the militias would enforce compliance. Jefferson, by then out of government, had warned Washington that using military force to fix what could be solved by negotiation would place him at the head of a political party that pushed the use of military force, and would diminish his stance of being above party. Washington, however, agreed with Hamilton, Knox, and Attorney General James Bradford that maintaining the authority of the government necessitated vigorously putting down any attempt at evading the laws. When Pennsylvania's governor, Mifflin, Washington's old nemesis, refused to call out his state's militia Washington summoned others, though not without pushback. A dozen years after the end of the Revolutionary War, many veterans were not willing to war against their fellow citizens. Some soldiers had to be conscripted, and there were minor draft riots. The force would include more Americans than had been at Yorktown, and would be more numerous than another army then in Ohio, led by Anthony Wayne, which had just defeated the Miami and their British allies at the Battle of Fallen Timbers.

The militia-based army crossing Pennsylvania was led by "Light-Horse" Harry Lee. Hamilton justified it in articles under yet another pseudonym, and helped it by obtaining a bridge loan of one million dollars from the BUS, and a second million to be disbursed later. The costs of the marching militias far exceeded both loans, so Hamilton found a third million by switching another loan from its original purpose, building naval vessels to counteract the "pirates" off the Barbary Coast of Africa. The western tax protesters had emotional support from beyond the "democratic societies" earlier established for cheering on France's Revolution. These became vocal and active on behalf of the protesters, metamorphosing into such powerful critics of Federalist policies that Washington and Hamilton were moved to denounce them and their newspapers as antidemocratic.

Ahead of the militias Washington sent Bradford and several jurists as negotiators. They met with the more moderate protest leaders, Gallatin and newspaper editor Hugh Brackenridge (a college friend of Madison's), and reached a deal to avoid bloodshed and revise the excise law. When local voters did not wholeheartedly ratify the deal, the jurists informed the administration that it was "absolutely necessary that the civil authority should be aided by a military force in order to secure a due execution of the laws." Only then were the militias dispatched. En route in Carlisle, the soldiers killed two men suspected of having set up a liberty pole; Washington offered to turn over the culprits for prosecution. After he had traveled some with the army, he returned to Philadelphia for a new session of Congress, leaving Hamilton and Lee with the troops. Information was already reaching them, in midstate, that resistance was disappearing, but they marched on.

In Pittsburgh they encountered no substantive opposition. Initially Lee, at Hamilton's urging, made mass arrests, including Gallatin and Brackenridge. Observers believed that had Washington been present, such indiscriminate arrests would not have been made. And shortly Lee pardoned and released all but twenty insurgents—those released included Gallatin and Brackenridge. The remaining prisoners were chosen more as examples than for their complicity. Brought to Philadelphia, they were paraded through the streets on Christmas Day. Only twelve stood trial for treason, and only two were convicted and sentenced to death. Washington pardoned them.

Meanwhile Jay had been negotiating in London. The British contended that neither the United States nor Great Britain had adhered to the strictures of the 1783 accords, implying that both were at fault. This was a false pretense, for although Americans had not repaid prewar British debts, those were not very large, and the British had done incalculable damage by restricting American trade and by not vacating the Midwest forts. Moreover, since the war's end the British had seized hundreds of American commercial ships and impressed thousands of sailors. So what Jay touted as concessions from the British in the 1794 Treaty of Amity, Commerce, and Navigation were no more than what the British had promised a decade earlier and had not previously honored. Britain did agree to pay eleven million dollars for damages to American shipping—most of it owned by Federalist stalwarts such Derby, Gray, and Girard—in exchange for being once again authorized to collect around three million dollars in prewar debts from Americans. The countries granted each other most-favored-nation status; in doing so the United States in effect repudiated its special trade relationship with France. Matters left unaddressed in the treaty included British compensation for American slaves freed during the war, and continued high-seas impressment.

Although Washington knew that the treaty was near to capitulation, he also knew that it would keep America out of a war that the country could not win. Yet sensing trouble in having the Senate ratify the treaty, he delayed submitting it. When he did so he would not have Hamilton at his side, since the latter planned to resign at year's end.

Mutterings of dissatisfaction with the administration, which had grown louder, centered on the president's use of a sledgehammer to sink a tack—a large army to put down a mild insurrection—and now meshed with anger over the Jay Treaty's provisions. The combination pushed into the antiadministration camp such formerly stalwart Federalists as New Hampshire senator John Langdon and Stephen Girard. The Philadelphian, using the celebrity and respect earned from his heroics during the yellow fever epidemic, in March 1794 chaired a meeting of merchants and shipowners that sent letters to the administration protesting the government's unwillingness to push for the return of vessels seized by the French and the British. When the letters brought no satisfaction, Girard, Langdon, and others who had been Federalists since the Constitutional Convention began to rethink their allegiance and become active anti-Federalists.

Before Hamilton left office he obtained a final loan of two million dollars from the BUS, and submitted to Congress his *Report on a Plan for Further Support of Public Credit*. Often overlooked, it marked a turning point in America's economic affairs because, after taking a victory lap for "a State of our finances prosperous beyond expectation, [that] solicited the public councils to enter with zeal and decision on measures commensurate with the greatness of the interests to be promoted," Hamilton recommended changes to previous policies, just the sort of changes that critics had been advocating for years. He tweaked tariff and tonnage rates, and in a deep bow to the Whiskey Rebellion–makers recommended that rural producers should pay less tax per gallon than urban ones, to balance extra transport costs. The most stunning change to his previous position was his statement that the national debt needed more rapid retirement—for five years, he had been adamant about carrying that debt in full. Yet even as he recommended accelerated repayment, he omitted any mention that the debt had grown to $83 million.

Congress did not know that fact either, but as Hamilton was leaving, Gallatin was returning as the representative from western Pennsylvania. Given access to a few state papers he calculated that the national debt had risen by $5 million in five years. "Gallatin is a real treasure," Madison wrote Jefferson, "sound in his principals, accurate in his calculations, and indefatigable in his researches. Who would have supposed that Hamilton could have gone off in the triumph he assumed with such a condition of the finances behind him?" Jefferson and Madison commissioned Gallatin to do more research, which he soon published as *A Sketch of the Finances of the United States*. It accused the government of having paid $11 million too much for assumption because it used as a basis the face value rather than the market value of the state certificates. Gallatin decried carrying the debt intact, citing the experiences of Spain, the Netherlands, and Great Britain, which had done so to the detriment of their economies. He further charged that America's sale of debt-related notes had done nothing for the economy other than to enable the already wealthy "to consume more, to spend more, and they have consumed and expended extravagantly."

There comes a moment in every pendulum's arc when it slows to a halt before reversing direction and heading toward the opposite apogee. In the spring of 1794, events signaling such a change in direction included Hamilton's resignation; his acknowledgment that the country no longer needed to keep the debt intact to stay united; Gallatin's persuading of the Federalist-controlled House to withhold funding for certain operations until it received adequate assurances on their financial impact; and his instituting of regular Ways and Means Committee oversight of executive branch financial actions. The old direction toward the benefit of the already wealthy was replaced by a new one whose aim was voiced in a toast given at a young men's Republican Society in New York: "Less respect to the consuming speculator, who wallows in luxury, than to the productive mechanic, who struggles with indigence."

As the pendulum picked up speed in its journey toward more emphasis on the poor sharing in the country's economic benefits, a particularly glaring excess of "the consuming speculator" came into public consciousness. A year earlier four development companies had bribed Georgia assemblymen to sell them thirty-five million acres west of the state, in areas near the Yazoo River, that would eventually be the states of Alabama and Mississippi, for the ridiculously low sum of five hundred thousand dollars. Wholesale batches of lots were soon resold to outsiders, primarily based in the North and among them a few prominent men such as Wilson, Nathan Prime, and Greenleaf, who sold them a third time to still others. John Adams reported to

Abigail that Greenleaf "has taken Advantage of the Gullability of the Boston Speculators in whose Estimation Dollars seem of no more Value than Cents ought to be to make an enormous hall of fishes to the amount of half a Million of Dollars by a very Artful Sale of shares at a monstrous Price in a purchase he made . . . at a very trifling one." Requests by Georgians to President Washington to do something about the mess went unheeded, so Senator James Jackson, a Georgia Democratic-Republican, resigned to return home and address the issue. Elected to the assembly, Jackson led the repeal of the sales legislation and attempted to sell the lands to the federal government. But then Jackson and his associates, fearing that the speculators would take their case to the Federalist Congress, put off the transfer until after the turn of the century, hoping that by then Democratic-Republicans would be in control.

The Washington administration avoided the Yazoo land mess because it needed to deal with recent developments in Europe that were negatively affecting America. In the Netherlands the exiling of the prince to London effectively foreclosed further Dutch investment in America. That forced Morris, Greenleaf, and Nicholson, who had been planning to sell their acreage to Dutch investors, to consolidate their holdings into the North American Land Company, so they could more easily sell shares to Americans. A second worry was the Barbary Coast "pirates," who for years had been seizing Americans in the waters off western Africa and the adjoining Mediterranean, now held 115, and were demanding one million dollars in ransom. Jefferson had long argued against paying such a ransom, but Washington was willing to do so.

Then Washington had to submit the six-month-old Jay Treaty for ratification by the Senate. He attempted to keep its terms secret, but a leaked copy was published and spurred a Jefferson-directed attack that ridiculed the treaty's provisions, as well as Jay, Hamilton, and Washington as individuals, for being too pro-British. Had the treaty come to the Senate from any hands but Washington's, it would have courted rejection for its abdicating to the Royal Navy the defense of American commercial shipping. Populist anger at this and other concessions occasioned torchlight rallies and the memorable slogan: "Damn John Jay! Damn everyone that won't damn John Jay! Damn everyone who won't put lights in his windows and stay up all night damning John Jay! " Jay commented that he could find his way across country by the glow of his burning effigies. In Philadelphia, Girard was among the leaders of protests against the Jay Treaty: "France is our avowed friend and in the hour of adversity was our vigorous and undaunted advocate. Great Britain is the universal foe of liberty," a handbill proclaimed. Wolcott sniffed that those in attendance at a protest meeting were "an ignorant mob, of the class which is most disaffected and violent." However, on the dais with Girard were Shippen, Peter Muhlenberg, and Thomas McKean, Pennsylvania's chief justice.

The BUS and BoNA gathered four hundred signatures on a letter urging ratification. "Many Persons signd," Butler wrote to Madison, "not from inclination or Approbation, but a dread of being refused Discounts at the Banks if they did not Sign." The senators, a group significantly entwined with the BUS, approved the treaty by precisely the required two-thirds majority. (Bingham, a new senator, voted yea.) But the House held up funding for the treaty during the rest of 1795.

Political outfall from the fight first claimed James Monroe, recalled from France for being overly sympathetic to the French, and then Edmund Randolph. The previous October in a letter home, the new French minister in the United States had painted Randolph's activities as pro-French. The British intercepted that missive, and as 1795 wore on teased the letter to Wolcott, then summarized it to him, and then sent it. Wolcott would discuss it with Washington only in person. After he and Timothy Pickering did so, Washington handed it to Randolph. Randolph might have dismissed it as secondhand gossip, but he was flustered and provided only an unsatisfactory explanation; he was also made to feel so uncomfortable that he resigned on the spot.

The Jay Treaty's importance has obscured two other economically important treaties signed during the Washington administration. In a 1795 Madrid pact, Thomas Pinckney won from Spain the right of American commercial use of the Mississippi River and control over a large territory of what would become Mississippi; Congress ratified the Treaty of Madrid in just one week. A treaty with the ruler of Algiers concerned trade routes carrying a sixth of America's wheat and flour, a fourth of its dried and pickled fish, and a large fraction of its rice. That trade was among the reasons why Washington and Congress agreed to pay the million in ransom that had been demanded. Wolcott obtained a loan from the BUS, and the bank, in turn, arranged to sell 6 percent notes to the London-based merchant bank, Barings & Company, and to have them pay the pirates. The United States agreed thenceforth to pay twenty thousand dollars annually in exchange for free shipping access to Algiers and to the adjacent African, Atlantic, and Mediterranean coasts, and for the Algerian ruler to prevent the other "pirate" entities, Tripoli, Tunis, and Morocco, from committing future kidnappings. This treaty, according to the economic historian Hannah Farber, had an important effect on American credit:

> In order for the United States to pay Algiers in specie, many parties had to accept American credit, including the first Bank of the United States, British stock buyers, and several transnational merchant-banking houses. Once they extended credit to the United States, these parties, like Algiers, became stakeholders in the success of the American Mediterranean trade.

In early 1796 proadministration forces rallied support for funding the Jay Treaty by stoking fears of a war with Great Britain. Insurer associations in New York and Massachusetts threatened to stop underwriting American commercial voyages if the treaty was not funded. Democratic-Republicans in the House were against funding but, as a Maryland representative wrote, "his constituents were desirous that it should be carried into effect, and he found himself bound to lay aside his own opinion, and act according to their will." Gallatin too succumbed to such pressure. Eventually Muhlenberg, also a Democratic-Republican, broke a tie in a committee on a funding bill that then narrowly passed the House; Muhlenberg's brother-in-law was so outraged that he stabbed him.

The French reacted to funding the Jay Treaty by giving carte blanche to privateers to seize American ships, and by refusing to accept the credentials of the newly arrived U.S. emissary, Charles Cotesworth Pinckney, brother of Thomas.

A provision of the Jay Treaty, obligating Great Britain to allow free trade between Canada and the United States, signaled opportunity to John Jacob Astor, a successful but still struggling Manhattan merchant. Astor handled furs from the West and musical instruments made by his uncle's company. Crossing to London, he made a deal with his much larger fur-trading competitor, the Northwest Company. Because the British were just then hampered in shipping furs from Canada directly to Europe, the Northwest Company would send them to Astor in New York for reshipment in American bottoms. Astor's net worth soared to $250,000, elevating him to the upper tier of the country's wealthy.

In the modern era it is a commonplace that presidential elections often turn on the state of the economy. By such a measure 1796 should have been occasion for an upset, since the year began with an ominous spiking of inflation, due to war between France and Great Britain. Wholesale prices that in 1793 had been at 102, by early 1796 were at 146. Benjamin Rush estimated 150 business failures in Philadelphia and—under Pennsylvania's constitution of 1790, which reversed the 1776 one's abolition of imprisonment for debt—a surge of jailings.

The defaulting of so many private loans forced Willing and the BUS board to address the bank's overinvolvement with the government: It had lent the United States far more than the government could readily repay, and it had allowed the government simply to roll over its loans. For the coming year the BUS decided that the government must repay a previously borrowed $1.4 million, and that the bank would not simply let the amount ride or, as it had been doing, roll over future loans. One congressman proposed that in order to retire all extant loans, the Treasury obtain a jumbo, a five-million-dollar one from the BUS, by pledging the sinking fund as collateral.

An alarmed Hamilton wrote Wolcott: "If this goes through & is sanctioned by the President the fabric of public Credit is prostrate & the country & the President are disgraced." Fortunately the BUS board had no interest in a jumbo. But when Wolcott tried to float new bonds to obtain money to pay off the BUS, no one wanted them, and that forced him to do what critics had recommended for years: Sell the government's shares of BUS stock back to it. That happened in the fall, the BUS accepting back 2,160 shares for $1.8 million. The BUS board was so pleased that it let the remainder of the government's loans slide.

A year earlier the District of Columbia commissioners had demanded that Morris, Greenleaf, and Nicholson pay the installment due on their purchases. The trio had been given below-market prices in exchange for erecting buildings and making capital improvements. They had not done enough, nor could they pay, so legal proceedings were begun. The partners then stopped employing the workforce developing the buildings, roads, and sewage canals. By July 1796, to keep creditors at bay Greenleaf sold his partners his one-third interest in the North American Land Corporation. Morris and Nicholson each paid Greenleaf with personal notes that Greenleaf used to pay some of his debts, and that were then resold. With each succeeding resale, these notes lost value. Morris was in such trouble that he begged Washington to appoint a commissioner to make a treaty with the tribes that had sold him the northern Pennsylvania acres, so he could sell them instead of continuing to hold them. "The loss of another year . . . would be ruinous to my affairs," he explained. Washington's responses exhibit a pained tone. In one he refused to appoint a commissioner, saying the Senate would need to agree. In another he told Morris: "I am so thoroughly impressed with the ruinous consequences wch must result to the public buildings from a delay of the payment which the Comrs have requested, that I should think my official conduct reprehensible if I did not press them on you urgently." Washington asked Morris to prove the critics wrong by restarting the buildings, for too many worthy artisans had been thrown out of work and innocent people ruined financially. Morris did not have the money to restart construction, and legal proceedings became more insistent.

Washington had decided not to stand for a third term but had said nothing publicly, lest the news complicate treaty negotiations. Then a scoop on his retirement was published by Benjamin Franklin Bache, a Franklin grandson and the ardent Democratic-Republican publisher of the Philadelphia-based *Aurora*.

Washington shortly confirmed his retirement plans in his "Farewell Address," printed (rather than delivered) in September and composed from drafts by Hamilton and from what Madison had penned four years earlier, all rewritten by Washington. Our mythology has overlooked that farewell's celebration of how America's disparate regions were combining economically to make a whole greater than the sum of its parts. Instead the focus has been on Washington's warning that "It is our true policy to steer clear of permanent alliance with any portion of the foreign world." Readers of his address had no doubt that Washington was referring to France, but his caution could as well have applied to Great Britain, for the United States was even more entangled with that country than with France, due to our overreliance on tariff income from British imports, and on the Jay Treaty.

The president's imminent retirement made it necessary for the country to once again defy its critics' expectations of failure, as it had done twice before at important junctures: when Washington had refused to become a king and the country continued as a confederation of states, and again when, despite dire predictions, the Constitution successfully transformed that loose association into a functioning, democratic republic. Now, with Washington very publicly retiring, America needed to defy expectations of failure a third time, by prevailing even though it would next be governed by a less adored, less charismatic, but no less democratically elected successor.

Doubts about America's survival persisted because the campaign of 1796 was so messy and vicious. As was usual at that time, Adams and Jefferson did not campaign openly, but Adams's partisans tarred

Jefferson's with being pro-French and Jefferson with being an atheist and a coward during the Revolution, while Jeffersonians labeled Adams and his proponents as pro-British monarchists and lackeys of the wealthy. For the first time in American history, a foreign power, France, openly attempted to influence the outcome. The strength of the antiadministration forces made an Adams win far from assured. Hamilton's animosity to Adams had grown to the point that Hamilton tried to press southern Federalist electors to vote only for vice-presidential candidate Thomas Pinckney, since that would lower Adams's electoral vote count. When the New England Federalists learned of the ploy, they had their electors do the opposite. The result was that Adams, with 71 electoral votes, edged Jefferson with 68, but because of Hamilton's failed maneuver on Pinckney, Jefferson was selected as vice president. As for Congress, the Federalists had enough strength to return to power in both houses.

It remained an open question as to whether the American system of democratic governance could survive with a vice president at odds with the president, with Hamilton meddling, with rising inflation, with losses due to privateering, with scandalous land sales—and, most of all, without Washington at the helm.

Part Five

———⬡⬡⬡———

Parties, Populism,
and Striving for
Economic Independence,
1797–1813

14

Adams: Necessary Transitions

*J*ohn Adams's long view of America was expressed in his memorable 1780 letter to Abigail:

I must study Politicks and War that my sons may have liberty to study Mathematicks and Philosophy. My sons ought to study Mathematicks and Philosophy, Geography, natural History, Naval Architecture, navigation, Commerce and Agriculture, in order to give their Children a right to study Painting, Poetry, Musick, Architecture, Statuary, Tapestry and Porcelaine.

Adams's version of the American dream positioned it not as we think of it today—a quest for material riches and comfort—but as a three-generation-long process of growth toward enabling each American to pursue fulfillment.

Adams's own fulfillment had been enabled by Abigail's adroit handling of the family finances as he devoted himself to public service. Speculating in bonds and state paper, she reaped 28 percent a year and at redemption a profit of 400 percent; and when Maine land was offered for sale, with the proviso that one person could buy only five lots, she enlisted relatives to buy many more for the family. Even so, John Adams was far less wealthy than his predecessor or his immediate successors, and he took it as an imperative that his presidency must demonstrate that a nonwealthy man could lead the United States just as competently as a wealthy man.

Reasoning that anyone who followed Washington as president would be viewed askance, Adams retained Wolcott at Treasury, Pickering at State, and James McHenry at War. But as Jefferson soon wrote to Gerry: "The Hamiltonians by whom [Adams] is surrounded are only a little less hostile to him than to me." When Adams sought to send Madison to Paris to replicate what Jay had done in London—find a way to make peace rather than let events cascade toward war—even Hamilton agreed. But Wolcott told Adams that sending Madison would inflame both parties, and threatened to resign. Taking him to mean that McHenry and Pickering also would resign, Adams backed down. "I see a Scene of Ambition, beyond all my former suspicions or Imaginations," he wrote Abigail. "An Emulation which will turn our Government topsy turvy. Jealousies & Rivalries have been my Theme and Checks and Ballances as their Antidotes till I am ashamed to repeat the Words: but they never Stared me in the face in such horrid forms as at present."

Events did not favor him. In Great Britain, when fear of a possible French invasion caused a run on the banks, Britons seeking a monetary safe haven eagerly bought American stocks and bonds, raising their prices; when the Bank of England realized that too much cash was leaving its coffers, it shut its credit doors. That action "quickly unraveled . . . the delicate web of Atlantic credit," writes the financial historian Richard H. Chew: "The result was a severe decline in the value and volume of American exports, the sudden collapse of U.S. wholesale prices for agricultural products, and hard times for the broader economy." The downturn was accelerated by French naval attacks on American shipping, the seizure of three hundred vessels in a short span. In late 1796 America's GNP, after five years of sustained expansion, dropped into negative territory. Over the next two years it would average only .13 percent. The downturn exposed that the previous period (an average 3.2 percent GNP increase for five years) had been an overexpansion. According to the economic historians Nicholas A. Curott and Tyler A. Watts, the BUS's pumping of 43 percent more credit into the economy was so inflationary that it "led entrepreneurs to overinvest in transportation improvements, banking, manufacturing, and other capital-intensive projects. Furthermore, the expectation of inflation induced individuals to bet on continued price increases by borrowing money to purchase real estate."

One early casualty of the downturn was the North American Land Company. Although Morris, Nicholson, and Greenleaf obtained mortgages on some properties, including one from the BUS on the thirty thousand acres that Morris had complained to Washington about, even the BUS could not cover the ten million dollars in Morris and Greenleaf's personal notes. Since those notes were already in the pockets of hundreds of Americans, their owners also suffered as the notes continued to lose value. Then the federal district commissioners obtained court orders to arrest the trio. The law required warrants to be served on individuals yet forbade servers from entering a home, so the three took refuge in their manors. Morris was troubled to learn that Wilson had been jailed for similar nonpayment, although Wilson's son had bailed out the associate justice. When the public learned that Morris could be jailed, his debtors and creditors made more forced sales of land and other assets, deepening the Panic of 1797. Morris went to prison, where Washington dined with him and offered to have Mrs. Morris and the family stay at Mount Vernon until the difficulties were cleared up. The family chose to remain near Morris. The ripples from his failure injured those who had invested with him, including Hamilton, Jay, Willing, Coxe, and Gallatin—five thousand dollars of Gallatin's, which nearly bankrupted him.

Bingham lost forty thousand dollars when a man entangled in the Morris web defaulted on a Bingham loan. Yet Bingham emerged from the Panic of 1797 as the wealthiest American and largest landholder. But Coxe, similarly owed considerable money by Morris and Nicholson, was forced by his inability to collect back into dependence on his family, although still titular owner of 350,000 acres in Pennsylvania and 400,000 in North Carolina. Since Coxe could not pay Church, who had been his partner, he had to face the formidable legal talent of Church's brother-in-law Hamilton.

Knox was a victim of the downturn; and because Lincoln had put up his property as collateral for Knox's Maine lands, Lincoln's property was attached by the Massachusetts Bank. Lincoln assured Adams: "There has not one penny [from public coffers] gone to pay any of the notes nor will any ever go from me for that purpose." Not fired as port collector, he used his fees to work his way out of debt and reclaim his property.

Like the Panic of 1792, the Panic of 1797 was halted by a single factor: in this instance, impending war. Adams resisted his cabinet's pressure to declare war on France, but did build up the navy, establishing a separate department that bought and constructed ships. This put money into just those coastal cities whose exports had been most adversely affected, and also brought victory at sea, as American ships soon captured dozens of French privateers without the loss of a single U.S. vessel.

Hamilton's bargain with Monroe, by which Hamilton had avoided public exposure of his extramarital affair, came apart in 1797 when Democratic-Republican newspaper editor James Thompson Callender published some details. Hamilton, certain that Monroe had leaked the materials, challenged him to a duel that Burr helped to prevent, but Hamilton still felt the need to present his side of the story. In a pamphlet he included enough details of the affair and subsequent blackmail to absolve him of the charge of misusing his government position, but he also certified his culpability on the other matters. Callender observed that Hamilton had done more to bring himself down than "fifty of the best pens in America could have."

Adams had sent emissaries to France in the hope that Foreign Minister Charles Maurice de Talleyrand, who had spent years in exile in the United States, would be receptive to a peace overture. But Marshall, Gerry, and C. C. Pinckney were startled that three Talleyrand agents demanded $250,000 in advance before any negotiation. The Americans refused to pay, and France did not accept their credentials. The "Quasi-War" with France continued.

Adams and his cabinet did not learn of these machinations until the spring of 1798. Pickering and McHenry demanded an immediate declaration of war, and the Democratic-Republicans in Congress insisted on the release of all correspondence. Adams would not declare war but did agree to raise an army and to release the correspondence with Talleyrand's agents, although only after substituting X, Y, and Z for their actual names. The XYZ Affair exploded in the headlines. Congress revoked the 1778 treaties with France and authorized attacks on French warships and privateers: "Millions for defense but not one cent for tribute" became the slogan of the day, one that ignored the United States having recently paid a one-million-dollar tribute to the Barbary pirates. In Salem, Derby and Gray put up ten thousand dollars apiece to construct a new fighting ship to donate to the navy. Also in reaction, Congress that summer passed four Alien and Sedition Acts, without the participation of Adams, who believed the acts were too draconian. He signed them anyway, the first one deliberately on July 14, the anniversary of the storming of the Bastille.

The acts affected French immigrants by tightening citizenship requirements and by making deportation easier; and they brushed back press criticism of the government by criminalizing the issuance of seditious statements, defined as those that were even modestly critical of the government or the president. Federalists had been specifically targeting immigrants since 1790, when Fenno had ranted in his *Gazette* against refugees from Haiti; and targeting newspapermen since Freneau began his rival paper a year later. Moreover, in the eyes of the poor and other citizens leaning toward the Democratic-Republicans, these acts seemed evidence that the wealthy in control of the country were attempting to amass even more power. News that the acts would become law drained capital from the country, as a dozen boatloads of French émigrés fled the United States, including moneyed ones associated with Lafayette's brother-in-law. However, after the acts went into force, the authorities did not deport a single alien.

As for sedition, the government used the acts mainly to prosecute Democratic-Republican newspapermen and politicians. The best known of the two dozen publishers prosecuted was Bache; and the most prominent politician, Congressman Matthew Lyon of Vermont. Both had criticized Washington, Adams, and the Adams administration's missteps with France and Great Britain. Bache's unforgivable sins, though, were charging that Washington had accepted a bribe during the war and, after Washington's retirement, offering a prayer for his speedy demise. Lyon was an unexpected Democratic-Republican, having followed the usual Federalist entrepreneur path of developing several mills on his land and becoming moderately wealthy. He stood accused of "scandalous and seditious writing [with] intent and design to excite against the . . . Government and President the hatred of the good people of the United States." By the rhetorical standards of the 1796 election, the calumnies that Lyon had written and published in his newspaper were very mild—such as that Adams had an "unbounded thirst for ridiculous pomp, foolish adulation, and selfish avarice." As with Bache, Lyon's prosecution had a political cause: He had spat in the face of a Federalist in the House and later responded to the man's cane attack by defending himself with the fireplace tongs. Convicted, fined, and jailed for four months, Lyon during confinement won reelection to Congress, doubling his previous vote. Bache died in prison of yellow fever before trial; his successor at the *Aurora,* William Duane, was subsequently jailed under the acts, as was Callender.

History has justly derided the Alien and Sedition Acts, but in doing so has failed to take note of something positive that Congress passed at the same time, a tax plan as progressive and as protective of the poor as any before or since. Eighteen months earlier Wolcott had recommended a tax on property to fund the army. The debate over it became a remarkable colloquy, a search for the best ways to exempt the poor from the tax and to ensure that the richest would pay the most. The resulting levy "struck a blow for equality," writes the economic historian Clement Fatovic, because it "enshrined the principle that the rate of taxation should be based on the ability to pay." The structure of the tax was also an acknowledgment by these wealthy legislators of a basic American notion, embraced during the Revolution and Early Republic eras but that has since been shunted aside: that this country depended as much for its survival and growth on the thriving of the nonwealthy as it did on the enrichment of its merchants and bankers.

The bill exempted property valued at under one hundred dollars, which meant virtually all simple dwellings, and levied less than one dollar of tax on the majority of the country's properties—those valued between one hundred and five hundred dollars. Beyond those properties valued at more than five hundred dollars, taxes went up sharply. Owners of slaves were charged fifty cents apiece for those aged from twelve to fifty. Since assessing the tax required measuring the property, instructions to assessors included counting the number of windowpanes, giving the levy the nickname "windowpane tax." It raised two million dollars rather easily, in part because of its justness and universality, and in equal part because taxpayers knew that the proceeds were to be used to support the new army.

That army had been judged necessary because of credible rumors that the French might try to seize the Gulf Coast or Canada. Adams asked Washington for advice on how an army should be led—by new generals or old ones—and Cincinnatus considered himself summoned from his plow and accepted its command. He did so in part to mitigate fears that this new army would be used as the government's weapon against its citizens, as armies were routinely used in Europe. Knowing the frailty of his own health, Washington insisted on having capable subordinates to take over, and asked for Knox, Pinckney, and Hamilton. Hamilton informed Washington he would not serve unless he was second in command. Washington gave in, and eventually Adams had to as well. Problems arose as Hamilton finagled supplies and funding from Congress, siphoning off money intended for other uses, and when he encountered roadblocks in getting the army paid, he asked several banks to advance money to him and bill the government for repayment. Hamilton began to fantasize that if war broke out, his army and the Royal Navy would together seize all of France and Spain's Caribbean and South American colonies.

Hamilton's obsession with the new army enabled Burr to pull off a coup in New York, the establishing of a bank. At that time the thoroughly Federalist banks in New York regularly denied loans to Democratic-Republicans. So Burr craftily petitioned the state to start a water company, capitalized at two million dollars; in the wake of a 1797 yellow fever epidemic, it was needed to supply fresh water. Hamilton had come around to the belief that Burr might switch parties and become a Federalist, so he accompanied Burr to the mayor's office to plead for the water company, and even contributed a memo on draining the swamps. At the last moment in the legislative process, Burr inserted a clause that allowed the Manhattan Company to use excess capital for other investments. "The Federalists dozed right through this deception because they knew of the Republican antipathy for banks and also because Burr had cleverly decorated the board with eminent Federalists," writes the Hamilton biographer Ron Chernow. The Manhattan Company then spent one hundred thousand dollars to erect a water supply system, and the remainder of the two million to start a bank that had many hallmarks of "democratic" institutions. The financial historian Perkins points out that some of its shares were reserved for openly avowed Democratic-Republicans, and that it also followed similar banks elsewhere in the United States whose "charter terms sometimes dictated that certain middling groups receive minimal access to credit facilities—for example, 20 percent of all the loan portfolios might be required to be mechanics or farmers." Burr became a hero to Democratic-Republicans. Party chieftains overlooked his egregious sin of not fulfilling the Manhattan Company's obligation to bring in unpolluted water—it took water from old wells. Hamilton's brother-in-law Church dueled with Burr over that outrage, but because Burr's set of pistols were not properly prepared, the duelists did not damage each other.

In September 1798, British admiral Horatio Nelson so thoroughly dismantled the French navy at the Battle of the Nile that there was no possibility of the French mounting a seaborne invasion of the United

States in the coming years. Adams learned this while at home, tending to an ailing Abigail; when McHenry pleaded that the president return to Philadelphia and hurry up the preparations for the Hamilton-led army, he retorted: "At present there is no more prospect of seeing a French army here, than there is in Heaven."

Fear is a more galvanizing political motivator than hope. That there was still grave danger of a French invasion was a message successfully spread by Federalist candidates for Congress in 1798; it worked best in the South, offsetting political gains by the Jeffersonians in the Northeast and the Midwest. The resulting, slightly increased Federalist majorities in Congress masked growing discontent.

Western newspapers now openly railed against the Adams-led Federalists in terms that echoed those earlier used by Jefferson, Madison, Gallatin, Freneau, Bache, and Lyon. William Manning, a farmer, tavern owner, and small-time trader in rural Massachusetts, writing as Labourer, summed up in *The Key of Libberty* the arguments of the less cultured but no less passionate patriots. Although publishers shied away from issuing the book, fearing indictment under the Alien and Sedition Acts, Manning's sentiments were widely shared. He charged that there was a near-complete split in the country between "those that Labour for a Living and those that git a Living without Bodily Labour," namely "the merchant, phisition, lawyer & divine, the philosopher and school master, the Juditial & Exeutive Officers & many others." The Federalists, Manning charged, had consistently used "arts & skeems" to control voting, employing such usual wealthy-man threats as to call in debts, remove patronage, and kick a recalcitrant voter out of his tenancy. The wealthy few, he continued:

> cant bare to be on a leavel with their fellow cretures, or submit
> to the determinations of a Lejeslature whare (as they call it)
> the Swinish Multitude are fairly rep-resented, but . . . are ever
> hankering & striving after Monerca or Aristocracy whare the
> people have nothing to do in maters of government but to se-
> port the few in luxury & idleness.

Gerry had remained in France to continue negotiations after his colleagues had returned home. When he did repatriate, he informed Adams of Talleyrand's softened demands, and had his report seconded by Adams's son Thomas, also home from Europe, and by communications from American officials abroad. Adams then informed Congress that he was going to send another delegation to France. A Federalist attempt to head off the mission was stopped by Bingham, who saw such a fight as politically unwise, and by Adams's willingness to enlarge a single-man emissary to three men. By then the leading French general, Napoleon Bonaparte, Talleyrand, and a few others, had ousted the Directory and had installed themselves as the new government. Adams slowed U.S. war preparations, especially after listening to people along his route to Philadelphia complain of having to pay the windowpane tax atop many others to maintain an army that might not be needed.

The previous fall there had been a pocket of resistance to that new tax in northeastern Pennsylvania, populated by German immigrants who likened the tax to those they had hated in their homelands. Democratic-Republicans used their anger to flip a seat. Their tax protests never attained the breadth and intensity of those against the whiskey tax, but there were liberty poles, voluntary associations of tax refusers, and other activities reminiscent of American rebellious glories dating back to Stamp Tax days. In reaction in February 1799 the authorities arrested twenty men. Revolutionary War veteran and auctioneer John Fries then put together a group to spring these neighbors from prison. Amicable negotiations ensued, and the prisoners were released. The president authorized the dispatch of an army unit, even though the *Aurora* reported that "the insurrection in Northampton is cooled down to an ordinary process of law, to which all the parties have voluntarily submitted"—including Fries, who announced his willingness to be arrested. Hamilton insisted on enlarging that force, declaring: "Whenever the government appears in arms, it ought to appear like a Hercules and inspire respect by display of strength." Five hundred soldiers easily arrested thirty-one insurgents, who were then put on trial. Fries and two others were convicted of treason. Some Federalists celebrated their expected hanging. Pickering wrote that making examples of "such high handed offenders are essential to ensure future obedience to the laws . . . and to suppress future insurrections. . . . And as painful as is the idea of taking the life of a man, I feel a calm and solid satisfaction that an opportunity is now presented [to] crush that spirit." Adams delayed the executions.

In Salem, in September 1799, a few months after his wife's death, Elias Hasket Derby died at the age of sixty. The couple had barely occupied the mansion they had built for their old age. Derby's estate was estimated at a million dollars, then the largest ever for an American. James Wilson and William Duer also died that year; once among the country's wealthiest men, both died heavily in debt.

In December 1799, Congress began its final session in Philadelphia before government operations were moved to the District of Columbia. On December 18 stunning news arrived: George Washington had died three days earlier, after a brief illness. In a congressional resolution that today might raise eyebrows, the Senate and House conveyed their condolences to Adams, a gesture acknowledging the need to celebrate what Washington had fought for through support of his elected successor. Adams's hand was strengthened by that and by Washington's removal from the scene. Shortly a New England congressman introduced a motion to curtail the Hamilton-led army. There was a widespread worry that Hamilton could become America's Bonaparte and, like Bonaparte, lead military legions against dissenting parts of the country. That concern was based on arguments made in articles written by Hamilton in 1798 that a standing army was necessary to control the "treason that lurk[ed] at the core" of the Jeffersonians.

The still-Federalist Congress then passed the Bankruptcy Law of 1800, mainly to forestall Democratic-Republicans passing one that would be too lenient on debtors. This law covered only involuntary bankruptcies involving high-dollar amounts and merchant debtors. The noninclusion of smaller debtors, thereby condemning them to continued imprisonment, almost doomed the act, which passed by only one vote. (It did enable Morris and others to start the long process of buying their way out of jail for a few cents on the dollar.) The same Congress passed the Land Act of 1800, which helped people of modest means seeking to settle in the Ohio territories. It halted large-scale land sales to speculators, and mandated direct sales to private individuals in lots of 320 acres, for two dollars an acre. Half a square mile was more than many families could farm, so shortly the obligatory acreage was reduced to 160.

In the spring of 1800 news came from Paris that negotiations were going well. Adams was elated. His cabinet downplayed the information, and Congress renewed an act forbidding trade with France even as it reduced the annual budget for the army from four million dollars to three. That would still put the budget in the red, so Congress raised tariffs and authorized Wolcott to take out new loans. He decided that the country would be better off selling bonds, as the government now owed considerable money to the BoNA and the Bank of New York as well as to the BUS. In what Perkins calls "the first true test of the government's status as an issuer of new securities," European buyers refused to take the new bonds at 5 or even 6 percent, so Wolcott was forced to issue them at a money-losing 8 percent.

A few blocks away from where Congress was dealing with these issues, Fries and his two associates were retried, once again found guilty, and sentenced to hang. Then Adams pardoned the conspirators, as Washington had done with the whiskey-tax rebels. When McHenry sought to protest, Adams accused him of disloyalty and of serving Hamilton, "the greatest intriguant in the World—a man devoid of every moral principle." McHenry resigned. Adams then requested Pickering's resignation. When Pickering refused, Adams fired him and replaced him with John Marshall, a staunch Federalist who had tried to effect reconciliation with France and who had also decried the Alien and Sedition Acts.

Adams believed that his reelection would be aided by the prospects of peace with France, the Fries pardons, the recovering economy, and the axing of the unpopular McHenry and Pickering. He discounted that he would be equally hurt by the issues of an unnecessary army, the windowpane tax, the Alien and Sedition Acts—which few people knew that he had opposed—and by residual distrust of his main supporters, the coastal cities' merchants and bankers. The Hamiltonian position on the election was that the country would be as badly off under Adams as under Jefferson, and he attempted to back Pinckney, although Pinckney was only on the Federalist ticket for vice president.

The eventual outcome of the national election was decided in the late spring state elections. With Morris still in jail, the Pennsylvania Democratic-Republicans were in a good position to elect a slate pledged to Jefferson, and they did. Then the critical state became New York. There Burr's influence in New York City helped to flip the state's legislature from a Federalist to a Democratic-Republican majority, assuring that in the fall the New York electors would vote for Jefferson. The Democratic-Republicans then made Burr the party's vice-presidential candidate. When the New York results became known, Adams told Jefferson at lunch: "You are to beat me in this contest." Jefferson responded that it was not their personalities that divided their fellow citizens but "two systems of principles on the subject of government." Adams agreed, and hoped that they could remain friends.

But continued friendship became impossible as the ensuing campaign escalated into unforgivable vitriol, expressed not only by partisans of Jefferson and Adams but also by Hamilton. His opposition to Adams was crystallized in a letter to Theodore Sedgwick, Speaker of the House: "If we must have an *enemy* at the head of Government, let it be one whom we oppose, & for whom we are not responsible." He extended that thought in a fifty-four-page letter to a private circle of Federalists, which bashed Adams in phrases fully as offensive as those that had caused the jailing of Bache and Lyon for sedition. The letter leaked, and after portions were printed, Hamilton was forced to release the entire missive. Its venom against Adams further split the Federalists and emboldened the Jeffersonians.

On August 30 a slave rebellion in Richmond, led by blacksmith

Gabriel Prosser, was postponed due to rain, and as a coconspirator waited for clear skies to resume the operation he told his owner about it. The owner got word to Governor James Monroe, and the state militia soon apprehended three Prosser brothers and twenty-three others. John Randolph, sitting in on interrogations, heard rhetoric echoing that of the American and French Revolutions and referencing a continuing uprising in Haiti. The plotters were speedily tried and hanged. According to documents that later surfaced, Prosser had believed an incoming Republican administration would treat slaves better than the Federalists had.

The November 1800 elections swept away Federalist control of the presidency, the House, and the Senate. Adams would later remark that his sending negotiators to France was "the most disinterested, prudent, and successful conduct in my whole life," though he believed it had cost him the election. His defeat had more to do with the seismic shift in political sentiment that rejected the catering to the wealthy long embraced by the Federalists as the sole path to economic growth.

But since the Electoral College tallies showed Jefferson and Burr tied with seventy-three votes each, the election was thrown into the House, which was still controlled by Federalists. Some told Jefferson that if he did not replace all Federalist appointees, or mothball the navy, or fully pay off the public debt, they would declare him president. He refused, not wanting to tie his hands. Hamilton became alarmed. He argued in multiple letters to Federalist congressmen that Burr was "the most unfit and most dangerous man . . . the most un-principled . . . who, while despising, has played the whole game of democracy"—in short, a disrupter who had no respect for the institutions of government and could do a lot of damage to what they had patiently built. Jefferson, he asserted, would not casually overturn a dozen years of progress, so they should vote for Jefferson.

On the first thirty-five ballots, before Hamilton's letters reached their addressees, enough congressmen continued to vote for Burr to deny the presidency to Jefferson, whom they had been lambasting for years as the prime enemy. On the thirty-sixth ballot, however, Hamilton's pressure resulted in abstentions by representatives from

Delaware and South Carolina who had previously voted for Burr, which moved their states into the "no result" column, providing Jefferson with enough of a margin in the House to certify him as the third president of the United States of America, and Burr as the vice president.

Before the new, Republican-dominated Congress took office, the Federalists sought to assure continuing control of the judiciary. Chief Justice Oliver Ellsworth retired so that Adams could install his successor. John Jay declined to take the post again, explaining that the Supreme Court did not have "the Energy weight and Dignity which are essential to its affording due support to the national Governmt." Adams instead nominated and Congress approved John Marshall as chief justice. The Federalists next passed a Judiciary Act that relieved Supreme Court justices of some circuit court duties and created six new judicial districts with sixteen new judges. Adams then appointed these "midnight judges" (including Wolcott) from a list of those pledged to uphold Federalist principles and prevent the state courts, which were more Democratic-Republican in nature, from deciding too many cases.

After that, cooperation between the factions of defeated Federalists ceased. Adams and Sedgwick, sharing a coach back to Massachusetts after Jefferson's inauguration, did not utter a word to each other during the several days' journey.

15

Jefferson: The Pendulum Swing

*B*y 1801 the United States of America was substantially larger than it had been in 1776, in terms of land area, population, and wealth, and it had weathered two changes in presidents and an expansion in its number of states without losing its commitment to democracy. According to the statisticians Jeffrey H. Lindert and Peter G. Williamson, "America was an even more egalitarian place in 1800 than in 1774," mainly because "the gaps between the richer urban regions and the poorer rural hinterlands [had] declined." The major cities had grown, although not as much as Great Britain's because America's had almost no machine-driven factories to hold workers in place and much open land to attract them. The Northeast had become more characterized by multiple small farms producing a variety of crops for sale to the region's larger cities as well as for sustenance—more of the farms had entered the market economy. In the South the trend had been in the opposite direction, concentrating landownership and slaveholding in fewer hands and in plantations that almost exclusively produced crops for export. Those two largely different economies were replicated in the newly settled areas, those that became Ohio and Michigan featuring relatively small farms and few slaves, and those west of the Carolinas and Georgia transformed into very large, multislave plantations. The added representatives from those new southern areas had expanded the clout of slaveholders in Congress.

A generation of entrepreneurs, born around the time of the Revolution, was coming into its own. Henry Clay of Kentucky became the last law pupil of George Wythe, the teacher of Jefferson and Marshall. John C. Calhoun ran the family farm in South Carolina so well that he was given the management of five others; he studied law on his own and dreamed of attending Yale. Andrew Dexter, Jr., who had graduated college in Providence in 1798, by 1801 was a rising Boston trader who bought and sold competitively with more experienced ones. The Appleton brothers, Samuel and Nathan, formerly shopkeepers in Ipswich, from a base in Boston were buying European dry goods at auction and selling them to Americans for potash and pearl ash that they then resold in Great Britain. "Happy America!" Nathan would shortly write in his diary, "where the poorest of your sons, *knows* that by industry & economy, he can acquire property and respectability, and has ambition enough to make the attempt—which seldom fails of success."

The most important gift a president can bequeath a successor is peace. Adams's emissaries returned to America early in the Jefferson administration with a treaty that ended the Quasi-War. The second most important gift is fiscal stability. Wolcott provided that by working to restrict the debt total to within 1 percent of what it had been when he took over from Hamilton, an eighty-three million dollars that now represented a significantly smaller fraction of the GNP. This diminished obligation, plus the vacating of British forts in the West, permission from Spain to conduct more commerce on the Mississippi, higher tariffs, and a resultant boost in government income, positioned the American economy for new growth.

Jefferson pursued that growth through financial policies quite different from Hamilton's, and he governed in a style deliberately opposite to Washington's. Where Washington had worn beautiful clothes to meetings, traveled in coaches, held formal dinners, and only engaged the public at brief levees, Jefferson was casual in his dress, refused to ride in coaches, made unaccompanied horseback trips around the District of Columbia, and often answered the door at the president's mansion and received anyone who showed up, regardless of status. An aristocrat by birth, owning one of the larger fortunes in the country and having spent years in France interacting with a society that valued aristocratic accoutrements, as president he rejected the trappings of wealth and nobility. His charm and approachability in formal and informal meetings became legendary. He shaped all the important legislation, but in a manner that left no fingerprints, introducing bills through legislators to reinforce the notion of legislative supremacy as basic to democracy.

Jefferson is mythologized as the promulgator of democratic ideas who was clueless about economic matters—but he had as much background in economic theory as Hamilton, having also read the works of British economists Adam Smith and David Ricardo, and the French physiocrats, and he respected Turgot enough to display a bust of the French economist at Monticello. Jefferson has similarly been derided as the naive champion of the agrarian, of the lone farmer-family as the basic unit of the American economy when the future lay with manufacturing—but in 1801, in a country still above 90 percent rural, and where arable land was rapidly being opened and farmed, it was reasonable to champion the agrarian. As for the associated charge that he was against manufacturing, cities, and capitalist development, by 1801 he had left behind the antipathy to manufacturing he had expressed in 1785 and was himself a manufacturer of nails, albeit with slave labor, and in his presidential addresses to Congress recommended encouraging and nurturing manufacturing. He also accepted cities as necessary, the more so as he understood how much of his political support came from city dwellers.

As for capitalism, Jefferson, Gallatin, and Madison were all for it, but they had long asserted that the majority of Americans had not been much helped by Federalist trickle-down initiatives based on the idea that enabling the wealthy in entrepreneurial ways would spur them to employ many people, who in turn would spend more and thereby assist the livelihoods of still others. The country had spent a dozen years on that path; Jefferson and his allies now sought to boost American capitalism in ways that more directly benefited that large majority of the populace who lacked bankable assets. They believed that capitalism in a thoroughly democratic country must go beyond encouraging the accumulation of monetary capital and marketable goods to the establishment of markets for exchange of those goods, and to the enfranchisement of labor so that laborers had some choice as to where and how to be employed. To accomplish these goals, they believed, mandated an immediate slashing of the national debt, an equal slashing of taxes, and a redirecting of government income toward infrastructure, so that more goods could move more freely about the country, thus energizing commerce, and toward education, so as to enhance all levels of production. The Jeffersonians' economic plans were as ambitious and as radical as Hamilton's had been, and in 1801 more attuned to the country that the United States of America had become.

Gallatin has been retroactively deprecated, too, because what he did as secretary of the treasury seems less momentous than what Hamilton had done. The two secretaries had both been immigrants to the United States who had lost fathers at an early age, had to scramble to make their living and an impact on their new country, and were extremely well qualified for their cabinet posts. But Gallatin, born into a wealthy family, had given up his patrimony to come to the New World, and was imbued with beliefs, derived from close studies of Rousseau and Voltaire, that the well-to-do had an obligation to help the poor get ahead. In America he had known poverty as a small trader in coastal Maine, and since then, though he had prospered modestly, he neither aspired to regain his position among the privileged nor especially curried their favor. "The fact is," he wrote in 1798, "I am not well calculated to make money,—I care but little about it, for I want but little for myself, and my mind pursues other objects with more pleasure than mere business." As a leader of the agrarian whiskey-tax revolt, and as a political activist who had a senatorial seat wrested from him but was returned to Congress by the people, he never lost sight of the needs of the poor. Serving them and championing democracy were tenets he shared with the wealthy slave-owning heirs, Jefferson and Madison. To assure Senate approval of Gallatin's nomination, Jefferson delayed it until the Republican Congress was seated in December.

In choosing some people for high office, every president disappoints others. Tench Coxe was irate because he was not in the Jefferson cabinet. Although he thought Madison and Gallatin eminently qualified, he had expected at least to be secretary of the navy, having helped Jefferson win the crucial state of Pennsylvania. Given a secondary post, Coxe wrote to Jefferson in a manner that his biographer calls "self-defeating . . . prompted by his unmitigatable despair as he saw his . . . laboriously contrived political career demolished by a few strokes of Jefferson's pen." His income was not enough to offset his many debts to his former partners Frazier and Church, and to his London factors. To shield his hundreds of thousands of acres from creditors, he had to make it appear that friends and relatives owned them.

In 1800 John Jacob Astor had begun doing what nearly every self-made wealthy person in the history of the United States has done—anticipate a trend and use his wherewithal to take advantage of it. Astor took the approaching peace as reason to buy shares in the *Severn*, bound for China, laden with thirty thousand sealskins, other furs, and Appalachian ginseng root. As the new administration was settling in, the *Severn* returned with silks, satins, spices, porcelain, and tea; Astor used the profit from selling them to buy out some of his partners and return the *Severn* to Asia. By continuing this pattern of voyages and steadily increasing his ownership, he shortly amassed enough money to purchase the large Manhattan home of Rufus King, who moved to London as ambassador. And he and his friend DeWitt Clinton, the governor's nephew, regularly bought Manhattan real estate parcels in the expectation of the island's increasing settlement.

For Stephen Girard, too, the onset of peace with France and Great Britain brought a plethora of opportunities to employ his expertise, credit, diligent and exhaustive research, and his connections, as well as his monetary capital. With his wife in a mental institution and no children to care for, he seldom took a day off, hiring people willing to work with him on Sundays. He researched prices on five continents and determined which goods would be the most valuable in each port. He entered the China trade with commissioned ships that he named for philosophers—*Voltaire, Rousseau, Helvetius,* and *Montesquieu*—and indulged himself only in having a noted sculptor create their figureheads. One typical letter to a representative aboard one of his ships directed him to sell Charleston cotton in Antwerp, buy gin in London, sell it in Brazil, bring coffee from there to Liverpool, and take British fabrics into the Mediterranean to sell for goods to trade in India, and then go to China to buy tea and spices before returning home. The two-year odyssey of that one ship trebled Girard's investment, and he had many out at once.

William Gray's fortunes rose by similar strategies; his letters to his captains evince the same attention to the marketability of goods at certain times. "A cool, discerning man who does not form his opinions hastily," Pickering had said of Gray, who had once been a soldier in his regiment. "For merchantile talent and extent of business, [he is] the first merchant in the United States."

As for Bingham, who was even wealthier, just as Jefferson was taking office he brought on board a ship bound for the Caribbean his very ill wife, Anne, in hopes of restoring her health, badly damaged by the birth of their son. It was to no avail. She died upon reaching the islands. The brokenhearted Bingham made plans to have the Willings rear his infant son, and booked passage for Europe.

The key to the Jeffersonian reforms was to decrease government spending to enable the use of government income to rapidly pay down the national debt and to eliminate direct taxes. And Jefferson took steps to accomplish both goals. With Gallatin's expert assistance the Jeffersonians cut military budgets, and then dropped entirely those recent sources of rebellion, the windowpane tax and the whiskey excise tax, which then permitted the axing of the few thousand government employees who had collected and administered those taxes. They also replaced the Bankruptcy Act of 1800 with one that better protected smaller debtors, and went beyond rescinding the Judiciary Act of 1801 to eliminate some of the new judicial districts and the "midnight judges" who presided over them, including Wolcott. They further refused to deliver commissions—William Marbury, a justice of the peace, sued Madison when his commission failed to arrive.

States and cities began to feel the influence of the new priorities and policies. For decades the Brown family had held such sway in Rhode Island that they controlled the only bank in the state; when another bank tried to form, the Browns called the loans of the would-be founders and pressured the legislature to prevent its charter. But after the Republicans came to power, the legislature chartered the Republican-backed Roger Williams Bank in Providence, and Jefferson cited that bank to Gallatin as an example: "I am decidedly in favor of making all the banks republican by sharing [government] deposits among them in proportion to the dispositions they shew. . . . It is material to the safety of republicanism, to detach the mercantile interest from it's enemies, and incorporate them into the body of it's friends." Shortly other state governments discovered that they could derive a lot of income by not acquiescing too readily to petitions for state charters of banks. Virginia first sought to extract from the Bank of Virginia the right to buy a fifth of its shares with a loan from the bank, and then demanded that the shares be given it at no charge. The would-be bank incorporators felt they had no choice but to agree.

For years Gallatin had insisted that the country's curse was carrying the national debt intact, and that "no class of citizens would be more benefitted by [its] extinction than the poor." In the Jefferson administration's first fiscal year, he applied more than seven million dollars of the ten-million-dollar income to debt reduction, and estimated that at such a clip the debt could be halved by the end of a second Jefferson term. This entailed considerable sending of money to the owners of that debt, and in the ensuing years a lot of it was sent out of the country that way, since many owners of the debt were foreign. However—and this has been less noted—about two million dollars a year was disbursed into the hands of American debt owners, who promptly invested it in U.S. entities, thereby providing capital to the economy at a rate comparable to what the BUS and other banks had pumped in during the 1790s. Jefferson's stimulus was nearly as large as Hamilton's had been, but has been forgotten.

Jefferson was fortunate in that the government's income was rising. The previous Congress had hiked tariff rates to 12 percent, so that the Dutch, Spanish, and Northern European traders who were doing more business in America were generating more tariff income than in previous years. Those European traders, blocked from direct commerce with other European markets by the continuing war between France and Great Britain, sent goods to the United States, paid the modest duties, and reshipped them in American bottoms to Europe. Most American owners of those bottoms leapt at the chance for easy profits from such arrangements; only a few, such as Gray, refused to rent out their ships for that purpose.

Under Jefferson and Gallatin the growth of GNP was steady, around 3 percent, about the same as that during the Hamilton and Wolcott years. But the new growth was of somewhat different character, for a lot of it took place not only in the usual components of the GNP—the stock of money and the aggregate value of goods—but in the sharply rising number of people employed and in their percentage of the total population. The newly employed included many independent farmers, factory workers, and seamen. It also featured more women, who were now earning wages rather than, as in the past, toiling unpaid in the home and on the farm.

Under Jefferson as well, the wealthy increased their wealth, and not at the expense of the poor—both groups gained. The wealthy continued to prosper because the growth of the country still depended heavily on the liquid capital they could provide in quantity. In the first decade of the new century—the Jefferson era—manufacturing grew so much that it reversed the previous negative ratios of American-made to British-made goods in many categories: Domestic production of candles and soap eclipsed imported ones by five to one. There was a similar reversal in the production of sugar. American-made textiles increased from half of what was used in American homes to two-thirds. Gallatin would calculate, from figures provided by the states, that by decade's end American income from internal manufacturing was $120 million annually, as large as the export trade. In other words, the movement of the pendulum in the direction of giving preference and aid to what would uplift the poor was good for the wealthy too, did not hurt the overall economy, and expanded America's capacity for capitalism as robustly as Hamilton's program had.

Gallatin was adamant that the main reason for growth under Jefferson was the same as it had been under Washington and Adams: the rejection of government attempts to control businesses, which remained

> perfectly free and unfettered, every species of trade, commerce, art, profession and manufacture, being equally opened to all, without requiring any previous regular apprenticeship, admission, or license. Hence the progress of America has not been confined to the improvement of her agriculture, and to the rapid formation of new settlements and States in the wilderness.

That Hamilton invention, the Bank of the United States, did suffer under Jefferson, in two ways, one of them inevitable—the establishing of dozens of other banks able to do what the BUS once monopolized. But Jefferson also gave it a whack by insisting, over Gallatin's objections, on reducing government ownership of the BUS, loans from it, and the amount of federal funds kept in it. The government's deposits were redistributed to multiple regional banks that were then able to use the deposits as the basis for expanding their loans, which enhanced local economies.

Gallatin assured the BUS board that there was no intent to close the bank, but Willing was not convinced. The bank's clout continued, however, because it was the clearinghouse for other banks' notes; should the BUS choose not to cooperate with a local bank, that bank would struggle, and so local banks followed the BUS lead and replicated Willing's cautious policies.

A secondary facet of Hamilton's financial structure troubled Gallatin: the sinking fund. He discovered that it was not, as Hamilton had encouraged people to believe, an actual fund held in reserve but merely an accounting device earmarking future tariff receipts for its purposes. Gallatin wanted no deception or obscurity in handling the public trust. Thereafter, as he constructed the government budgets he specifically set aside and sequestered some incoming funds for the inevitable rainy day.

Hamilton was publicly and relentlessly critical of each and every step taken by Jefferson and Gallatin to reduce the debt, eliminate taxes, downsize the military, rely less on the BUS, redirect government income, and provide transparency to financial operations. While Gallatin publicly admired the pillars of Hamilton's economic system—for instance upholding the BUS even as Jefferson undermined its participation in government affairs—Hamilton never conceded that anything done by the Democratic-Republicans resulted in a positive for the country. Hamiltonian Federalists echoed his partisanship; but in Salem, when they sought to vote to have the town stop employing anyone associated with Gray's trading rivals, the Crowninshield family, who had become Republicans, Gray, still a staunch Federalist, opposed the measure as unseemly and it was dropped.

While Jefferson had been secretary of state, he had protested paying tribute to the Barbary Coast pirates, preferring to have America best them militarily. Washington and Adams had paid the tribute. But soon after Jefferson's inauguration, and without discussing it with his cabinet or Congress, he dispatched a navy squadron to the area. America's treaties with the fiefdoms had been unraveling, and just prior to the arrival of the squadron, Tripoli, the best-armed of the four fiefdoms that made up the Barbary Coast, had informed the American attaché it would declare war if the United States did not immediately furnish a new warship, back payment of tribute, and sign a new treaty at triple the price. For emphasis the bashaw's soldiers overran the American compound. The U.S. squadron attempted diplomacy; when that failed, they prevailed in firefights. Thereafter the squadron was able to convoy American ships to their destinations. The United States paid no further tribute, and Jefferson's aggressive use of the American military defused criticism leveled at him for curtailing the military budget.

The entente with the Barbary Coast fiefdoms continued until March 1804, when the American squadron suffered the egregious loss of the frigate *Philadelphia,* captured with three hundred men. Jefferson then raised the navy appropriation to build new ships. To obtain money for that purpose, Gallatin had Congress ratchet up the tariffs to 15 percent, and directed the money from the extra percentage into a separate Mediterranean fund. Navy lieutenant Stephen Decatur led a contingent of marines on a daring overland mission to scuttle the *Philadelphia*; the marines' success aroused Americans and made Decatur a hero. Even so, a Jefferson attempt to obtain permission from Congress to build more ships and strengthen the army failed to pass, because the Republican majorities refused to go along with their president's experience-driven change of heart on military preparedness.

In 1802 James Jackson and other Georgians were finally able to have their state transfer title to the Yazoo area lands to the federal government, for $1.25 million. The Compact of 1802 produced howls from northern speculators who had paid money for some of those lands, and from Matthew Lyon, now a congressman from Kentucky. While he did not himself own any Yazoo land, he wanted titles to all such contested acreages validated rather than nullified by Congress. John Randolph, Jefferson's cousin and chairman of the House Ways and Means Committee, wanted no rewards for speculators or for bribe-taking state legislators, and attempted to deny both sets by introducing legislation to invalidate all claims made under the state law. During a debate Randolph called Lyon a jackal feeding on other people's entrails, and Lyon replied that "these charges have been brought against me by a person nursed in the bosom of opulence, inheriting the life services of a numerous train of the human species, and extensive fields, the original proprietors of which property, in all probability, came no honester by them than the purchasers of Georgia's land." Although Randolph's invalidation measure was defeated, he did block private sales.

"There is on the globe one single spot, the possessor of which is our natural enemy," Jefferson wrote of New Orleans in 1802, because through it "the produce of three-eighths of our territory must pass to market." The crisis over New Orleans began in 1798, when Spain revoked the right of American traders to deposit goods in New Orleans for reshipment elsewhere. Adams had been prevented from dealing with access to New Orleans by the Quasi-War. When Jefferson took office he and Madison learned of a secret treaty in which Spain ceded to France New Orleans and other Louisiana parcels. Should France rule New Orleans, Jefferson wrote: "The impetuosity of her temper, the energy and restlessness of her character" would cause "eternal friction with us." So he and Madison refused Napoleon's request to assist in reconquering Haiti, lest the French then use Haiti as a base for controlling New Orleans. They sent Chancellor Livingston to Paris to buy New Orleans for two million dollars. Napoleon was not interested, and Talleyrand tried to tell Livingston that Spain still owned the city.

The obvious importance of New Orleans allowed the Federalists to make political hay by chiding Jefferson for slimming the navy and army when a potential war with France loomed. The administration then sent Monroe, a former emissary to France, to assist the elderly Livingston. Monroe departed with alacrity, only slightly hampered by his net worth having already been diminished by the expense of governing Virginia; he sold household furnishings to obtain funds to travel to Paris and to prepare for the even larger expenses that would arise in replacing Rufus King as ambassador to Great Britain.

In Paris the Peace of Amiens that had ended the war between France and Great Britain was threatening to evaporate, and France was also gearing up to send an expedition to take possession of New Orleans. Livingston threatened to have an American force reach that city first and take possession. The French minister "*seemed alarmed at the boldness of the measure and told me he* would answer my note but that it would be evasively," Livingston reported home. "I told him I Should receive with pleasure any communication from him, but that we were not disposed to triffle—that the times were critical." Negotiations began. Napoleon bypassed Talleyrand because of the foreign minister's bribe demands in the XYZ Affair, and put them in the hands of François Barbé-Marbois, who had served in the Philadelphia legation prior to the French Revolution and was married to an American.

Monroe and Livingston were nonetheless startled when France offered to sell the entire Louisiana Territory for $11.25 million, plus forgiveness of French debts to America of $3.75 million. The price was less than three cents per acre and included virtually everything north and west of the Mississippi River, clear up to Canada at the northern end and to the Rocky Mountains at the west, excluding only Texas. Napoleon wanted some things that were easy to grant— permanent trading positions and navigation rights in New Orleans and the lower Mississippi—and one very tough thing, immediate payment. Livingston and Monroe, believing that waiting for instructions from home might lose the opportunity to buy, agreed to the terms.

News of the Louisiana Purchase arrived in America in July 1803. Jefferson, Madison, and Gallatin grasped its economic potential and set out to finance the purchase in ways that would not unduly delay the paring down of the national debt. The Federalists raised predictable objections to the cost and governability of the new territory. They also feared that the new states eventually created from the purchase would likely vote for the Republicans, which would further decrease New England's waning influence on the government. Hamilton gave the Louisiana Purchase his grudging approval but charged that the chance to buy it was merely a by-product of the Haitian insurgents' successful resistance to the French forces sent to overwhelm them, rather than of any "wise or vigorous measures on the part of the American government." But detractors could not deny Livingston's observation when he signed the deed: "The United States take rank this day among the first powers of the world."

Gallatin obtained from the BUS a pledge to lend the government what was owed to Americans by France, and Bingham became involved in the other financing. With his son-in-law, Alexander Baring, scion of a British banking family, Bingham arranged for the Barings Bank and its trading partner, Hope and Company of Amsterdam, to provide the immediate cash demanded by Napoleon. In a deal overseen by Gallatin, the United States gave 6 percent notes to the London and Amsterdam banks. Though a higher rate than Gallatin wished to pay, he calculated that the potential tariffs from New Orleans traffic would enable the United States to handle the purchase price and the repayments within a decade—a very short time for such a monumental acquisition. It was the most significant economic move of the Jefferson presidency, and one fully as important to America's future as the establishing of Hamilton's banking and credit system had been in the 1790s.

Recognition of the purchase's economic potential helped the treaty pass the Senate easily. The House more narrowly approved, for Randolph opposed it as too expensive, and was joined in his dissent by Federalists and some states' righters.

The Lewis and Clark expedition to explore the Louisiana Territory began before the purchase. In 1802 Jefferson obtained congressional approval of and appropriation for a Corps of Discovery to explore the entire area west of the Mississippi, in response to threats of spreading British, French, and Spanish influence. He had long sought such an expedition, in the 1780s backing an unsuccessful one and in 1793 persuading Washington, Adams, and other colleagues to put up personal funds for a French expedition that ended in failure. He now arranged for his private secretary, Meriwether Lewis, to receive instruction from prominent scientists of the American Philosophical Society in the skills that the expedition would need. For Lewis's coleader he chose the experienced Indian-country soldier George Rogers Clark. Jefferson's instructions ordered the examination and documentation of the topology, geology, flora, fauna, Native American tribes, and atmospheric conditions of the region, with an eye toward its future economic exploitation.

Gallatin's report to Jefferson that he had asked the Bank of the United States to open a branch in New Orleans brought a raging presidential response, that the BUS was "one of the most deadly hostilities existing, against the principles and form of our Constitution." But Gallatin convinced him that a BUS office would facilitate tariff collection, and Jefferson acceded to this reasonable point. It was emblematic of Jefferson's pragmatism, a trait that mythology has refused to acknowledge, and that was also on display as he worked with the Federalists to resolve constitutional issues with the purchase, mainly to prevent the matter ending up in the bailiwick of the Supreme Court, whose chief justice, John Marshall, a distant cousin of Jefferson's, had become a principal enemy.

The cousins had studied with the same law teachers, and Marshall had taken over Jefferson's law practice when Jefferson became governor, but Marshall had been on the front lines in the Revolutionary War and Jefferson had not, and for a long time the two had been quite philosophically opposed. By 1803 Marshall as chief justice had already done damage to the Republicans in his decision in *Marbury v. Madison*. William Marbury had sought a writ of mandamus from the Court to compel Madison to issue his certificate of appointment (by Adams) as a justice of the peace. Such writs were in the Court's jurisdiction, according to Article 13 of the Judiciary Act of 1789. Reasoning that Madison would likely ignore any writ from the Court, but that not to issue one would declare the Court's powerlessness, Marshall found a third way: He declared void that part of Article 13 expanding the Court's jurisdiction as "repugnant to the Constitution." This ruling arrogated to the Supreme Court the power to determine the constitutionality of any legislative act.

During Jefferson's first two years as president, slave traders escalated their purchases and sales in the United States, in the expectation that on January 1, 1808, as per the Constitution, Congress could close down the slave trade. In Jefferson's 1785 *Notes on Virginia*, he had begun to disavow slavery as a "commerce [of] the most unremitting despotism on the one part, and degrading submissions on the other." Having since become more outspokenly abolitionist even as he continued to be a slaveholder, in 1803 he backed a revision of the slave-carrying law that markedly narrowed the ability of American-owned vessels to transport slaves, to the point of forbidding American sailors from serving on foreign ships engaged in that trade. In 1804 Congress debated extending the Northwest Territory's ordinance against slavery into the area near St. Louis, but pressure from the area's whites forced Congress to cede the matter to local authorities, who then enforced slavery. Jefferson tried again in an annual message to Congress: Taking note of the 1808 sunset date of the prohibition on new slavery laws, he urged immediate passage of a measure to "withdraw the citizens of the United States from all further participation in those violations of human rights . . . which the morality, the reputation, and the best of our country have long been eager to proscribe." Congress agreed to stop importation as of January 1, 1808, but did not even attempt to deal with slavery as an institution or with slaves as a form of property. Aware of that deadline, in 1807 Great Britain passed An Act for the Abolition of the Slave Trade, but did not formally end slavery within its empire.

In 1804 there were several notable deaths of titans of American wealth whose money and influence had been important to the country during the Revolution and early years of the Republic. Jeremiah Wadsworth died at sixty-one after a decadelong illness; during that final decade he had helped create the Hartford Bank and the Hartford and New Haven Turnpike, both of which were virtual monopolies and coined money, and he had taken ownership positions in a Massachusetts turnpike venture and in canals, aqueducts, and other quasi-public facilities. At the time of Wadsworth's death, the mess surrounding the Nathanael Greene estate had not yet been fully resolved. William Bingham also died that year, at fifty-two. At his death the *Pilgrim* matter was unresolved, as were problems with his Maine holdings. His executor quickly settled these. Bingham's estate was $3.5 million—triple the size of Derby's in 1799. For the next 160 years, the trust that Bingham established paid out steadily, and in 1964 distributed its remaining $838,000 to 315 heirs.

Robert Morris did not die in 1804 but by then had withdrawn from the scene. Upon leaving prison his debts were decreed to be $2,948,711. His creditors divided his assets. Morris believed that the North American Land Company's holdings were still worth many millions, but most were sold for seven cents per acre. The BUS, his major creditor, took possession of many assets, among them the thirty thousand acres in mid-Pennsylvania and adjacent New York that he had complained about to Washington in 1796. The bank did nothing with that tract, lacking an understanding that the coal already discovered beneath its surface might soon become very valuable as fuel for steam engines. Morris and his wife lived modestly, and his health declined until his death, at seventy-two, in 1806.

The most notorious death of a financier in 1804 was that of Alexander Hamilton, fatally shot in a duel with Vice President Burr. In

Hamilton's last known letter, to Sedgwick, he expressed his "growing distaste for Politics," and counseled Sedgwick and other New England Federalists against forming a separate confederacy and breaking away from the union over the Louisiana Purchase: "Dismemberment of our Empire will be a clear sacrifice of great positive advantages, without any counterballancing good; administering no relief to our real Disease; which is DEMOCRACY, the poison of which by a subdivision will only be the more concentered in each part, and consequently the more virulent." Hamilton's removal from the scene helped quell the fervor for a separate confederation being pushed by Pickering, Cabot, Wolcott, and a few others, but the notion persisted.

Burr was not at first censured for his role in Hamilton's death—duels were fairly common, although illegal—and was permitted to resume his duties as vice president. However, the Republicans could not countenance him on the ticket in 1804 and replaced him with George Clinton. In that election Jefferson was attacked for his policies and his private life—his long-term liaison with his slave Sally Hemings, first revealed during the 1802 elections, was one focus. Despite the attacks Jefferson won reelection by an overwhelming majority, sweeping fifteen of seventeen states, and the Republicans increased their dominance in the House to 114 versus 28 Federalists, and in the Senate by 27 to 7.

On March 4, 1805, Jefferson in his second inaugural address touted the nation's economic progress during his first term. His most important achievement, he declared, was "the suppression of unnecessary offices, of useless establishments and expenses, [which] enabled us to discontinue our internal taxes," commenting:

> The remaining revenue on the consumption of foreign articles, is paid cheerfully by those who can afford to add foreign luxuries to domestic comforts. . . . being collected on our seaboards and frontiers only, and incorporated with the transactions of

our mercantile citizens, it may be the pleasure and pride of an American to ask, what farmer, what mechanic, what laborer, ever sees a tax-gatherer of the United States? These contributions enable us to support the current expenses of the government, to fulfil contracts with foreign nations, to extinguish the native right of soil within our limits, to extend those limits, and to apply such a surplus to our public debts, as places at a short day their final redemption.

If peace continued, he planned to apply the excess government income to infrastructure projects, and if war should break out, to the military.

Shortly after this speech Adams sent a letter to Rush, an early Revolutionary who to Adams's dismay had become a Republican. He posed "a few questions to your conscience, since I know you have one." "Is the present State of the Nation [r]epublican enough? Is virtue the principle of our Government? Is honor? Or is ambition and avarice adulation, baseness, covetousness, the thirst of riches, indifference concerning the means of rising and enriching, the contempt of principle, the Spirit of party and of faction, the motive and the principle that governs?"

The ways in which the Jefferson administration might have answered these questions to reassert American core principles were soon compromised by the onrush of war. Open hostilities resumed between Great Britain and France. Shortly, British ships intercepted American commercial vessels in the Atlantic on the suspicion that they might be carrying goods to France, and prevented others from trading with the French Caribbean; and the French reciprocally boarded American vessels to determine if they were trading with Great Britain. And Spain, with French assistance, saw fit to contest the American assertion that the Louisiana Purchase had included West Florida. The dispute over Florida grew so rancorous that Jefferson contemplated war with Spain. In September, Gallatin responded to his request for an estimate of its costs with a long memo, composed while his son was dying. While delay would give Spain time to reinforce their military in West Florida, such a war would cost $11 million and entail new taxes. If peace could be extended through 1809, $3.5 million a year could be accumulated for building up the navy or for diplomatic efforts. Jefferson's war resolve softened.

Then came reports of the Battle of Trafalgar in October 1805. Just off the southwest coast of Spain, Admiral Nelson resoundingly defeated a combined French and Spanish fleet. Although Nelson did not survive the encounter, his victory established Great Britain's complete naval supremacy. It became clear that the Spanish could not defend the Floridas from the sea. Jefferson's message to the new Congress, in December 1805, was belligerent: He reported that he had given "orders to our troops on [the Spanish Florida] frontier to be in readiness to protect our citizens, and repel by arms any similar aggression." Three days later he sent a confidential message asking Congress for a two-million-dollar appropriation, with the use unspecified but implying that it would go to buy West Florida through the intercession of France. This latest Jefferson attempt to have Congress appear as the originator of legislation ran afoul of Randolph, chair of the Ways and Means Committee. Since negotiations had failed, Randolph asked, why should the United States pay ransom? He would champion two million dollars for war preparations, but only if Jefferson would directly request it. Jefferson refused. Randolph pronounced himself no longer a Republican or a Federalist but a third "something," a "tertium Quid." Thereafter more legislators referred to themselves as Quids.

Randolph bungled the impeachment of Supreme Court Justice Samuel Chase and interfered with the resolution of the Yazoo land fraud. Chase had traduced the usual politically neutral behavior of the bench by attacking all things Republican even when he was instructing juries, as he had done since presiding over Alien and Sedition Act trials. Randolph took a lead role in the Senate's prosecution—and did a terrible job: Chase was acquitted. In the Yazoo lands controversy, Randolph argued that Georgia had the right to take whatever actions it pleased, even to negate a prior act of its legislature, and the federal government had no right to intervene. He rejected compromises that would have ceded most of the land to the government while arranging for investors to settle in the remainder.

In December 1805, at Austerlitz, the French defeated the Russian and Austrian armies, causing the dissolution of what remained of the Holy Roman Empire; shortly afterward Great Britain formed a Fourth Coalition against France with Prussia, Russia, Saxony, and Sweden. American commercial shipping was increasingly targeted by both sides.

Benjamin Lincoln, the Federalist port collector of Boston, again offered his resignation, presuming that Jefferson would want a Republican to supervise the outposts that would provide early warning of foreign attacks. Jefferson asked him to stay on: In early 1807 having a Federalist in that position served to deflect growing sentiment that the Northeast should break away from the Union.

A few yards from Boston's bay, Andrew Dexter, Jr., that enterprising young man from Providence, was erecting the tallest commercial building in America. Having earlier decided that what the port city needed was an imposing exchange building to enable it to regain the lead in commercial transactions (which it had ceded to New York, Philadelphia, and Baltimore), he planned a seven-story building known as the coffee house, and to finance it began buying up outlying banks rushed into existence in the prior decade that were now teetering. He acquired ones in Pittsfield, Massachusetts; Glocester, Rhode Island; Bucksport, Maine; and Detroit, Michigan, so he could have them issue notes that he could use to pay his construction bills. When Congress refused a charter for Dexter's planned takeover of the Detroit bank, he sent his father and brother to Detroit to reorganize it as a private company; and to have that new entity look more solid, he had them drag along tons of iron bars and an iron vault door. Few accepters of the new bank's notes noticed that these did not pledge redemption by the bank, only by its officers and stockholders, and they were wholly ignorant that Dexter held 9,999 of its 10,000 shares. But then whispers began: In Boston's *Columbus Centinel* an anonymous writer asked: "Who aids and countenances the emission of . . . Bank Notes which are no better for the public than blank paper?" and answered, "A certain office in Boston [the public entity erecting the coffee house], which by reason of the *'miserable falling off* of its deposits, is reduced to the practice of *every expedient* to increase them. At this office the bills are palmed upon the ignorant and unwary." The anonymous writer may have been Nathan Appleton, who when visiting his in-laws in the Berkshires had gleaned evidence that Dexter's Pittsfield Bank was badly overextended.

On August 17, 1807, off Manhattan, Robert Fulton began the run of the *North River Steamboat of Clermont*, up the waterway later known as the Hudson River toward Albany, in a partnership with Robert Livingston, who had obtained from New York State the right to operate a steamboat on that route. The two had been working together since meeting in France; as both knew, the potential for profit went beyond the encouragement of steamboats: success would give a boost to agricultural and industrial production near the Hudson, and to the plans already on drawing boards for canals to connect the Hudson to the Great Lakes and the Midwest. On August 18 Fulton's boat reached Albany, having spent thirty-two hours en route over the 150 miles, including an overnight stay at Clermont, Livingston's home.

Fulton had delayed his boat's maiden voyage for a month to devote his energies to perfecting explosive torpedoes, the need for which had soared because relations with Great Britain had radically deteriorated, perhaps past the point of no return, due to the British assault on the USS *Chesapeake* on June 22, 1807.

The attack had come about as a result of a series of events dating back to early 1806, when Jefferson had sent Monroe and Thomas Pinckney to London to negotiate a pact to replace the lapsed Jay Treaty. The United States specifically sought to stop British impressment and to have Great Britain observe American neutrality. At the end of 1806, the negotiators had signed a draft treaty. On March 3 a copy reached the British envoy in Washington, who showed it to Madison, who read it and was aghast. One provision had the United States agreeing that Great Britain could take action against France and ships heading for France in retaliation for a recently enacted French decree that forbade European nations' importing British goods. This was an overt denial of America's right as a neutral to trade with France. The draft also contained absolutely no restrictions on British impressment. Jefferson refused to submit the Monroe-Pinckney treaty to the Senate for ratification.

And then came the incident involving the *Chesapeake*. For years British vessels seeking supplies had routinely been putting into American ports, thereby providing opportunities for desertion. In early 1807 letters circulating among the British vessels near North America specifically reported four deserters aboard the *Chesapeake*. On June 22, off the coast of Norfolk, HMS *Leopard* ordered the *Chesapeake* to halt and be searched. The *Chesapeake* refused, and the British fired enough cannon rounds to kill three sailors and wound eighteen others, including the captain, who then lowered his colors. The *Leopard* removed the four—two African Americans, an American-born white man, and one British-born man who had previously served in British ships.

U.S. reaction was immediate, including Fulton's postponement of his steamboat test to try to improve his torpedoes. On Bastille Day, Jefferson wrote to the economist Pierre-Samuel du Pont de Nemours:

> Never since the battle of Lexington have I seen this country in such a state of exasperation . . . and even that did not produce such unanimity. The federalists themselves coalesce with us as to the object [of our negotiations with Great Britain], tho' they will return to their trade of censuring every measure taken to obtain it. "Reparation for the past and security for the future" is our motto.

Jefferson added information on his current greatest distraction: "Burr's conspiracy. . . . One of the most flagitious of which history will ever furnish an example."

Burr was on trial for conspiring with the British and Spaniards to seize territory in the Southwest and in Mexico to create an independent country: "There is not a man in the US who is not satisfied of the depth of his guilt, [but] such are the jealous provisions of our law in favor of the accused & against the accuser, that I question if he can be convicted." At the trial in Richmond, Chief Justice Marshall narrowly defined treason as the commission of an overt act. None had occurred, since Burr's collaborator James Wilkinson had informed Jefferson of the conspiracy before it came to fruition, and so the jury acquitted Burr. He soon left the country.

That the *Chesapeake* incident presaged war sooner or later was obvious to astute international merchants such as Girard, Gray, and Appleton, who took steps to protect their interests. Girard directed Barings to use his deposits to buy American bonds and corporate stock; he became a major stockholder of the BUS. Gray shipped home from overseas depots and put into storage his large stocks of Russian, Indian, and Chinese teas and spices. Should war break out, his warehoused goods would become even more valuable. Appleton did the same.

Jefferson was alarmed enough to ask Gallatin for a memo of what would be needed in case of war. On July 25 Gallatin submitted a very extensive list, since "we must expect an efficient [British] fleet on our coast late this autumn, with perhaps a few thousand land forces, for the purpose of winter operations in the South. Their great objects of attack will be one of four places according to seasons & circumstances. New York, Norfolk, Charleston (or perhaps Savannah) New Orleans." His listing of what would be needed in case of war ranged from saltpeter to heavy cannons, "muskets, pistols, swords," a new fort on the James River to protect "the immense deposits of produce at Petersburgh & Richmond," an immediate narrowing of the channel in New York Harbor to prevent invasion, and so on. For all-out war Gallatin envisioned thirteen thousand men on land and sea including those engaged in supply, at a cost of $18 million a year. He estimated that $8.5 million could come from current income, another $2.5 from new taxes, and the remaining $7 million through loans. Some preparations must be made immediately, and:

If we have peace, one or two millions of dollars thus expended will not be felt & our readiness thus displayed will have a favorable effect on all our foreign relations. If we have war, and we shall have waited without doing this, the President will be charged with neglect, & the more so, as the law had not only authorized the embodying of the militia, but made a large appropriation for the expence.

Jefferson, taken aback by the high potential costs of war, decided to pursue diplomacy until Congress met again. By early winter, when it returned, there had been no sign of a British invasion, and the cold had halted most seagoing activity. The longtime Speaker of the House was absent, and the new one took the opportunity to appoint new committee chairmen, notably replacing Jefferson's critic Randolph as head of the Ways and Means Committee. As one result of this leadership realignment, Congress did not challenge Jefferson's current strategy for dealing with the British. Both the executive and legislative branches chose to believe that the crisis with Great Britain could be defused by an updated version of nonimportation. It was expected to diminish the commercial incomes of Great Britain and France, and if that did not spur them to allow American commercial vessels to trade freely, the United States could then resort to an embargo. If an embargo was ineffective, the United States could invade Canada, Nova Scotia, and Jamaica and hold them until the British acceded to American demands.

Gallatin was certain that neither nonimportation nor an embargo would hurt Great Britain or France nearly as much as they would hurt American shippers. While the president's inner circle was debating, bad news arrived from London: The British had not only not apologized for the *Chesapeake* incident, they had doubled down on their right to impress sailors. Along with that came word that France was going to detain all American vessels to make certain that no American armaments were getting through to Great Britain. Jefferson, feeling that he had no choice, asked Congress to pass a total embargo on American shipping so that American vessels would not become prey for British or French raiders. The Senate agreed immediately, and the House did after a few days, by a margin of 2 to 1. On December 22, 1807, Jefferson signed the embargo: "As to the hope that it may . . . induce England to treat us better," Gallatin wrote Jefferson, that was "entirely groundless," and he warned, in a caution that ought also to have reverberated through the years: "Government prohibitions do always more mischief than had been calculated; and it is not without much hesitation that a statesman should hazard to regulate the concerns of individuals as if he could do it better than themselves."

16

Madison:
A War for Economic Freedom

The Embargo of 1807 was a policy reluctantly entered into, a stopgap to forestall more dramatic actions that could lead to war. It was hard on American shipping and on the enterprises that provided the ships' cargoes, the tobacco, rice, and cotton plantations of the South and the forestry, fishing, and grain fields of New England. In Boston, after only two weeks of the embargo, crowds of unemployed sailors, dockworkers, and warehousemen marched to the governor's mansion and demanded jobs or food. Governor James Sullivan told them he could provide neither.

The embargo's effect was dramatic: During 1807 exports had reached $108 million; exports for 1808 would be $22 million. A matching drop in incoming goods drastically reduced the government's income from tariffs. But the larger economy continued to perform well. Between 1807 and 1812, America's GDP would keep growing at a good rate, due to the steady growth of America's population (an added 250,000 people a year), and to further expansion of settlement into new areas, and to higher productivity from increased mechanization in factories.

But that rapid growth was threatened by British and French constraints on trade, and in the last year of the Jefferson presidency it became increasingly clear that economic independence might not be achievable without a second war of independence against Great Britain. In early 1808, in the hope that better American compliance with the embargo would exert more economic pressure on Great Britain, the Jefferson administration tightened the restrictions on American fishing vessels and intercoastals, requiring both to post bonds before sailing. That did not much alter American compliance, nor discourage Great Britain and France from impressments and ship seizings. Shortly the administration would report to Congress that in recent years the Royal Navy had impressed 4,028 American citizens and discharged 936, leaving 3,092 still in British service; a later accounting showed that of the ten thousand American sailors impressed since 1775, only a thousand had been born in the British Isles.

Federalists loudly blasted the embargo as an attempt at catering to France, undertaken by a president whom they continued to accuse of being a Jacobin. They attacked Republican merchants who supported the embargo, such as Stephen Girard, and Federalist merchants who did so contrary to the party line, such as William Gray, who provoked Federalist ire by his contention that making an embargo was within the constitutional rights of the president and Congress. A Salem newspaper accused Gray—employer of more seamen in Salem than anyone else—of profiting from others' suffering: "Having an immense property in France and countries subject to France he is in favor of that policy which will preserve peace with Napoleon, and having a good stock of Indian, Russian, and Italian goods on hand, he is daily growing richer by the Embargo." Gray answered that in the first six months of the embargo he lost 10 percent of his net worth. And shortly he began providing two barrels of flour a week and financial assistance to sailors and others thrown out of work. His detractors next accused him of giving out spoiled flour and counterfeit money. Reelected as a Federalist to the state assembly, he served dutifully but then moved his home to Boston. Once there, he changed his party affiliation to Republican and let his name to be put forth for lieutenant governor on a ticket headed by another apostate from Federalism, Elbridge Gerry.

John Jacob Astor did not like the embargo and communicated his distaste for it to Gallatin, but he also saw in it an opportunity to persuade the government to help his fur trade and thwart the British from extending their fur trade all the way to Oregon. He would do so by establishing a series of fur-trading posts throughout the Louisiana Purchase, from the Mississippi River westward toward the Pacific Ocean. To get the government's backing for this, he first explained his notion to his fellow real estate buyer, New York's mayor DeWitt Clinton, in hopes that DeWitt would communicate it to his uncle George, the vice president, and that George Clinton would pass it on, with approval, to Jefferson. When the Clintons showed enthusiasm, Astor wrote to Jefferson: "I take the Liberty of addressing Direct to you—for without the entire approbation of goverment I am sure the buissness Could not succeed neither would I wish to engage in it." Jefferson considered it "highly desirable to have that [fur] trade in the hands of our own citizens [and] oust foreign traders who so much abuse their privilege by endeavoring to excite the Indians to war on us," and pledged "every reasonable patronage & facility in the power of the Executive." Hastening to Washington, Astor met with Jefferson, Gallatin, Madison, and Secretary of War Henry Dearborn, whose responsibilities included Native Americans. With their pledges of military support in hand, Astor gathered his resources and began establishing a chain of outposts from the Mississippi River westward, while sending ships around South America to the Columbia River to secure the Pacific end of the outpost chain. However, the enterprise proceeded more slowly than he imagined.

In mid-1808 Astor also used his growing understanding of how to push the levers of government to enable one of his ships to break the embargo. He persuaded a New York congressman to ask the president to allow a Chinese national, Punqua Wingehong, to sail for home on an outgoing ship: "He is desirous of returning to Canton, where the affairs of his family and particularly the funeral obsequies of his grandfather, require his solemn attention." Jefferson obliged, and—despite letters of protest in the New York papers and on Wall Street—Punqua boarded Astor's *Beaver* for a voyage to China, the only ship permitted to sail for that destination during the embargo. The voyage netted Astor two hundred thousand dollars.

The largest amount of money made by anyone in America in 1808 was one million dollars, by one of the newest Americans, David Parish. Son of a Scottish businessman, Parish had been born in Germany, and by the turn of the century had moved to Amsterdam and become a resourceful trader, known for taking risks to amass a fortune. In 1806, acting on a tip from Talleyrand, he took a huge one, crossing to Philadelphia as agent for a syndicate awarded the task of transferring a large quantity of gold bullion, then in Mexico and belonging to Spain, into Napoleon's hands. Parish's connection with the Barings Bank won for the syndicate a pledge that the Royal Navy would not interfere with a neutral American vessel carrying the gold. The gold-transfer adventure took two years, but in mid-1808 Parish received his million-dollar part of the commission. Having already decided to remain in the United States, Parish used a third of his windfall to buy two hundred thousand acres in New York from Gouverneur Morris and others looking to get rid of them, and began developing a territory between the Thousand Lakes and Lake Ontario.

A perhaps inevitable casualty of the 1807–1808 embargo was the house of cards created by Andrew Dexter from country banks' notes to fund the seven-story Exchange Coffee House in Boston. In the spring of 1808 the building was nearing completion and had tenants waiting to move in, although not as many as Dexter had hoped. Financial problems began to surface, and would emerge fully as the building opened and began to do business. Nathan Appleton, whose adherence to the respectable merchants' code of financial conduct based on mutual trust was steadfast, had become irate about the violations of that trust by many rural banks' lending practices. He soon focused on Dexter's Farmers' Exchange of Gloucester, whose notes he believed to be fraudulent; that bank's actions, he would later write, were "evil [and] of a magnitude too serious to be unregarded." He expanded his concern to all of Dexter's banks, and during 1808 got in touch with sixty-three firms that had used notes from Dexter's banks, and asked each for one hundred dollars so he could send "runners" to these banks and try to obtain specie for their notes. The merchants also signed a joint letter warning those banks that if demands for immediate payment were not met, the signers would cease accepting the notes as tender. A pseudonymous letter in the *Columbus Centinel* laid all this out. Shortly a reporter showed up on the doorstep of the Gloucester Farmers' Exchange and tried to cash some notes. He was refused. A larger investigation soon revealed that behind its $760,000 in notes were just $86 in gold and silver. Then the merchants and banks in Boston and in other large cities refused to honor Dexter's country bank certificates, and his entire fraudulent enterprise collapsed.

Because of the growing likelihood of war, Gallatin recommended reducing the percentage of government income applied to paying down the debt, and raising that for military preparedness. They had already reduced that debt from $83 to $45 million, and since it had also shrunk as a percentage of the GDP, the debt was no longer adversely affecting economic enterprise. The government's income as a percentage of the GDP was just 1.59 percent, a historic low. Though the Jeffersonians are often cast as liberals, they had successfully accomplished a goal of conservatives in all eras: slimming the government. However, the need to use the government's income for non-debt-reduction purposes now took over, spurring a realization by Jefferson, Gallatin, and Madison that without resurrecting some old taxes and levying new ones, they could not obtain enough to raise military preparedness high enough for the American forces to reach the strength necessary to counter the British.

In later years, the lack of government income to equip and arm troops would be cited as a failing of the Jeffersonians. But the country's problems with preparedness went beyond the availability of funds. A principal difficulty was that the United States no longer had a pool of seasoned, capable generals. Its high command featured such men as James Wilkinson, a wholehearted participant in the Burr conspiracy until the last moment, and whose move of two thousand soldiers to a malaria-infested camp near New Orleans killed or permanently disabled most of them. The army had fewer than four thousand men, and the navy only five frigates and three sloops. Plans for proper outfitting had also lagged; for instance, Eli Whitney had not yet filled his 1798 contract to deliver ten thousand rifles.

The drastic shortfall in current government income undercut a new Gallatin report to Congress on *Public Roads and Canals* that was as visionary and predictive as Hamilton's *Report on Manufactures*, and suffered a similar fate. Like Hamilton's report, Gallatin's recommended actions that because of circumstances could not be implemented when they were first made. Gallatin sought to establish new federal-state partnerships and public-private ones to build American infrastructure. Canals would link America's internal waterways, with turnpikes alongside of the rivers and man-made waterways crisscrossing the country. The price tag would be twenty million dollars. If the United States could allocate two million per year—a not-unreasonable sum, given the size of previous budgets—it could be paid for in a decade. But the embargo-hampered budget made even that initial funding impossible.

Election season arrived. Despite growing public outcry over the economic effects of the embargo, and of challenges for the Republican nomination from Vice President Clinton and Ambassador James Monroe, and from the Quids refusing to cast votes, Madison was nominated by the Republican caucus. After Madison's nomination Jefferson began to let go of the reins of government, ostensibly to avoid hampering the freedom to act of the presumptive next president. The election lacked the fireworks of the previous two; the Federalists, without a Hamilton to lead them, settled for C. C. Pinckney as their presidential candidate, and Rufus King for vice president. Madison received fewer electoral votes than Jefferson had, and Clinton won some New York electors and Monroe some in the South, but the end result was a Madison landslide, and Clinton continuing as vice president. While Republicans lost twenty-three seats in the House, they still maintained a sizable majority and did not lose any net seats in the Senate.

During the next hundred days, prior to the end of Jefferson's term, he was even less active, resisting Gallatin's entreaties for direction on how to replace the failed embargo. Finally, after the lame-duck Congress had defeated a resolution to license American privateers, it passed a replacement, a Non-Intercourse Act that would lift the embargo for all American ships not bound for British or French ports. Jefferson gave in and signed it into law on March 1, 1809, three days before the end of his term.

Madison was the third very wealthy Virginia planter to become president. He was well prepared for the position, having chaired committees in the Continental Congress dealing with international commerce, worked closely with Washington in the postwar period, been a state legislator, the main constructor of the Constitution and of the Bill of Rights, a floor leader in the House of Representatives, and secretary of state during eight years of international challenges. In his 1809 inaugural address, Madison reiterated the predilections he had embraced over the years, pledging himself and the American populace

> to cherish peace and friendly intercourse with all nations having correspondent dispositions . . . to hold the Union of the States as the basis for their peace and happiness; to support the Constitution, which is the cement of the Union, as well as in its limitations as in its authorities . . . to observe oeconomy in public expenditures; to liberate the public resources by an honorable discharge of the public debts; to keep within the requisite limits a standing military force, always remembering that an Armed and trained militia is the bulwark of the Republic. . . .

He cautioned that the "unrivalled growth of our faculties and resources" had come while the United States was at peace and Europe was at war, but that recently Europeans, "in their rage against each other, or impelled by . . . principles of retaliation" had caused the dramatic downward change. It was an acknowledgment that the country over which Madison would preside, and the international world it inhabited, were much more complex and the economy more complicated than when Washington had been president. Madison's challenges came at him from many quarters, and near simultaneously. Among others, he had to deal with a Congress that was not inclined to yield to his leadership. For instance, he decided to retain Gallatin as secretary of the treasury because too many senators were against having Gallatin become secretary of state. Since Madison intended to function as his own secretary of state, he acceded to political pressure to elevate Robert Smith, then secretary of the navy, even though Smith had resisted the embargo and been a thorn in Jefferson's side. To replace Smith he chose Paul Hamilton, a veteran and former governor of South Carolina, but not a seafarer. For secretary of war, Madison picked Revolutionary War physician and former Boston congressman William Eustis. These cabinet officials became almost as adverse to him as the Hamiltonians had been to Adams.

Their first undermining of Madison came in their vigorous resistance to the Non-Intercourse Act; however, the populace was with Madison on that, which gave him and Gallatin time to tackle other issues. For Gallatin the most serious of these was the charter of the Bank of the United States, due to expire in 1811. If, as seemed increasingly likely, the country went to war, the United States would need a stable financial system and a central bank to handle the challenges. So in March 1809 he submitted a report to the Senate on the Bank of the United States that included a strong recommendation for recharter.

Although today scholars know a fair amount about the operations of the BUS, at that time the public knew very little of them. Hamilton and Wolcott had supervised the bank's operations but had told Congress almost nothing of them. Even Gallatin, who had been much more open about other Treasury operations, had not bothered Congress with many details of the BUS. In March 1809, worried that reflexive Quid and Republican animosity to the bank might allow its charter to expire just when the country would need it most, Gallatin made additional detailed reports on the BUS, and recommended a renewal of the BUS charter, contingent on major changes to make the

BUS more like a central bank, more responsive to the government, and less dependent on foreign stock owners. In Gallatin's recharter plan, the federal and state governments, not private investors, would select the bank directors. The BUS would be required to lend the federal government three-fifths of its capital, expanded from ten to thirty million dollars, and to cap the interest rate on those loans. Stock in the bank would be issued to the states to reduce the percentage of foreign BUS ownership, then 18,000 of 25,000 shares. To help the states purchase this stock, the bank would provide low-cost loans, plus an annual dividend of 8.5 percent. These changes would make the bank vastly more democratic in operation and ownership. Also of importance was that in 1809, in contrast to 1791, when the BUS had first opened and only four state banks were in operation, there were now eighty, with more chartered each month.

In Congress the battle lines were immediately drawn, with those in the Republican majority who favored recharter on one side, but on the other, several different factions that united on this single issue: Republicans whose districts included at least one local bank and who were pressured by those banks to vote against recharter; older Republicans whose antipathy to the bank had continued through the decade; Quids who had fought it all along; and the remaining Federalists, who were only a quarter of the Senate and a third of the House but who continued to oppose anything proposed by the party of Jefferson. The strength of the opposition resulted in Gallatin's recommendation being consigned to a committee.

Gallatin had developed a friendship with the British envoy, and that worthy agreed to recommend to London some easing of the Orders in Council on shipping and impressment. Madison signed a preliminary document on June 19, and news of it traveled quickly through American port cities, spurring the departure of six hundred commercial ships. However, while these vessels were still at sea, London rejected the agreement, recalled the helpful envoy, and sent a new one who was so anti-American that shortly he and the secretary of state were communicating only through letters. The Madison administration requested this envoy's recall, but it was clear that the British were not inclined to ease tensions with the United States, or to cease their decimation of American shipping.

The third branch of government, the judiciary, was beginning to assert its latent power. In 1810 the case of *Fletcher v. Peck*, regarding the Yazoo lands, finally reached the Supreme Court. In 1800 the Bostonian speculator John Peck had bought some land sold by Georgia to one of the land companies; parts of that tract had first been owned by Prime and by Greenleaf. In 1803 Peck resold some to fellow speculator Robert Fletcher to provide the basis for a legal case; soon afterward Fletcher sued Peck for breach of contract, claiming that Peck did not have the right to sell because Georgia had rescinded the earlier sale to the land companies. The Supreme Court had to decide whether a Georgia legislature could invalidate a law made by a previous one. The Marshall Court was unanimous in ruling in Peck's favor—that the second Georgia legislature had no right to rescind the law of the first, since the Constitution's contracts clause upheld the validity of a contract once made. The decision ratified the Supreme Court's power to overturn state laws, and cleared the way for the development of the Yazoo lands. It also resulted in the speculators reaping over more than four million dollars on an investment of five hundred thousand.

Madison had to report to Congress in 1810 that during the previous year various entities in Napoleon's empire had seized and were holding 127 American ships. In reaction to this and to continued British seizures, the administration adopted a new measure that would allow British and French merchandise to be brought into the United States if carried in American ships. Napoleon then promised to withdraw his Milan and Berlin decrees that were preventing the United States from trading with Europe—provided Great Britain withdrew its

Orders in Council. Napoleon knew that the British would prevent him from having to keep his promise.

These contretemps were signals to Stephen Girard, who knew more about European history than his American contemporaries. By early 1810 he came to believe that there was little chance for the United States to avoid becoming embroiled in a war, and decided to hurry the repatriation of his assets. He ordered money and goods shipped from stashes in Hamburg, Riga, and Copenhagen, first to London, and from there to the United States. Some, including German linens and British manufactures, he had loaded on his ship the *Good Friends*, and instructed the captain to wait with it off Amelia Island, Florida, until repeal of the Non-Intercourse Act, so it could be legitimately landed. Of his repatriated $1,235,000, in addition to the goods there were $20,000 in silver, U.S. government loan notes, and BUS stock.

In the spring of 1810 the congressional committee considering the BUS recharter released its report. To the surprise of some representatives, they recommended it. But the opposers managed to block a recharter bill until after the 1810 elections. In that election the Republicans increased their majority in the House by fourteen seats. However, some 45 percent of the new Congress consisted of men elected to it for the first time, the majority of them under the age of forty—young enough to have been toddlers during the Revolutionary War. Though many of these new representatives were not as tied to old partisan beliefs as their elders, and were amenable to arguments in favor of rechartering, the recharter bill now had important new opponents, among them Henry Clay, then a senator from Kentucky, as well as Vice President Clinton and former president John Adams. Madison, long a detractor of the bank, was notably silent during the recharter debate, as was Jefferson, but Republican newspapers continued to argue against recharter. Adams expressed the feelings of many who objected in a letter to Benjamin Rush, which Rush then quoted verbatim to Jefferson in an attempt to demonstrate to the two former presidents that they still agreed on many things and ought to resume their friendship. Adams wrote:

The banking infatuation pervades all America. . . . There is no honest bank, but a bank of deposit. A bank that issues paper at interest, is a pick pocket, or a robber. . . . An Aristocracy is growing out of [the banks] that will be as fatal as the feudal Barons, if unchecked. . . . Think of the number, the Offices, Stations, wealth, piety and reputations of the persons . . . who have made fortunes by the banks, & then you will see how deeply rooted the evil is. The numbers of debtors who hope to pay their debts with this paper, united with the Creditors who build palaces in our cities, and Castles for Country Seats, by issuing this paper, form too impregnable a phalanx to be attacked by Any thing less disciplined than Roman Legions.

Despite the obvious importance of having some sort of national bank for the government to rely on in case of war—a war that many could see approaching—popular feeling was turning against it. As recharter moved toward votes in the House and Senate, Astor sent his son-in-law to meet with Gallatin. The treasury secretary memorialized the meeting in a note to Madison: Astor and his friends would put up two million dollars for the government's use if the bank was not rechartered. In this instance, the son-in-law emphasized to Gallatin, "profit was not [Astor's] object, and that he would go great lengths, partly from pride & partly from wish to see the Bank down." Astor wanted the bank "down" because he, along with other prominent New York–based financiers (and Girard), had had unpleasant clashes with its board, which after the death of Thomas Willing had become even more conservative.

In the House, on January 24, 1811, the bank recharter was defeated 65–64. In the Senate, debate lasted into February and resulted in a 17–17 tie, broken by Clinton, who defied his party and president by voting to let the charter expire. Serious economic consequences began immediately. Over the next year seven million dollars of investment in the bank was returned to investors, two-thirds of it exiting the United States; also, the state banks, filling the void created by the absence of the BUS, raised the amount of loan paper in circulation from twenty-eight to forty-five million dollars—a quite inflationary infusion.

The bank's stock fell, and Girard took advantage of the depressed share price to buy many more shares, become the largest single shareholder, and take a seat on the board. When Pennsylvania refused a new charter for the BUS, Girard was in position to purchase most of the BUS's assets, and at bargain prices, among them the thirty-thousand-acre tract in mid-Pennsylvania that the bank had taken over when Morris had been declared bankrupt, and on which coal had been discovered. Girard also bought the bank's imposing Philadelphia headquarters and in it opened his private Girard Bank, depositing in it $1.2 million of his own, making it one of the largest banks in the country. A historian of the Girard Bank writes that opening his own facility "allowed Girard to capitalize the value of his BUS shares at par, continue to collect dividends on the same, and profit from the discount and interest resulting from the earning assets of his bank." While Pennsylvania state law could prohibit any unincorporated association of individuals from opening a bank without a license, it could not prevent a single individual from doing so. Girard hired the former BUS cashier and rented out its offices to the BUS trustees so they could complete the dissolution of the bank's property—much of which Girard continued to purchase at fire-sale prices. The established Philadelphia banks tried hard to kill Girard's enterprise.

In March 1811 Secretary of State Smith entered Madison's office and began speaking of Adams's firing of Pickering, referencing a just-published excerpt from Adams's memoir. Madison understood this as a signal that Smith had realized he was about to be fired, and told Smith why: that his department "laboured under a want of the harmony & unity, which were equally essential to its energy and its success," and that he had made "representations calculated to diminish confidence in the administration committed to me." To replace Smith, Madison appointed James Monroe. This was unexpected, as the two had been estranged since Jefferson's refusal to submit the Monroe-Pinckney treaty to the Senate. Monroe had reconciled with Jefferson but not with Madison, a friend of many years. But when Madison asked Monroe to take over at State, the younger man was so eager for the post that he resigned as Virginia's governor; thereafter Monroe and Madison resumed their closeness. Having been emissary to France and to Great Britain, Monroe was well suited to attempt to prevent war with those countries. In 1811 he was somewhat successful in pushing France toward lessening its seizures of American shipping and opening its European and Caribbean ports, but he got nowhere with Great Britain.

The American public drumbeat for war against Great Britain grew louder, especially after an incident in which the USS *President* in a firefight nearly destroyed HMS *Little Belt*. Republicans said the incident demonstrated British aggression, while Federalists seized on the unresolved question of whether the *President* had fired first, to argue that the Republicans were provoking a war. Moderates then hoped that an American apology for firing on the *Little Belt* would be matched by a British apology for having attacked the *Chesapeake* in 1807, but nothing of the sort could be arranged.

American martial spirits were further stoked by reports of the Battle of Tippecanoe, on November 7, 1811. A thousand army troops, mostly militia, led by Indiana Territory governor William Henry Harrison, had traveled to the area at the confluence of the Tippecanoe and Wabash Rivers to have a serious conversation with Native Americans led by Tecumseh and his brother, known as the Prophet, to get the Native Americans to stop trying to evict American settlers from the area. The Native Americans were from a half-dozen tribes, and had weapons and income from the British. When Tecumseh was temporarily absent, several hundred tribesmen attacked the American forces. Harrison's men repulsed the attackers and then burned their encampment. Harrison played up the victory as breaking the Tecumseh confederacy, but Tecumseh had merely moved into Canada, where he convened an even-larger band of Chippewa from the Niagara area, Menominee from Wisconsin, Sioux, Winnebago, and others. Seizing on the Battle of Tippecanoe, the West's young representatives in Congress, notably Henry Clay and Felix Grundy of Kentucky, became "war hawks."

Madison, detailing the recent depredations of France and Great Britain in his next address to Congress, asked Congress to act: "With this evidence of hostile inflexibility in trampling on rights which no Independent Nation can relinquish, Congress will feel the duty of putting the United States into an armour, and an attitude demanded by the crisis, and corresponding with the national spirit and expectations." He recommended expanding the army and navy, and preparedness.

Congress did not respond with alacrity. And as they were dallying, in mid-December a series of earthquakes began in New Madrid, Missouri, of a magnitude that would later be estimated at more than 7.5 on the Richter scale, leaving fissures in the earth several miles long, throwing up deadly sulfurous fumes, and toppling thousands of chimneys and setting many buildings aflame. The quakes were felt as far away as Augusta, Annapolis, and Detroit. The series lasted intermittently into February 1812, caused the Mississippi River to run backward for a while and the evacuation of dozens of towns, and impeded for years the development of towns and businesses along the river.

During the first months of 1812, Great Britain continued to seize American vessels, many of them deliberately within sight of the American coast, even though it made little sense for Great Britain to have its Royal Navy do this, on two counts. First, British merchants' livelihood depended on robust American trade, which was already depressed because of the operation of the Non-Intercourse Act and would be further impacted by added seizures of vessels, and second, because the action gave to Napoleon's France an opening to offer to America a lessening of France's strictures on American commerce and a way to continue to make money from international trade.

In the District of Columbia, the Republican-majority Congress increasingly called for war, led by Clay, who had left the Senate, ran for and won a seat in the House, and was then elected its Speaker, and by Secretary of State Monroe. But Federalists were just as loudly calling for an accommodation with Great Britain. Most of the antiwar Federalists were from New England, but the sentiment extended to people in other areas that were heavily reliant on transoceanic commerce. New York City and environs, Delaware, and Maryland. Pennsylvania, having large western areas with no connection to export, remained firmly Republican, as did southern and western states, even though the South's economy was suffering because it could not export its cotton, tobacco, and rice. Gallatin, in an attempt to ensure that if war came it could be conducted so that the nation "may be burdened with the smallest quantity of debt, perpetual taxation, military establishment, and other corrupting or anti-Republican habits or institutions," had floated a first sizable loan in June 1811. Eight months later, it was all used up, and in February 1812 Congress authorized him to take out another eleven million dollars.

On May 11, 1812, an event occurred that might have changed the course of the war: An assassin killed British prime minister Spencer Perceval. His replacement, Robert Jenkinson, Lord Liverpool, soon took the opportunity of the change in government to alter policy toward the United States. On June 6, the new British government decreed a relaxation of the Royal Navy's blockade of American shipping and a withdrawal of the Orders in Council.

By then, however, Madison had already sent to Congress a message detailing Great Britain's bad conduct and refusal to negotiate; he did not formally request a declaration of war, but did assert that Great Britain was in "a state of war against the United States," and explained what that meant: "It has become, indeed, sufficiently certain that the commerce of the United States is to be sacrificed, not as interfering with the belligerent rights of Great Britain . . . but as interfering with the monopoly which she covets for her own commerce." The peoples' representatives agreed. The House approved a declaration of war by a 2–1 margin, and the Senate ratified it. On June 18, 1812, Madison signed the legislation and war was declared. He would only later learn that by then Liverpool had dispatched a vessel to America bearing news of the withdrawal of the hated Orders in Council. Had this been known in Washington, war would have been avoided.

Gallatin calculated that funding the war would require $20.8 million in the war's first year—almost twice the amount of previous year's entire federal budget. Should the war continue into 1813, the second-year budget would be $32 million. Accordingly he and Madison asked Congress to reinstitute all the old internal taxes.

The pendulum that had been aiming toward the aiding-the-poor end of its arc now slowed markedly, and began to descend toward a stasis or equilibrium point.

Congress did not respond well to the administration's demand for reinstating taxes, putting off their imposition for at least a year and instead doubling the tariffs, which could not produce enough money to pay the bills. Congress in fact adjourned without passing any measures to fund the war it had declared. Gallatin was partly to blame, having divulged the information that the current year's income was high due to a lucky windfall of five million dollars, from the return to American ports of those six hundred commercial ships that had been dispatched during an interlude when peace seemed at hand. Similar income would not be available in the future, Gallatin knew, and tried to float a ten-million-dollar loan.

This was a crisis point. Would the banks rise to this challenge and sell the loan bonds to their customers? Would the wealthy do their part in what was already being billed as the second war of independence?

The answers were not heartening, in part because there were not yet enough Republican-backed banks, their chartering having been prevented by legislatures in states controlled by the Federalists, or by such antiadministration stalwarts as George Clinton. A larger part of the impasse had to do with the existing Federalist banks being able to find ways not to cooperate with Gallatin. This was especially so in the Boston area, from which Gallatin had hoped to raise $724,000. William Gray, recently the Republican lieutenant governor of Massachusetts and the president of the State Bank of Massachusetts, took three hundred thousand dollars' worth, while letting it be known, as his biographer would write, that "he did not believe individuals should be wealthy and not help the government in time of need." Governor Elbridge Gerry could not do the same, since his fortune had become seriously depleted by having pledged his own property as collateral for his brother, who had since gone bankrupt. The Boston-Salem area was home to many wealthy men, but most were Federalists, and they let the rest of the area's loan quota go unsubscribed.

Philadelphia's quota was larger, and Gallatin was pushing Girard to take one million dollars of the loan, but Girard did not like the terms and as he pointed out, the United States was then suing him for $910,456 for his *Good Friends* exploit. Girard offered to underwrite five hundred thousand dollars, but only if the loan proceeds were then lodged in his just-created bank. Gallatin felt he could not do that, and Girard did not participate. Astor left his promise of 1811 mostly unfulfilled, although he continued to furnish Gallatin with the most detailed estimates of British forces in Canada, obtained through his trading network.

Further evidence of divisiveness in America, in regard to the war, came in Baltimore, just days after war was declared: The publisher of the *Federal Republican*, Alexander Hanson, decried the war against "Mother England . . . the last hope of civilization, law and order," and a mob accusing him of Toryism then destroyed his printing press. Weeks later, when Hanson attempted to resume publishing, armed Federalists defending his office fired into an attacking mob, killing two. Hanson and some defenders were taken to jail, where the mob broke them out to assault them; in the chaos "Light-Horse" Harry Lee and another Revolutionary War general were wounded so grievously that they never recovered.

Actual fighting between the United States and Great Britain began in July. U.S. strategic objectives were to capture parts of Canada to either be incorporated into the United States or held as bargaining chips; and at sea, to attack British shipping and isolated Royal Navy vessels in the Atlantic and Caribbean, thereby ramping up economic pressure to settle the war. Despite the clear superiority of the Royal Navy, it was so engaged fighting France in so many other corners of the world that it could deploy only a small fraction of its resources to the American theater of operations, and had to divide those among coastal details and protecting the St. Lawrence River and the Great Lakes. On land, American militias outnumbered the British and their Native American allies in Canada, but were not very professional or organized. The ranking American commander in the upper Midwest, Brig. Gen. William Hull, the territory's governor, undertook a poorly conceived three-pronged American invasion of Canada, with units from the four American forts on the border—Fort Michilimackinac, between Lakes Michigan and Huron; Fort Dearborn, in what later became Chicago; Fort Detroit, and Fort Niagara. The invasion faltered for multiple reasons including the refusal of several New England states to send militia to Hull. There were reciprocal British attempts on the inadequately garrisoned American forts. Detroit and Michilimackinac were lost to attackers, and Hull then decided to abandon Dearborn.

At sea that summer, American naval forces were more successful. Privateers took hundreds of British commercials, and in naval actions from the Azores, to the Canary Islands, the mouth of the St. Lawrence, and Lake Ontario, the U.S. Navy scored notable victories. The most latterly famous was between the USS *Constitution* and HMS *Guerriere*, four hundred miles southwest of Halifax, Nova Scotia. In a bloody encounter of boarding parties and entangled ships, British cannonballs appeared to bounce off the American ship's sides, earning it the nickname "Old Ironsides," and the *Constitution*'s cannons disabled the *Guerriere*. which eventually had to be blown up and sunk. The *Constitution* made it into Boston with two hundred prisoners, to general acclaim even in deep Federalist territory. Gray paid for some of its repairs and refitting.

By the late fall of 1812, there was enough enthusiasm and optimism for American prospects in the war to make Madison feel he might earn a second term. He just barely squeaked by, with 50.4 percent of the popular vote and less than 60 percent of the electoral vote. Gerry became vice president; his fortune had been so diminished that he was unsure if it would cover the expenses of the position that the government did not provide.

In the spring of 1813, the shipping magnate and rum producer Francis Cabot Lowell, impressed by the seventeen textile mills in Rhode Island, and having memorized the plans for a British power loom on his last prewar voyage to England, began to gather investors to fund a competitive textile factory in Waltham, west of Boston on the Charles River. It would take in raw cotton and put it through the several weaving and other manufacturing processes necessary to produce various kinds of cloth. Previously those operations required several different mills, one for each step of the process. Lowell could count on investment from his family, but to amass enough for this capital-intensive project he solicited Appleton and Thorndike. Within a few years they would move the enlarged operations to the new model city of Lowell, Massachusetts.

That spring Gallatin was looking forward to going to Russia. Madison had offered him the opportunity of traveling to that country, which was seeking to mediate an end to the war. Gallatin had eagerly accepted, but felt he could not take up that post until he had placed the new sixteen-million-dollar loan that had been authorized. By March 13, 1813, he had managed to obtain pledges only for $3,956,400, and warned Madison: "We have hardly enough money to last till the end of the month." From the whole of New England, just $500,000 had been pledged, a large chunk of that from Gray; and in Philadelphia, while Girard had pledged $100,000 and his bank's customers an additional $22,000, the other city institutions had only agreed to take $150,000. As the Albany Argus newspaper put it, the Federalist plan was to "starve the government into peace, to withhold all aid and assistance which would facilitate a vigorous prosecution on our part."

This was remarkable. Even though their country was at war, the Federalist bankers' antipathy to the Democratic-Republican administration was so intense that they were choosing to withhold their funds from the prosecution of the war. Clearly, money was needed if the United States was to win the war of economic independence— this was not the Revolutionary War, when troops willingly served without pay; nearly forty years later, troops demanded regular pay, and supplies had to be purchased with currency that maintained its value. Should the United States not find the money to continue the war, the country might have to prematurely sue for peace. That was what the New England Federalists wanted, but their reasoning was unsound, for if peace came, there was no assurance that their trade with Great Britain would profitably resume.

Gallatin had to resort to placing newspaper ads inviting investors to suggest deals with the government, so long as those deals were above one hundred thousand dollars. David Parish had previously declined to participate, but now he confided to his friend Alexander Dallas, district attorney for Pennsylvania, and very close to Gallatin, that if "a serious intention exists in the part of the executive to bring this War to close as soon as it can be done with honour," he might be able to put together a syndicate to take the remainder of the loan. Receiving encouragement, he got in touch with Astor, Girard, and the leaders of a few banks in New York and Philadelphia. There was resistance from the old Bank of North America and from the Bank of New York. Girard told Parish that he would come in, but only if his previous condition of having the proceeds of the loan deposited in his bank was met, for "should it be otherwise, the Chartered Banks of Philadelphia will continue to refuse my Bank Notes, which would, of course, compell me to pay in Specie the installments of the [federal] loan as they came due . . . and compel me to reduce my banking oper- ations to a small scale." Girard was also wary because just then he was pleading with Monroe and Madison to be permitted to pay $180,000 to the British to ransom his *Montesquieu*. Madison soon agreed to Girard's request, and Girard paid the British and got his ship back.

On April 2 Parish learned that some potential bond-purchasers who had previously said yes to him were now saying no, so he ap- proached Astor about taking a larger position in the loan. He also threatened the Bank of New York: It must participate or he would take his and his friends' accounts elsewhere. The Bank of New York agreed to be a secondary purchaser. Negotiations among Girard, Parish, and Astor continued, as did theirs with Dallas and with Gallatin, who hastened to Philadelphia to close the deal.

On April 6, at Dallas's Philadelphia home, he, Gallatin, Girard, and Parish, the last having in hand Astor's pledge, had a momentous meeting and made a compact. Theirs was an extraordinary and a thoroughly American collaboration, and it is worthy of note that all five of the participants were immigrants. Each had chosen to emigrate to the United States as an adult; and since becoming successful had stayed because of their love for the country, its ideals, and the conditions that it continued to provide for amassing wealth. Astor's and Girard's fortunes were now large enough to put them on a level with all but the wealthiest men in Europe. The current war had already hurt them, and they stood to lose much more should America not prevail. Parish's iron foundries and other facilities near Lake Superior had been damaged by British raids; Astor's fur business had been greatly impacted, and with Manhattan an obvious target of invasion his extensive real estate holdings were at risk; while Girard's ships were being seized, compromising his main sources of income.

Parish, Girard, and Astor jointly pledged to take more than ten million of the sixteen-million-dollar loan, but not at the 6 percent that Gallatin had offered. Rather, they agreed to pay in eighty-eight dollars a share and in return receive an annuity that would yield them thirteen years of annual payments that would eventually total the full one hundred dollars per share. The pledged amounts were more than the trio's current combined private fortunes, and as such involved considerable risk for them. Nonetheless, they put up ten million dollars, received the certificates, kept more than a million dollars' worth of the certificates apiece, and resold the rest. The big purchasers were insurers in Philadelphia, and banks and brokers in New York, and merchants in Baltimore, who all resold the certificates in smaller batches to hundreds, perhaps thousands, of individuals. A list of the occupations of some of the individuals to whom Girard's bank sold the bonds included:

boarding school operator, clerk, conveyancer, attorney, widow, sea captain, gentleman, clergyman, bookbinder, financier, commodore, sailmaker, Navy Agent, bricklayer, stove merchant, physician, stock broker, goldsmith and jeweler, brewer, grocer, oil and colourman, shoemaker, storekeeper, iron merchant, distiller and refiner, Collector of the Port, merchant taylor, auctioneer, mahogany merchant, and flour merchant.

The historian of the Girard bank Don R. Adams, Jr., calls what Girard, Parish, and Astor did "the commencement of investment banking in America." It was also a ratification of the nonwealthy's willingness and ability to actively fund the country's activities.

Girard, Astor, and Parish had wished to keep their involvement a secret. However, a Federalist clerk in the Treasury Department stole a document about it from Gallatin's desk, and it was soon publicized. Girard, Astor, and Parish came under fire. Nonetheless the deal held. The money enabled the United States to keep armies in the field and ships afloat during a very difficult 1813, and the loan–purchase structure of middlemen and small-batch buyers set the pattern for absorption of further loans. Astor, Parish, and Girard continued to pitch in individually, and became public advocates for a new Bank of the United States, to buy big loans at wholesale and sell them at retail.

By late fall of 1813, the first British intimations of peace were received. It would take until August 1814 before settlement talks began, and in the interim, and for six months after talks began, the war continued. During this period the British burned portions of Washington, D.C., after which the war in America became a stalemate.

Finally, on December 24, 1814, that stalemate, combined with the peace in Europe achieved at the Congress of Vienna, produced the accord signed at Ghent, ending the War of 1812. It was followed by the Battle of New Orleans, which defeated a British attempt to take the city that was so important to American commerce. Although the treaty merely reestablished the territorial status quo ante, for Americans it was a victory for economic independence. After Napoleon was defeated at Waterloo in June 1815, the Royal Navy no longer had a need to impress American sailors, which assisted American shipping, as did the official withdrawal of the Orders in Council. A further lowering of British commercial barriers took place based on the British realization that trade with America was more and more essential. The end of the War of 1812 also brought to a close British support of Native American resistance, which led to more settlement of the lands west of the original thirteen states.

Political independence had been achieved in 1783. But it was only in 1813, fifty years after active resistance to Great Britain began, that the United States of America achieved economic independence. The syndication of the government bond issue and the establishing of the Lowell manufacturing combine completed a remarkable reversal of the elements that in colonial days enforced economic infantilization. Where once a half-dozen investors could not legally form a venture, now corporations bloomed like wildflowers. Where once banks were forbidden, now each state had many, and the banks offered credit to tens of thousands of people. Where once a journeyman had almost no possibility of ever owning property and climbing out of near-poverty, now more than half the electorate owned property, and the gap in wealth between the 1 percent and the remainder of the populace had narrowed and was continuing to do so. Where once the Continental Congress could not find buyers for a bond proposal, now thousands of Americans bought bonds even in the midst of a war. Where once the country was unduly dependent on imported manufactures, now more than half of what was needed was made within it, and interstate commerce outweighed exports and imports. Capitalism and democracy would ever vie for dominance in the United States of America, but the country was now ready to take advantage of the industrial revolution and was firmly on the path to becoming the world's economic colossus.

Acknowledgments

This book, my third about the Revolutionary Era, is the beneficiary of research conducted for the two earlier books in libraries and depots from Boston to Charleston and from New York to California. My particular thanks, on this one, to the New York Public Library for its unmatched research collections and for providing access to difficult-to-obtain early American documents, and to librarian Melanie Locay for the use of the Frederick Lewis Allen Room. My researches at the Phillips Library of the Peabody Essex Museum, the Connecticut Historical Society, the American Antiquarian Society, and the American Philosophical Society, among other depots, were also assisted by knowledgeable staff members. Salisbury's Scoville Library helped me by borrowing books from other depots in the state of Connecticut.

I want to also salute the searchable online archive of 182,000 letters and other documents of the founding fathers at https://founders .archives.gov, the necessary starting point and standard reference for the founders' thoughts and deeds; and the many years of issues of the *William and Mary Quarterly*, whose articles frequently and insightfully investigate economic matters.

Friends and family read portions of this work and made helpful comments. They include Tom Key, Hank Lowenstein, Bruce McEver, Anne McNulty, Peter Petre, Michael Ratner, Rich Reifsnyder, Shelby White, my sons Noah Shachtman and Daniel Shachtman, and my wife Harriet Shelare. My editor, Charles Spicer, and my longtime agent, Mel Berger, were always of assistance. To all of them, my continuing gratitude. What errors remain in the book are mine alone.

Tom Shachtman
Salisbury, CT, May 2019

Notes

The Notes mainly cite direct quotes from participants; their spelling, punctuation, and grammar have deliberately not been modernized. References cited only once are credited in the Notes, while those that appear more often are abbreviated in the Notes and provided in full in the Bibliography. Letters and papers of Washington, Adams, Jefferson, Franklin, Hamilton, and other founders are from https://founders.archives.gov, unless otherwise indicated. WMQ = *William and Mary Quarterly*; PMHB = *Pennsylvania Magazine of History and Biography*; JER = *Journal of the Early Republic*.

1. Offensive Acts

3 *"I like rich wine."* Hancock letter, Nov. 12, 1767, in Unger, *Hancock*, 68.

3 *"Though Mr. Hancock may not."* Ibid., 119.

4 *"Heard a noise."* Kirk, in Editorial Note, Hancock case, *Legal Papers of John Adams*, vol. 2, 179–180. Online at: https://rotunda.upress.virginia.edu/founders/default.xqy?keys=ADMS-print-05-02-02-0006-0004 -0001.

4 *"Shutting their eyes."* Stephen Hopkins, "An Essay on the Trade of the Northern Colonies," in Jensen, *Tracts*, 3–16. See also Hopkins, *The Rights of Colonies Examined* (Providence: William Goddard, 1765).

4 *"To over-awe and terrify."* *Massachusetts Gazette*, June 20, 1768, in B. Carp, *Rebels Rising*, 49.

5 *American port protests.* Nash, *The Urban Crucible*; Carp, *Rebels Rising*; Jesse Lemisch, "Jack Tar in the Streets: Merchant Seamen in the Politics of Revolutionary America," *WMQ* 25, no. 3 (July 1968, 371–407).

5 *To force the colonies to pay.* Staughton Lynd and David Waldstreicher, "Free Trade, Sovereignty, and Slavery: Toward an Economic Interpretation of American Independence," *WMQ* 68, no. 4 (October 2011): 605.

6   *British MP had even cited.* Ferguson, *Power of the Purse*, 20.
7   *Gave the colonists leverage.* Andrew Shankman, "Toward a Social History of Federalism: The State and Capitalism To and From the American Revolution," *JER* 37 (Winter 2017): 625–626.
7   *"I have come to a Serious."* Hancock to Barnard & Harrison, Oct. 14, 1765, JH letter book, 1762–1783.
9   *"I go to church and come home."* Laurens, in Wallace, *The Life of Henry Laurens*, 2.
10   *"In grandeur, splendor of buildings."* Quincy, Jr., in Sellers, *Charleston Business*, 17.
10   *"Cocksure about the rightness."* Sellers, viii.
10   *"A glorious opportunity."* Laurens, October 11, 1765, in Wallace, 116.
10   *"I am in your power."* Laurens, in ibid., 119.
11   *"Their value to the mother country."* Baron de Kalb, in Shachtman, *How the French*, 17.
11   *"On liberal principles."* Letter to Hancock, in Tyler, 99.
11   *"Forbidden to make a hat."* Jefferson, "Summary View."
12   *"Kingdom . . . has always bound."* Pitt in Dickinson, *Letters from a Farmer in Pennsylvania*, no. 2, 1768, in Jensen, *Tracts*, 138.
12   *"Splendour and glory."* A. Smith, *Wealth of Nations*, vol. 4, section vii, c. 81.
12   *One-third of Great Britain's total foreign trade.* Crowley, *Privileges of Independence*, 13.
12   *Surpassed Britons in per capita income.* Lindert and Williamson, *Unequal Gains*, 8, 39.
12   *7 percent of the populace.* Allan Kulikoff, "The Progress of Inequality in Revolutionary Boston," *WMQ* 28, no. 3 (July 1971): 375–412; Fatovic, 21; Kulikoff, "The American Revolution and the First Great National Depression," in Andrew Shankman, *The World of the Revolutionary American Republic: Land, Labor, and the Conflict for a Continent* (New York: Routledge Worlds, 2014).
13   *Was 16 percent more.* Lindert and Williamson, *Unequal*, 79.
13   *"Was based to a great extent."* Jean Jensen, in Jeanne Boydston, "The Woman Who Wasn't There: Women's Market Labor and the Transition to Capitalism in the United States," in Paul A. Gilje, ed., *Wages of Independence: Capitalism in the Early American Republic* (Lanham, MD: Rowan & Littlefield, 2006).
13   *Bartered products included.* Shachtman, *The Fourteenth Colony*, 9.
14   *"Effectually a tax."* Daniel Dulany, *Considerations on the Propriety of Imposing Taxes on the British Colonies* (New-York: John Holt, 1765).
14   *"Many of the little villages."* Otis, *The Rights of the British Colonies.*
15   *"Land, livestock, inventories."* Perkins, 54.
15   *"Principal Merchants, Factors."* Newell, *From Dependency to Independence*, 217.
15   *"You have given."* Burke, in Crowley, 31.
15   *"The greatest difficulty."* Steuart, *An Inquiry*, vol. 2, 120.

16 *"I should be glad to see."* Otis, *The Rights of the British Colonies.*
17 *A thousand families depended.* J. Adams, in Fowler, *Baron of Beacon Hill,* 225–230.
18 *"Extream Corruption."* Franklin to Joseph Galloway, Feb. 25, 1775.
18 *A fancy coach emblazoned.* Richard Washington to G. Washington, Nov. 10, 1757.
19 *"Threatened to undermine."* Breen, *Tobacco Culture,* xii–xiii.
19 *"The charity of the vessel."* Sellers, 195–196; Wallace, 138–143.
19 *"No fraud had been committed."* "Extracts from the Proceedings of the Court of Vice-Admiralty in Charles-Town," anonymous [Henry Laurens], 1768, in Jensen, *Tracts,* 185–206.
20 *"Those who call truth."* Ibid.
20 *"Behaved more like a pirate."* *New London Gazette,* July 21, 1769, in Maier, *From Resistance,* 15.
20 *"Painfull Drudgery."* J. Adams, *Diary and Autobiography,* vol. 3, 306.

2. Resistance Becomes Rebellion

22 *"What is this but taxing us."* Dickinson, *Letters,* no. 2, 1768, in Jensen, *Tracts,* 138.
22 *"In Freedom we're born."* Dickinson, in Edwin Wolf, Jr., *John Dickinson,* 6.
22 *"Dreading the evils."* Mason to Washington, April 28, 1769.
23 "A certain Degree." *Independent Advertiser,* March 20, 1749, in Breen, *Marketplace,* 184–185.
23 *"Cabinetmakers, spinners, weavers."* B. C. Smith, *The Freedoms We Lost,* 103.
24 *"Facing ruin."* *New-York Gazette,* in Marc Egnal and Joseph A. Ernst, "An Economic Interpretation of the American Revolution," *WMQ* 29, no. 1 (Jan. 1972): 29.
25 *"Romans we are not."* Henry Drinker to Abel James, Dec. 9, 1769, in "Effects of the Non-Importation Agreement in Philadelphia, 1769–1770," *PMHB* 14, no. 1 (Apr. 1890): 41–45.
25 *Men from Glasgow arrived.* Carp, *Rebels Rising,* 50–51.
26 *"There are not five Men."* Mason, in Broadwater, 53.
27 *"Foundation of American independence."* J. Adams, *Diary and Autobiography,* vol. 8, 384.
28 *"State the rights of the colonists."* In Beeman, *Our Lives,* 21.
29 *"A large and populous town."* Jefferson, "Summary View."
29 *"The power, but not the justice."* J. Warren, "Suffolk Resolves." www.drjosephwarren.com/2012/09/the-suffolk-resolves-draft/.
30 *"On my right hand."* G. Morris to John Penn, May 20, 1774, in Nash, *The Unknown American Revolution,* 100.
30 *"Clearly state."* In Beeman, *Our Lives,* 38.
30 *Bespoke suit with gold knee buckles.* Irvin, *Clothed in Robes,* 25.
31 *Other wealthy Americans.* Andrew M. Schocket, "Thinking About Elites in the Early Republic," *JER* 25, no. 4 (Winter 2005): 555.

31 *"A view of these acts."* Jefferson, "Summary View."

32 *"To the sword."* In Unger, *Hancock,* 184.

32 *"A brilliantly original."* Breen, *Marketplace,* 325.

33 *Reduced British imports.* Jacob M. Price, "New Time Series for Scotland's and Britain's Trade with the Thirteen Colonies and States, 1740–1791," *WMQ* 32 (Apr. 1975): 307–325.

33 *"We are trying by a Thousand."* J. Adams to Edward Biddle, Dec. 12, 1774.

33 *"Opulence, grandeur, and refinement."* Irvin, *Clothed in Robes,* 44.

34 Massachusettensis and Novanglus. Essays in Jensen.

34 *"[Westchester] Farmer,"* in Chernow, *Alexander Hamilton,* 58.

34 *"Will infinitely exceed the demands."* Hamilton, "The Farmer Refuted &c.," Feb. 23, 1775.

35 *"The New England governments."* George III to Lord North, Nov. 18, 1774. Letter 263, *The Correspondence of King George the Third with Lord North from 1768 to 1783* (London: John Murray, 1867).

35 *"The death warrant."* Wadsworth Papers, box 1, folder 1, letters from Pall Mall (London), February 20 and 28, 1775.

35 *"This is a Prelude to a Tragedy."* Ibid., folder 2, copy of Alex Brimmer to Colin Drummond, April 19, 1775.

3. Pledging Lives and Fortunes

37 *Authorized a two-million-dollar one.* Grubb, "State Redemption."

38 *"Developed increasingly warm friendships."* Unger, *Hancock,* 211.

39 *"The burthen falls chiefly on the poor."* A. Wayne, in Risch, 8.

39 *His recruiting posters.* Christopher Geist, "A Common American Soldier," *Colonial Williamsburg Journal,* Autumn 2004. Online at www.history.org /Foundation/journal/Autumn04/soldier.cfm.

39 *"Young, landless, and unskilled."* Charles Neimeyer, *America Goes to War: A Social History of the Continental Army* (New York: New York University Press, 1997), 8–26. See also Charles Royster, *A Revolutionary People at War: The Continental Army and American Character, 1775–1783* (Chapel Hill: North Carolina University Press, 1979).

39 *"Yeomen successfully pressured."* Gregory H. Nobles and Alfred F. Young, *Whose American Revolution Was It?* (New York: New York University Press, 2011), 212.

40 *"Butter, butter, butter."* Trumbull to Wadsworth, June 29, 1775, Wadsworth Papers, box 1, folder 4.

41 *"I am tired of trying to Please."* Wadsworth to Trumbull, August 19, 1775, ibid.

41 *"Artificial scarcity."* Washington to the Massachusetts Council, Aug. 29, 1775.

41 *"After Lexington and Concord."* Hedges, *The Browns,* 218–219; East, *Business,* 71.

42 *"Trimming off the rough edges."* Dolly Hancock, in Unger, 220.

42 *"We are reduced to the alternative."* John Dickinson's Composition Draft,

June 26–July 6, 1775, in the Founders Archive, includes Jefferson's original and annotations.

42 *"The further effusion of blood."* Dickinson, "Olive Branch Petition." http://avalon.law.yale.edu/18th_century/contcong_07-08-75.asp.

43 *"A man on the rise."* Rappleye, *Morris,* 36.

43 *Simultaneously being petitioned.* Carp, *To Starve the Army,* 31.

44 *"Could exceed in value."* Doerflinger, 242.

44 *"Being at the seat of government."* Billias, *Elbridge Gerry,* 123–126.

44 *William Duer.* Robert F. Jones, "William Duer and the Business of Government in the Era of the American Revolution," *WMQ* 32, no. 3 (July 1975): 393–416.

45 *Not ten men in his colony.* In J. Adams, Adams *Diary and Autobiography,* ii, 448–449.

46 *"There are no men."* Quoted in Rappleye, *Morris,* 37.

46 *"There was substantial conflict."* Nuxoll, v.

46 *"Insider trading, buyer and seller cartels."* Pierre Gervais, "Early Modern Merchant Strategies," *Economic Sociology* 15, no. 3 (July 2014): 19–20.

46 *"I have much in my power."* Morris, in Nuxoll, *op. cit.*

48 *"The cause of America is."* Paine, *Common Sense,* 1776. Online at: www.ushistory.org/paine/commonsense/.

48 *"People out of doors."* Irvin, *Clothed,* 13–14.

48 *Monograph on American honor.* C. B. Smith, *American Honor,* 1–11.

48 *"The Author's reasoning."* Laurens, in McDonough, 174.

49 *"Hackneyed in every Conversation."* J. Adams to William Tudor, Apr. 12, 1776.

49 *"Remember the influence of wealth."* "A Watchman," *Pennsylvania Packet,* June 24, 1776, in Schlesinger, 591.

49 *"They get all the profit."* "A Tradesman," in Rappleye, *Morris,* 63.

49 *"As if the same were the ships."* Cited in Beeman, *Our Lives,* 330–331.

50 *"The Ports are open you see."* Adams to Tudor, Apr. 12, 1776.

51 *As representatives of their states.* Maier, *American Scripture,* 150–153.

4. Blood, Property, and Profit

55 *"A distinct set of families."* Jefferson in Meacham, 121. Virginia abolished entail in 1776, primogeniture in 1785; in 1777 Georgia became the first state to abolish both.

56 *"It is the Happiness."* Cannon, in Nash, 270.

56 *"In such a manner as will."* Dickinson, *Essay of a Frame of Government* (Philadelphia: James Humphreys, Jr., 1776).

57 *Eligible 50 to 70 percent.* J. T. Main. "Government by the People."

57 *Enfranchise the 87.5 percent.* Donald Radcliffe, "The Right to Vote and the Rise of Democracy, 1787–1828," *JER* 33 (Summer 2003): 223.

57 *Trimmed the overweighting.* Paul Leicester Ford, "The Adoption of the Pennsylvania Constitution of 1776," *Poli. Sci. Quarterly* 10, no. 3 (Sep. 1895): 426–459.

57 *"The mob made a second branch."* In Robert F. Williams, "The Influences of Pennsylvania's 1776 Constitution on American Constitutionalism During the Founding Decade," *PMHB* 112, no. 1 (January 1988): 35.

57 *"That an enormous Proportion."* Franklin's revisions of the "Pennsylvania Declaration of Rights" [between July 29, 1776 and August 15, 1776].

57 *"Of all the radical steps."* Nash, *Unknown Revolution*, 271.

58 *Previously exempt speculative.* Fatovic, 31.

58 *"We ardently wish."* Cited in Williams, 34.

60 *"An act to prevent monopoly."* East, 203.

60 *"Was they real friends."* *Journal and Correspondence of the Maryland Council of Safety* 16 (1777): 17; reprint (Baltimore: Maryland Historical Society, 1897).

60 *"Natural and original principles."* P. Webster, *Political Essays*, 1791, iv.

61 *"If further occasional supplys."* Morris to Washington, Jan. 1, 1777.

62 *70 percent.* Lorenzo Sabine, *Biographical Sketches of Loyalists of the American Revolution* (Boston, C. C. Little and J. Brown, 1864), 12–13.

63 *"By which I lost £3,000 Sterling."* Derby to Thomas Lane, April 1, 1776, in McKey.

63 *"Your friend and employer."* Letter to Captain Collins, in E. H. Derby Shipping Papers. Hasket & John Papers, March 23, 1780.

63 *"Of all Prizes and Plunder."* Derby Shipping Papers, box 9, folder 9, Hasket & John papers, 1779–1780.

64 *Salt fish, shingles, whale oil.* Ibid.

64 *"Even after splitting."* Rappleye, *Sons of Providence*. 203.

65 *"The farmer cannot hire."* William Whipple, in Kulikoff, "First Great National Depression," 145.

65 *"Sits at the fountain Head."* N. Brown to S. Hopkins, Dec. 18, 1775, in Hedges, 221.

66 *"We shall be ready to transact."* Morris to Bingham, June 3, 1776, in Alberts, 20.

66 *"My scruples about Privateering."* Morris to Bingham, Apr. 25, 1778, in Rappleye, 105.

68 *"There is such a thirst for gain."* Washington to J. A. Washington, Nov. 26, 1778.

68 *"Not to control day-to-day management."* Carp, *To Starve the Army*, 42.

69 *Oxen could be used.* Sumner, *Financier*, vol. 1, 136.

69 *Drop in personal income.* Lindert and Williamson, *Unequal Gains*.

69 *"Fix the price of goods."* In Simeon E. Baldwin, *The New Haven Convention of 1778: Three Historical Papers* (New Haven: Tuttle, Morehouse & Taylor, 1882), 58.

69 *"I think every Step should be."* S. Adams, in Smith, *Freedoms*, 159.

70 *"A great cry against the merchants,"* A. Adams to J. Adams, July 31, 1777, in B. C. Smith, "Food Rioters." Online at: https://libcom.org/history/food-rioters-american-revolution-barbara-clark-smith.

70 *"Sirs: It is a matter of great."* Ibid.

70 *"The conviction that a fundamental."* Ibid.

70 *"The great merchants were seldom."* East, 204.

71 *"In our desultory state."* Washington to Mifflin, July 28, 1777.

72 *"Dissipation, extravagance, and total neglect."* Willing to Morris, in Rappleye, 124.

72 *"Unless some great."* Washington to H. Laurens, December 23, 1777.

72 *"We had in Camp."* Washington, Circular to the States, Dec. 29, 1777.

72 *"Conceal the true state."* Ibid.

5. Valley Forge Dreams

73 *Refusals to pay going market.* Wadsworth Papers, January–March 1778, box 4, folders 1–3.

73 *"Money is the sinews."* Greene to Washington, January 1778.

74 *"Subscribe to morrow."* H. Laurens to J. Laurens, Mar. 15, 1778, *Letters*, vol. 12, 558–561.

74 *"Did enhance the efficiency."* Doerflinger, 198.

74 *"The want of this Money."* Wadsworth to Mifflin, Jan. 11, 1778, Wadsworth Papers, box 4, file 1.

74 *"Two or three thousand pounds."* J. Huntington to Wadsworth, Jan. 18, 1778, ibid.

75 *"Taxation in each Colony."* Laurens to Isaac Motte, January 26, 1778, in *Letters*, vol. 12, 343–350.

75 *A different facet of its wealth.* Gregory D. Massey, *John Laurens and the American Revolution* (Columbia: University of South Carolina Press, 2000).

75 *"Compare their condition."* Greene to Washington, January 1778.

76 *"Drones and Incumbrances."* H. Laurens to Washington, May 5, 1778.

76 *Real agenda was to assign blame.* Fleming, *Washington's Secret War*, 129–165.

77 *"Inevitable Force of Evidence."* Committee at Camp to Laurens, Feb. 6, 1778.

77 *"I am willing to do."* Trumbull to Washington, July 19, 1777.

77 *"The number of little, piddling."* Committee at Camp to Laurens, Feb. 28, 1778.

78 *Compete for scarce resources.* Willard O. Mishoff, "Business in Philadelphia during the British Occupation, 1777–1778." *PMHB* 61, no. 2 (Apr. 1937): 165–181.

78 *"Almost open Trade."* In East, 180.

78 *"I never was in any employment."* In Cooke, *Coxe*, 28–31.

78 *"You plead in excuse."* H. Laurens to Morris, Jan. 11, 1779, in Morris, *Letters*, vol. 15, 34–39.

79 *"Whenever we find ourselves."* Committee of Commerce to Robert Morris, Feb. 21, 1778, in Rappleye, 141.

79 *"To undertake what I could not."* Wadsworth to Dyer, Jan. 28, 1778, Wadsworth Papers, box 4, folder 2.

79 *"We have got Col. Wadsworth."* James Lovell to S. Adams, Apr. 19, 1778, in Carp, *To Starve the Army*, 50.

79 *"I am persuaded You will not."* Wadsworth to Mass. Magistrates, March 28, 1778, Wadsworth Papers, box 4, folder 3.

81 *"Large Concerns and important Business."* Holker, July 4, 1778, in Rappleye, 160.

81 *"Disaffected inhabitants."* J. Laurens to H. Laurens, July 18, 1778, in W. G. Simms, *The Army Correspondence of Col. John Laurens* (New York: Bradford Club, 1867).

82 *"If the French are not supplied."* Wadsworth to H. Laurens, Oct. 17, 1778.

83 *"A great Number of unprincipled men."* Colt to Wadsworth, Oct. 26, 1778, Wadsworth Papers, Box 4, Folder 3.

83 *"Expel the poor."* Paine, "A Serious Address to the People of Pennsylvania," *Pennsylvania Packet,* December 1, 5, 10, 12, 1778. Online at: www .thomaspaine.org/essays/american-revolution/a-serious-address-to-the -people-of-penn.html.

84 *Beaumarchais's agent. Financier,* vol. 1, 178–179.

85 *"The common interests of America."* Washington to B. Harrison, Dec. 18–30, 1778.

86 *"The legislative body should."* "The Essex Result, Document 12," in Oscar and Mary Handlin, eds., *The Popular Sources of Political Authority: Documents on the Massachusetts Constitution of 1780* (Cambridge: Harvard University Press, 1966).

86 *"Too little acquainted."* J. Adams to James Sullivan, May 26, 1776.

86 *"The balance of power in a society."* Ibid.

87 *"However just and upright."* Greene to Wadsworth, April 14, 1779, in East, 87; Platt, 80–81.

6. Interlude: Assault on Fort Wilson

89 *"Most heinously criminal."* In Alexander, 593.

90 *"And in the darkest seasons."* Republican Society tract, in Rappleye, *Morris,* 178–179.

90 *"Distinguished for their wealth."* Rush, in ibid.

90 *"The whole country."* Constitutional Society tract, in ibid.

90 *"In the midst of money."* May 23, 1779, broadside, in ibid., 180.

90 *"The social compact or state."* Anonymous, attributed to Paine, in Foner, *Tom Paine and Revolutionary America* (Cambridge: Oxford University Press, 2005).

91 *"We have arms in our hands."* *Pennsylvania Packet,* July 1, 1779, in Alexander, 598–599.

7. Bricks Without Straw: The Path to Yorktown

94 *"We can no more support."* Greene, in Carp, *To Starve the Army,* 72.

94 *"My Credit is nearly sunk."* Ibid.

94 *Three factors exacerbated.* Buel, *In Irons,* chaps. 1–4.

95   *"Kind of imperceptible Tax."* Franklin to S. Cooper, April 22, 1779.

95   *"Not only choose, but absolutely compel."* Washington to B. Harrison, Dec. 18–30, 1778.

95   *"Indefinite power of emitting."* Madison, "Money," *National Gazette,* Philadelphia, December 19 and 22, 1791.

96   *"I am aware how apt the imagination."* Hamilton to——, [December–March 1779–1780].

98   *"Revise their laws."* In Grubb, "State Redemption," 26.

99   *"Some measure for introducing."* In Foner, *Paine and Revolutionary America,* 179.

99   *"While I admit, Sir."* Vergennes to Adams, June 21, 1780, in Giunta, *Emerging Nation,* 77.

100   *"The sentiments of the people."* Bingham to Jay, July 1, 1780, in Alberts, 85.

100   *"Here was the army."* Martin, *Memoir.*

101   *"Signal misfortune."* Bingham to Jay, July 1, 1780, in Alberts, 85.

101   *"To be established for furnishing."* Smith, *Wilson,* 142–144.

101   *"While the war was carried on."* Paine to Reed, June 4, 1780. Reed's agreement is in his repeating some of Paine's phrases in a June 5, 1780, letter to Washington.

102   *"That the faith of the United States."* Lewis, *A History,* 14–21; Konkle, *Willing,* 79–83.

102   Soon replicated in Boston. Bodenhorn, *State Banking.*

102   *"The public good required."* Hamilton to Duane, Sep. 3, 1780.

104   *"Won the bulk of the French."* Cutterham, "Revolutionary Transformation," 9.

104   *"French wheels."* Duer, in Jones, *King,* 69.

105   *"Undertakers without fortune."* Chastellux, Jean-François, Marquis de, *Travels in North-America, vol. 1* (Dublin: Colles, Moncrieffe, White, 1787), 29.

105   *"The business of this country."* Rochambeau to Ségur, Sep. 4, 1781, in Lee Kennett, *The French Forces in America, 1780–1783* (Westport, CT: Greenwood Press, 1977), 70.

105   Three million rations. Madison to Jefferson, June 23, 1780.

106   *"Without credit, there is no borrowing."* Steuart, vol. 2, 123.

106   *"Melting down."* Wilson, Dec. 19, 1780, in Seed, *Wilson.*

106   *"Aristocratic engine."* Journal of William Maclay, 270.

106   *"We are reduced to dry bread."* Wayne to Reed, Dec. 16, 1780, in John A. Nagy, *Rebellion in the Ranks: Mutinies in the American Revolution* (Yardley, PA: Westholme Publishing, 2016).

107   *"Complicated distresses."* Washington to Hancock, January 5, 1781.

108   *"Borne one-fourth of the entire."* Reed to Washington, May 17, 1781.

108   *"I believe I may venture."* Washington to Rochambeau, Jan. 29, 1781.

108   *"Considering the diffused."* Washington to J. Laurens, Jan. 15, 1781. For Hamilton input, see similar phrasing and reasoning in Hamilton to James Duane, Sep. 3, 1780.

109 *"Mr. Lawrens is worrying."* Franklin to Jay, Apr. 12, 1781.

110 *"This appointment was unsought."* Diary, Feb. 21, 1781, in *Papers*, vol. 1, 8–9.

110 *"I have great expectations."* Washington to John Mathews, June 7, 1781.

112 *"If it is not excessive."* Hamilton to Morris, Apr. 30, 1781, in *Papers*, vol. 1, 31–60.

112 *"Interweaved."* Morris to Hamilton, May 26, 1781.

112 *"In one general money connexion."* Morris to Jay, July 13, 1781.

113 *"Other Gentlemen of your Character."* Morris to Jefferson, July 13, 1781.

114 *"This was the first."* Martin, *Memoir*, 222–223.

114 *"Dizzying pace."* Platt, *Jeremiah Wadsworth*, 25.

8. Triumph, and the Costs of War

119 *"What else could be expected of us?"* Morris to Franklin, Nov. 27, 1781.

120 *"That great friend to sovereign."* G. Morris to Greene, Dec. 24, 1781, in Ferguson, 154.

120 *"Discriminatory policy."* Ferguson, 134.

120 *"We pay as much for three."* In Cutterham, "Revolutionary Transformation," 14.

121 *"Public credit has again."* Livingston to Jay, 1782, in Sumner, *Financier*, vol. 2.

122 *Commence a new blockade.* Buel, *In Irons*, 217–222.

122 *"I would not be surprised."* John Cruden, in Lauren Duval, "Mastering Charleston: Property and Patriarchy in British-Occupied Charleston, 1780–1782," *WMQ* 75, no. 4 (Oct. 2018): 604.

123 *"Our impatience to pre occupy."* John, Lord Sheffield, *Observations on the Commerce of the United States* (London: J. Debrett, 1782).

124 *"When I see such a number."* Washington to B. Lincoln, Oct. 2, 1782.

124 *Presented a petition.* Richard D. Kohn, "The Inside History of the Newburgh Conspiracy," *WMQ* 27, no. 2 (Apr. 1970): 187–220; and C. Edward Skeen and Richard H. Kohn, "The Newburgh Conspiracy Reconsidered," *WMQ* 31, no. 2 (Apr. 1974): 273–298.

124 *"We have borne all that men."* Henry Knox petition, Dec. 1782, in James E. Wensyel, "The Newburgh Conspiracy," *American Heritage* 32, no. 3 (Apr.–May, 1781).

124 *"A convulsion of the most dreadful."* St. Clair to Knox, Jan. 1783, in ibid.

124 *"The necessity and discontents."* Hamilton to Washington, Apr. 8, 1783.

125 *"Mushroom gentry."* Lincoln to Knox, Mar. 22, 1783, in Mattern, 143.

125 *"Take the direction."* Hamilton to Washington, Feb. 13, 1783.

125 *"Something so shocking."* Washington to Officers of the Army, Mar. 15, 1783.

126 *"A general and tolerably equal."* N. Webster, 1787, in Fatovic, xiv.

126 *Sinking of the average American's income.* Lindert and Williamson, "American Incomes, 1774–1860" (National Bureau of Economic Research Working Paper 17211, 2013), 3. Online at: www.nber.org/papers/w17211.

127 *"He that forgets and forgives."* Gadsen to Marion, Nov. 17, 1782, in Rebecca Brannon, *From Revolution to Reunion: The Reintegration of South Carolina Loyalists* (Columbia: University of South Carolina Press, 2016), 6.

130 *"To be the informer."* M. L. C. Woolsey to Wadsworth, May 28, 1785, in Platt, 125.

131 *"It is painful to us."* Brown, July 12, 1786, in Hedges, 297.

132 *"More national."* Kulikoff, *Agrarian Origins*, 109.

133 *"Damn the old musty rules."* Mercy Otis Warren, *Sans Souci, Alias Free and Easy, or An Evening's Peep into a Polite Circle* (Boston: Warden & Russell, 1785).

133 *Was a "projector."* Edward G. Lengel, *First Entrepreneur: How George Washington Built His and the Nation's Prosperity* (Boston: Da Capo Press, 2016). See also Joel Achenbach, *The Grand Idea, George Washington's Potomac and the Race to the West* (New York: Simon & Schuster, 2004).

134 *"Proportion of the wealthy."* Main, "Government by the People," 400.

134 *"Worse governed."* In ibid., 406.

135 *"Doing their duty."* Notes of proceeding of Congress for Dec. 4, 1782.

137 *"Required abandoning."* Jeffrey S. Pasley, "Private Access and Public Power: Gentility and Lobbying in the Early Congress," in Bowling and Kennon.

138 *Neighbors complained.* Richard H. McKey, Jr., "Elias Hasket Derby and the Founding of Eastern Trade," part 1, *Essex Inst. Hist. Coll.* 98, no. 1(January 1962): 1–25.

9. Targets of Ire

140 *"A deep laid contrivance."* Aedanus Burke, *Considerations on the Society or Order of the Cincinnati* (Hartford: Bavil Webster, 1783).

140 *"Sucked all of the available specie."* *Pennsylvania Gazette*, April 6, 1785.

140 *"To husbandmen."* Witherspoon, in Kulikoff, *Agrarian Origins*, 109.

140 *"Drained the countryside."* Terry Bouton, "Moneyless in Pennsylvania: Privatization and the Depression of the 1780s," in Matson, *Economy*, 221.

141 *"The merchant of moderate capital."* *Pennsylvania Gazette*, April 6, 1785.

141 *"Opposition to the state's emission."* Bodenhorn, "Federal and State Commercial Banking Policy in the Federalist Era and Beyond," in Irwin and Sylla, *Founding Choices*, 154.

142 *"Control of commerce."* Wilson, in Smith, *James Wilson*, 154.

142 *"An engine of destruction."* Whitehill, in ibid.

142 *"The parson lives on the sins."* P. Webster, *An Essay on Credit*, Feb. 10, 1786.

143 *"As great an amount."* Wadsworth to Colt, Feb. 6, 1784, in Platt, 138.

144 *"This formerly rude soil."* Jean de Crèvecoeur, *Letters from an American Farmer* (London: T. Davies, 1782), 54.

144 *"An ill-considered fiscal policy."* Perkins, 173–186.

144 *"Considering the prostrate situation."* Rufus King to John Adams, Oct. 3, 1786.

145 *"That they had shed their blood."* George Richards Minot, *The History of the Insurrections, in Massachusetts, in the year MDCCLXXXVI, and the rebellion consequent thereon* (Worcester, MA: 1788), 17.

145 *"Had lodged a formal plea."* Frank E. Manuel and Fritzie P. Manuel, *James Bowdoin and the Patriot Philosophers* (Philadelphia: American Philosophical Society, 2004), 206.

146 *"This high-handed offence."* Bowdoin, Proclamation of September 2, 1786. http://college.cengage.com/history/ayers_primary_sources/commonwealth_massachusetts_bowdoin.htm.

146 *"Annihilate all debts."* Humphreys to Washington, Oct. 25, 1786.

146 *"Ostensible object is the revision."* Henry Lee to Madison, Oct. 19, 1786.

146 *"Commotions of this sort."* Washington to Humphreys, Oct. 22, 1786.

146 *"Combustibles in every state."* Washington to Knox, Dec. 26, 1786.

146–147 *"Incroachments on the rights."* Jefferson to Madison, Jan. 30, 1787.

147 *"The pressure of the public voice."* Washington to Lafayette, June 6, 1787.

10. Curing the Defects

148 *"The evils issuing from these sources."* Madison to Jefferson, Oct. 14, 1787.

149 *"Into the hands."* Madison to Monroe, April 30, 1787.

149 *"Acknowledged merits."* Madison to Pendleton, April 22, 1787.

149 *"Indispensable."* Washington to Madison, Mar. 31, 1787.

151 *Thirty had seen active service.* McGuire, *To Form a More Perfect Union.*

152 *"Those indomitable spirits."* Stephen Mix Mitchell, in Klarman, *Framers' Coup*, 70.

152 *"The national property of small states."* Charles de Secondat, Baron de Montesquieu, *De l'esprit des lois* (Paris: P. Didot & Fermin Didot, 1803).

153 *"A free people are the most addicted."* J. Adams, *A Defence of the Constitutions of Government of the United States*, 1789.

153 *"If the multiplicity."* Madison, "Vices of the Political System of the United States," April 1787.

154 *"Creditors or debtors—Rich or poor."* Ibid.

155 *"The people . . . should have as little."* Sherman, quoted in Madison, "Notes on the Constitutional Debates," May 31, 1787. Online at: http://avalon.law.yale.edu/18th_century/debates_531.asp. For generations Madison's notes have been attacked for incompleteness and favoritism; recent analysis of the original handwritten notes has shown them to be the most accurate accounts available. See Lynn Lizzell, "Madison's Notes: At Last, A New and Improved Look." March 8, 2018, www.libertylawsite.org.

155 *"The evils we experience flow."* Gerry, in Madison, "Notes."

155 *"No government could long subsist."* Wilson, in ibid.

155 *"Admitted that we had been."* Mason, in ibid.

156 *"Enriched some free Americans."* Holton, 275.

156 *"One interest must be opposed."* G. Morris, in Madison, "Notes."

157 *"All communities divide themselves."* Hamilton, in Yates, *Notes of the Secret Debates*, http://avalon.law.yale.edu/18th_century/yates.asp.

157 *"Distinguished for their rank."* Dickinson, in ibid.

158 *Constituted a "framers coup."* Klarman, *The Framers' Coup.*

159 *"Sees the Union dissolving."* Hamilton in Yates, *Notes of the Secret Debates.*

160 *"Employ our own people."* Coxe, in Cooke, 102–105.

160 *"The diversity of opinion turns."* Franklin, in Madison, "Notes," 226–227.

162 *"It therefore astonishes me."* Franklin and G. Morris, in ibid., 651–655.

164 *"I never saw him so keen."* Alexander Donald to Jefferson, Nov. 12, 1787.

165 *"Merchant interests and private securities."* McGuire, *op. cit.*

165 *"Mechanics and manufacturers."* Hamilton, "Federalist 35."

166 *"The prosperity of commerce."* Hamilton, "Federalist 12."

11. Washington: Creating the Establishment

171 *"Neither Dignity, nor Authority."* J. Adams to Washington, May 17, 1789.

171 *"Gentlemen, consulting their own."* Washington to David Stuart, June 15, 1790.

172 *"Tho elected as a republican enemy."* Madison to Jefferson, May 23, 1789.

172 *"Not easily get out."* J. Adams to A. Adams, Feb. 17, 1793.

172 *"It is in vain."* Muhlenberg, quoted in "The First Congress, on $6 a Day," *New York Times,* March 2, 1989, A27.

173 *"A far cleverer fellow."* Morris to Washington in conversation, April 1789, as recalled by Washington family members, in Rappleye, 454.

173 *"The consumption of which are least."* P. Webster, "Sixth Essay on Free Trade and Finance, 1783," in *Political Essays,* 231–232.

174 *"Personal connections to the industries."* Pasley, 68.

174 *"I fear that the impost."* *Journal of William Maclay,* 11–12.

175 *"Favorable symptom."* Madison to Jefferson, May 9, 1789.

175 *"Bound us in commercial manacles."* Madison, in 1 Annals of Cong., 185–186, 204–206.

176 *"His situation is peculiarly distressing."* Derby to Congress, June 10, 1790, in E. H. Derby, 67–69.

177 *"Capital in mobilizable form."* Elkins and McKitrick, 116.

179 *42 percent.* Ferguson, 273–274.

179 *"It would be hard to aggravate."* Hamilton, in Crowley, *The Privileges of Independence,* 154.

180 *"A Crisis of public distress."* P. Webster, in Wright, *One Nation Under Debt,* 136.

181 *"The question Whether."* Jefferson to Madison, Sep. 6, 1789.

181 *"Somber, haggard."* Jefferson's Account of the Bargain on the Residence and Assumption Bills, 1792. Online at: http://founders.archives.gov /documents/Jefferson/01-17-02-0018-0012.

182 *"To bind down the public."* *Journal of William Maclay,* 15.

183 *"That if Congress took any measures."* Michael J. Stone, in *Annals of Cong., House, 1st Cong., 2nd Sess.,* 1227.

183 *"Slavery was a necessity."* Matthew Mason, *Slavery and Politics in the Early Republic* (Chapel Hill: University of North Carolina Press, 2006), 25.

184 *"Consciously created patent."* B. Zorina Khan, *The Democratization of Invention: Patents and Copyrights in American Economic Development, 1790–1920* (Cambridge: Cambridge University Press, 2005), 8.

187 *"Every power vested in a Government."* Hamilton, "The Final Version of an Opinion on the Constitutionality of an Act to Establish a Bank," Feb. 23, 1791.

12. Progress, Panic, and Paternalism

189 *"If a golden mountain."* James Sullivan, in Cowen, 36.

190 *"A legislative attempt to balance."* Bodenhorn, "Federal and State Commercial Banking Policy," 158.

190 *"A monetary impulse."* John Taylor to Washington, Jan. 14, 1794.

191 *"The uniform and universal tendency."* Articles of 1791, in James P. Walsh, "'Mechanics and Citizens': The Connecticut Artisan Protest of 1792," *WMQ* 42, no. 1 (1985): 75.

192 *"An amazing effect."* Noah Webster to James Greenleaf, October 13, 1791, in Cowen, 11.

192 *"Generally found the most attentive."* Letter to Coxe, sent to Jefferson, in Joseph R. Blasi, Richard B. Freeman, and Douglas L. Kruse, *The Citizen's Share: Reducing Inequality in the 21st Century* (New Haven: Yale University Press, 2014), 4.

193 *"Although often urged."* E. H. Derby, "Elias Hasket Derby."

193 *"In the transaction."* Ibid.

193 *"I can assure you."* Wolcott to Samuel Breck, Nov. 25, 1805, in Cowen, 61.

194 *"Used his offices."* Jones, *"The King of the Alley,"* 133.

194 *"Lives in the style."* Cutler, in Pasley, 90.

194 *"I have written you twice."* Knox to Duer, Jan. 27, 1791.

195 *"Extravagant sallies of speculation."* Hamilton to William Seton, Jan. 18, 1792.

195 *"Shopkeepers, widows, orphans."* Cited in Jones, 176.

196 *"Every existing bank."* Hamilton to Seton, Feb. 10, 1792.

196 *"'Tis time, there must be."* Hamilton to Duer, Mar. 2, 1792.

196 *"Cured by a few bankruptcies."* Wolcott to A. Wolcott, Sr., Jan. 30, 1792, in Cowen, 102.

200 *"While we have land to labour."* Jefferson, *Notes*.

200 *"The spirit of enterprise must be less."* Hamilton, *Report on Manufactures*, final version, Dec. 5, 1791.

201 *"Deplorable truth."* In Elkins and McKitrick, 283.

201 Congress approved them all. Douglas A. Irwin, "The Aftermath of Hamilton's 'Report on Manufactures'" (NBER Working Paper 9943, August 2003). Online at: www.nber.org/papers/w9943.

202 *"Broaches a new constitutional."* Madison to Pendleton, Jan. 21, 1792.

202 *"Disquietude."* Jefferson to Washington, May 23, 1792.

203 *"Encompassed on all sides."* Washington to Jefferson, Aug. 23, 1792.

203 *Economic philosopher Karl Polanyi. The Great Transformation* (New York: Farrar and Rinehart, 1944).

13. New Resistance to Authority

204 *"Withholding unnecessary opportunities."* Madison, "Parties," *National Gazette*, Jan. 12, 1792.

204–205 *"Be a fool indeed,"* Washington, in Jefferson, Jefferson's Conversation with Washington, July 10, 1792.

205 *"Possible that Mr. Jefferson."* Hamilton as "An American," in *Gazette of the United States*, Aug. 4, 1792.

205 *"Ravings."* Elkins and McKitrick, 285–287.

205 *"This exactly marks the difference."* Jefferson to Washington, Sep. 9, 1792.

205 *"Both of you are pure."* Washington to Jefferson, Oct. 18, 1792.

206 *"Such persevering and violent opposition."* Hamilton to Washington, Sep. 1, 1792.

206 *"Whereas certain violent and unwarrantable."* Washington, Proclamation of Sep. 15, 1792.

206 *"The people are stupid."* Madison, *National Gazette*, Dec. 20, 1792.

208 *"The ruin of Mr. Adams."* Cabot to T. Parsons, Oct. 3, 1792, *Letters*, 57–58.

210 *"Organ of discourse."* Hamilton, "Pacificus No. 1," June 29, 1793.

212 *"If particular nations grasp."* Jefferson, *Final State of the Report on Commerce*, Dec. 16, 1793.

212 *"To obtain reparation."* Hamilton to Washington, Apr. 14, 1794.

213 *"Didn't merely redistribute."* William Hogeland, *The Whiskey Rebellion*, 69, 7.

215 *"By formal public meetings."* Hamilton to Washington, Aug. 2, 1794.

216 *"Absolutely necessary that the civil authority."* U.S. Commissioners to Edmund Randolph, Aug. 17, 1794.

218 *"A State of our finances."* Hamilton, *Report on a Plan for Further Support of Public Credit*, Jan. 16, 1795.

218 *"Gallatin is a real treasure."* Madison to Jefferson, Jan. 31, 1796.

219 *"To consume more, to spend more."* Gallatin, *A Sketch*.

219 *"Less respect to the consuming speculator."* In Wilentz, *Chants Democratic*, 71.

220 *"Has taken Advantage."* J. Adams to A. Adams, Jan. 23, 1796.

221 *"France is our avowed friend."* Handbill of July 23, 1795, in Wilson, *Girard*, 150.

221 *"An ignorant mob."* Wolcott, in Alberts, *Golden Voyage*, 259.

221 *"Many Persons signd."* Butler to Madison, Aug. 21, 1795.

222 *"In order for the United States to pay Algiers."* Hannah Farber, "Millions for Credit: Peace with Algiers and the Establishment of America's Commercial Reputation Overseas, 1795–1796," *JER* 34, no. 2 (Summer 2014): 188.

222 *"His constituents were desirous."* In Todd Estes, *The Jay Treaty Debate, Public Opinion, and the Evolution of Early American Political Culture* (Amherst: University of Massachusetts Press, 2006), 184.

224 *"If this goes through."* Hamilton to Wolcott, May 30, 1796.

224 *"The loss of another year."* Morris to Washington, Aug. 25, 1796.

224 *"I am so thoroughly impressed."* Washington to Morris, Sep. 14, 1796.

225 *"It is our true policy."* Washington, "Farewell Address," Sep. 19, 1796.

14. Adams: Necessary Transitions

229 *"I must study Politicks and War."* J. Adams to A. Adams, May 12, 1780.

230 *"The Hamiltonians by whom."* Jefferson to Gerry, May 17, 1797.

230 *"I see a Scene."* J. Adams to A. Adams, Mar. 17, 1797.

230 *"Quickly unraveled."* Richard S. Chew, "Certain Victims of an International Contagion: The Panic of 1797 and the Hard Times of the Late 1790s in Baltimore," *JER* 25, no. 4 (Winter 2005): 367.

230 *"Led entrepreneurs to overinvest."* Nicholas A. Curott and Tyler A. Watts, "What Caused the Recession of 1797?" *Studies in Applied Economics* 48 (February 2016): 2.

232 *"There has not one penny."* Lincoln to Adams, in Mattern, 211.

232 *"Fifty of the best pens."* Callender, in Wood, *Empire*, 237.

234 *"Scandalous and seditious writing."* Indictment of Matthew Lyon, in Aleine Austin, *Matthew Lyon, "New Man" of the Democratic Revolution, 1749–1822* (University Park: Pennsylvania State University Press, 1981), 110.

234 *"Unbounded thirst for ridiculous pomp."* M. Lyon, in ibid., 108–117.

234 *"Struck a blow for equality."* Fatovic, 160.

236 *"The Federalists dozed right through."* Chernow, *Hamilton*, 588.

236 *"Charter terms sometimes."* Perkins, 276–277.

237 *"At present there is no more prospect."* Adams to McHenry, Oct. 22, 1798.

237 *"Those that Labour."* William Manning, *The Key of Libberty.* (Cambridge: Harvard University Press, 1993.)

238 *"The insurrection in Northampton."* B. F. Bache, in Paul Douglas Newman, "Fries's Rebellion and American Political Culture, 1798–1800," *PMHB* 119, nos. 1 and 2 (January/April 1995): 44.

238 *"Whenever the government appears."* Hamilton to McHenry, Mar. 18, 1799.

239 *"Such high handed offenders."* Pickering to Adams, May 10, 1799.

239 *"Treason that lurked at the core."* Hamilton, as "Titus Manlius," in "Hamilton on the Louisiana Purchase: A Newly Identified Editorial from The New York Post," *WMQ* 12, no. 2 (Apr. 1955): 269.

240 *"The first true test."* Perkins, 328.

240 *"The greatest intriguant."* Adams to McHenry, as reported to Hamilton, May 31, 1800, *Hamilton Papers*, vol. 24, 557.

241 *"You are to beat me."* Adams conversation with Jefferson, in Meacham, *Art of Power*, 327–338.

241 *"If we must have an* enemy." Hamilton to Sedgwick, May 10, 1800. (Emphasis in original.)

242 *"The most disinterested, prudent."* Adams to William Cunningham, Feb. 22, 1809.

242 *"The most unfit."* Hamilton to John Rutledge, Jr., Jan. 4, 1801.

243 *"The Energy weight."* Jay to Adams, Jan. 2, 1801.

15. Jefferson: The Pendulum Swing

244 *"America was an even more egalitarian."* Lindert and Williamson, *Unequal Gains,* 95.

245 *"Happy America."* N. Appleton, in Kamensky, *Exchange Artist,* 4.

247 *"The fact is I am not well calculated."* Gallatin to Lewis F. Lesdernier, May 25, 1798, in Dungan, 64.

248 *"Self-defeating."* Cooke, *Tench Coxe,* 397.

249 *"A cool, discerning man."* Pickering to E. Stevens, Nov. 29, 1799, in Gray.

250 *"I am decidedly in favor."* Jefferson to Gallatin, July 12, 1803.

250 *"No class of citizens,"* Gallatin, *A Sketch.*

251 *The GNP was steady.* Lindert and Williamson, chaps. 4 and 5.

255 *"These charges have been brought."* Lyon, in Austin, 141.

255 *"There is on the globe."* Jefferson to R. Livingston, Apr. 18, 1802.

255 *"The impetuosity of her temper."* Ibid.

256 *"Seemed alarmed."* Livingston to Madison, Apr. 13, 1803.

257 *New England's waning influence.* Thomas J. Farnham, "The Federal-State Issue and the Louisiana Purchase," *Louisiana History* 6, no. 1 (Winter 1965): 11.

257 *"Wise or vigorous measures."* Hamilton, *New York Evening Post,* July 5, 1803.

257 *"The United States take rank."* R. Livingston, in Farnham, "The Federal-State Issue," 11.

258 *"One of the most deadly hostilities."* Jefferson to Gallatin, Dec. 13, 1803.

259 *"Repugnant to the Constitution."* Marshall, in *Marbury v. Madison.* Online at: www.law.cornell.edu/supremecourt/text/5/137.

259 *"Commerce of the most unremitting."* Jefferson, *Notes.*

259 *"Withdraw the citizens."* Jefferson, to the United States Congress, Dec. 2, 1806.

261 *"Growing distaste for Politics."* Hamilton to Sedgwick, July 10, 1804.

261 *"The suppression of unnecessary."* Jefferson, Second Inaugural Address, Mar. 4, 1805.

262 *"A few questions to your conscience."* Adams to Rush, Feb. 6, 1805.

263 *"Orders to our troops."* Jefferson, Annual Message to Congress, Dec. 6, 1805.

265 *"Who aids and countenances."* In Kamensky.

266 *"Never since the battle of Lexington."* Jefferson to Dupont de Nemours, July 14, 1807.

267 *"We must expect an efficient."* Gallatin to Jefferson, July 25, 1807.

269 *"As to the hope."* Jefferson to Congress, Dec. 12, 1807.

16. Madison: A War for Economic Freedom

271 *"Having an immense property."* In E. Gray, *William Gray.*

272 *"I take the Liberty of addressing."* Astor to Jefferson, Feb. 27, 1808.

272 *"Highly desirable to have that trade."* Jefferson to Astor, April 13, 1808.

272 *"He is desirous of returning."* S. Mitchill to Jefferson, July 12, 1808.

273 *"Evil and of a magnitude."* Nathan Appleton, in Kamensky, 148.

276 *"To cherish peace and friendly."* Madison, Inaugural Address, Mar. 4, 1809.

281 *"The banking infatuation."* J. Adams, quoted in Rush to Jefferson, Jan. 2, 1811.

281 *"Profit was not [Astor's] object."* Gallatin to Madison, Jan. 5, 1811.

282 *"Allowed Girard to capitalize."* Donald R. Adams, Jr., *Finance and Enterprise,* 15.

282 *"Laboured under a want."* Madison, Memorandum on Robert Smith, Apr. 11, 1811.

284 *"With this evidence of hostile."* Madison, Nov. 5, 1811.

285 *"May be burdened with the smallest."* Gallatin to Madison, Mar. 12, 1812.

285 *"A state of war against."* Madison to Congress, June 1, 1812.

287 *"He did not believe individuals."* E. Gray, *William Gray.*

287 *"Mother England, the last."* A. Hanson, in "First Blood: The Baltimore Riots," National Park Service. Online at: www.nps.gov/articles/first-blood .htm.

289 *"We have hardly enough."* Gallatin to Madison, March 5, 1813.

289 *"Starve the government."* *Albany Argus,* in Kenneth I. Brown, "Stephen Girard's Bank," *PMHB* 66, no. 1 (Jan. 1942): 42.

290 *"A serious intention exists."* Parish to Dallas, in Donald R Adams, Jr., "The Beginning of Investment Banking in the United States," *Pennsylvania History* 45, no. 2 (1978): 104. See also J. Mackay Hitsman, "David Parish and the War of 1812," *Military Affairs* 26, no. 4 (Winter 1962–1963).

290 *"Should it be otherwise."* Girard, in Adams, *Finance and Enterprise,* 31.

292 *"Boarding school operator."* In Adams, "The Beginning," 114.

292 *"The commencement of investment."* Ibid.

Bibliography

Adams, Donald R., Jr. *Finance and Enterprise in Early America: A Study of Stephen Girard's Bank, 1812–1831.* Philadelphia: University of Pennsylvania Press, 1978.

Alberts, Robert C. *Golden Voyage: The Life and Times of William Bingham, 1752–1804.* Boston: Houghton-Mifflin, 1969.

Alexander, John K. "The Fort Wilson Incident of 1779: A Case Study of the Revolutionary Crowd." *WMQ* 31, no. 4 (Oct. 1974).

Beeman, Richard R. *Our Lives, Our Fortunes and Our Sacred Honor: The Forging of American Independence, 1774–1776.* New York: Basic Books, 2013.

———. *Plain Honest Men: The Making of the American Constitution.* New York: Random House, 2009.

Billias, George Athan. *Elbridge Gerry: Founding Father and Republican Statesman.* New York: McGraw-Hill, 1976.

Bodenhorn, Howard. *State Banking in Early America.* New York: Oxford University Press, 2003.

Bowling, Kenneth R., and Donald R. Kennon, eds. *The House and the Senate in the 1790s: Petitioning, Lobbying, and Institutional Development.* Athens: Ohio University Press, 2002.

Breen, T. H. *The Marketplace of Revolution: How Consumer Politics Shaped American Independence.* Oxford, UK: Oxford University Press, 2004.

———. *Tobacco Culture: The Mentality of the Great Tidewater Planters on the Eve of Revolution.* Princeton: Princeton University Press, 1985.

Buel, Richard, Jr. *America on the Brink: How the Political Struggle Over the War of 1812 Almost Destroyed the Young Republic.* New York: Palgrave Macmillan, 2005.

———. *In Irons: Britain's Naval Supremacy and the American Revolutionary Economy.* New Haven: Yale University Press, 1998.

Carp, Benjamin L. *Rebels Rising: Cities and the American Revolution.* New York: Oxford University Press, 2007.

Carp, E. Wayne. *To Starve the Army at Pleasure: Continental Army Administration and American Political Culture, 1775–1783*. Chapel Hill: University of North Carolina Press, 1984.

Chernow, Ron. *Washington*. New York: Penguin Press, 2010.

———. *Alexander Hamilton*. New York: Penguin Press, 2004.

Cooke, Jacob E. *Tench Coxe and the Early Republic*. Chapel Hill: University of North Carolina Press, 1978.

Cowen, David Jack. *The Origins and Economic Impact of the First Bank of the United States, 1791–1797*. New York: Garland Publishing, 2000.

Crowley, John E. *The Privileges of Independence: Neomercantilism and the American Revolution*. Baltimore: Johns Hopkins University Press, 1993.

Cutterham, Tom. "The Revolutionary Transformation of American Merchant Networks: Carter and Wadsworth and Their World, 1775–1800." *Enterprise and Society* 18, no. 1 (March 2017).

DeConde, Alexander. *The Quasi-War: The Politics and Diplomacy of the Undeclared War with France, 1797–1801*. New York: Scribner, 1966.

Derby, E. H., Esq. "Elias Hasket Derby." In *Lives of American Merchants,* edited by Freeman Hunt. New York: Derby & Jackson, 1858.

Doerflinger, Thomas M. *A Vigorous Spirit of Enterprise: Merchants and Economic Development in Revolutionary Philadelphia*. New York: W. W. Norton, 1987.

Elkins, Stanley, and Eric McKitrick. *The Age of Federalism*. New York: Oxford University Press, 1993.

Fatovic, Clement. *America's Founding and the Struggle Over Economic Inequality*. Lawrence: University of Kansas Press, 2015.

Ferguson, E. James. *The Power of the Purse: A History of American Public Financing, 1776–1790*. Chapel Hill: University of North Carolina Press, 1961.

Fleming, Thomas. *Washington's Secret War: The Hidden History of Valley Forge*. New York: HarperCollins, 2005.

Flower, Milton E. *John Dickinson, Conservative Revolutionary*. Charlottesville: University of Virginia Press, 1983.

Foner, Eric. *Tom Paine and Revolutionary America*. Cambridge: Oxford University Press, 2005.

Fowler, William M., Jr. *The Baron of Beacon Hill: A Biography of John Hancock*. Boston: Houghton-Mifflin, 1980.

Gallatin, Albert. *A Sketch of the Finances of the United States*. New-York: William A. Davis, 1796.

Giunta, Mary A., ed. *Documents of the Emerging Nation: U.S. Foreign Relations, 1775–1789*. Lanham, MD: Rowman & Littlefield, 1998.

Gray, Edward. *William Gray, of Salem, Merchant: A Biographical Sketch*. Boston: Houghton-Mifflin, 1914.

Grubb, Farley. "State Redemption of the Continental Dollar, 1779–90." *WMQ* 69, no. 1 (January 2012).

Handlin, Oscar, and Mary Flug Handlin. *Commonwealth: A Study of the Rule of Government in the American Economy: Massachusetts, 1774–1861.* Cambridge, MA: Belknap Press, 1969.

Hoffman, Ronald, John J. McCusker, Russell R. Menard, and Peter J. Albert, eds. *The Economy of Early America: The Revolutionary Period, 1763–1790.* Charlottesville: University of Virginia Press, 1988.

Hogeland, William. *The Whiskey Rebellion.* New York: Scribner, 2006.

Holton, Woody. *Unruly Americans and the Origins of the Constitution.* New York: Hill & Wang, 2007.

Irvin, Benjamin H. *Clothed in Robes of Sovereignty: The Continental Congress and the People Out of Doors.* New York: Oxford University Press, 2011.

Irwin, Douglas A., and Richard Sylla, eds. *Founding Choices: American Economic Policy in the 1790s.* Chicago: University of Chicago Press, 2011.

Jefferson, Thomas. *A Summary View of the Rights of British America.* Online at: avalon.law.yale.edu/18th_century/jeffsumm.asp.

———. *Notes on the State of Virginia.* Paris: 1785.

Jensen, Merrill, ed. *Tracts of the American Revolution, 1763–1776.* Indianapolis: Hackett Publishing, 2006.

Jones, Robert F. *"The King of the Alley": William Duer, Politician, Entrepreneur, and Speculator, 1768–1799.* Philadelphia: American Philosophical Society, 1992.

Kamensky, Jane. *The Exchange Artist: A Tale of High-Flying Speculation and America's First Banking Collapse.* New York: Viking, 2008.

Ketcham, Ralph. *James Madison: A Biography.* Charlottesville: University of Virginia Press, 1990.

Klarman, Michael J. *The Framers' Coup: The Making of the United States Constitution.* New York: Oxford University Press, 2016.

Konkle, Burton Alva. *Thomas Willing and the First American Financial System.* Philadelphia: University of Pennsylvania Press, 1937.

Kulikoff, Allan. *The Agrarian Origins of American Capitalism.* Charlottesville: University Press of Virginia, 1992.

Lewis, Lawrence, Jr. *A History of the Bank of North America.* Philadelphia: Lippincott & Co., 1882.

Lindert, Peter H., and Jeffrey G. Williamson. *Unequal Gains: American Growth and Inequality Since 1700.* Princeton: Princeton University Press, 2016.

Lodge, Henry Cabot. *Life and Letters of George Cabot.* Boston: Little, Brown, 1878.

Maclay, William. *Journal of William Maclay, 1789–1791.* Harrisburg, PA: Lane & Hart, 1880.

Madison, James. *Notes of Debates in the Federal Convention of 1787.* New York, W. W. Norton, 1966.

Madsden, Axel. *John Jacob Astor: America's First Multimillionaire.* New York: John Wiley & Sons, 2001.

Maier, Pauline. *Ratification: The People Debate the Constitution, 1787–1788.* New York: Simon & Schuster, 2010.

———. *American Scripture: Making the Declaration of Independence*. New York: Knopf, 1997.

———. *From Resistance to Revolution: Colonial Radicals and the Development of American Opposition to Britain, 1765–1776*. New York: Knopf, 1991.

Main, Jackson Turner. "Government by the People: The American Revolution and the Democratization of Legislatures." *WMQ* 23, no. 3 (July 1966): 391–407.

Martin, Joseph Plumb. *Memoir of a Revolutionary Soldier*. Mineola, NY: Dover Publications, 2006.

Matson, Cathy, ed. *The Economy of Early America: Historical Perspectives and New Directions*. University Park: Pennsylvania State University Press, 2006.

Mattern, David B. *Benjamin Lincoln and the American Revolution*. Columbia: University of South Carolina Press, 1995.

McCoy, Drew R. *The Elusive Republic: Political Economy in Jeffersonian America*. Chapel Hill: University of North Carolina Press, 1980.

McCraw, Thomas K. *The Founders and Finance: How Hamilton, Gallatin, and Other Immigrants Forged a New Economy*. Cambridge: Harvard University Press, 2012.

McDonough, Daniel J. *Christopher Gadsden and Henry Laurens: The Parallel Lives of Two American Patriots*. Sellinsgrove, PA: Susquehanna University Press, 2000.

McGuire, Robert A. *To Form a More Perfect Union: A New Economic Interpretation of the Constitution*. New York: Oxford University Press, 2003.

McKey, Richard H., Jr. "Elias Hasket Derby and the American Revolution." *Essex Institute Historical Papers* 97 (April 1961).

McMaster, John Bach. *The Life and Times of Stephen Girard. Vol. 1*. Philadelphia: Lippincott, 1918.

Meacham, Jon. *Thomas Jefferson: The Art of Power*. New York: Random House, 2012.

Morris, Robert. *Papers of Robert Morris, Vol. 1*. Pittsburgh: University of Pittsburgh Press, 1973.

Nagy, John A. *Rebellion in the Ranks: Mutinies in the American Revolution*. Yardley, PA: Westholme Publishing, 2016.

Nash, Gary B. *The Unknown American Revolution*. New York: Viking Press, 2006.

———. *The Urban Crucible: Social Change, Political Consciousness, and the Origins of the American Revolution*. Cambridge: Harvard University Press, 1979.

Newell, Margaret Ellen. *From Dependency to Independence: Economic Revolution in Colonial New England*. Ithaca: Cornell University Press, 1998.

Nuxoll, Elizabeth M. *Congress and the Munitions Merchants: The Secret Committee of Trade During the American Revolution*. New York: Garland Publishers, 1985.

Otis, James. *The Rights of the British Colonies Asserted and Proved*. London: J. Williams, 1765.

Perkins, Edwin J. *American Public Finance and Financial Services, 1700–1815.* Columbus: Ohio State University Press, 1994.

Platt, John D. R. "Jeremiah Wadsworth, Federalist Entrepreneur." Ph.D. thesis, Columbia University, 1955.

Polanyi, Karl. *The Great Transformation: The Political and Economic Origins of Our Time.* New York: Rinehart & Co., 1944.

Rappleye, Charles. *Robert Morris: Financier of the American Revolution.* New York: Simon & Schuster, 2010.

———. *Sons of Providence: The Brown Brothers, the Slave Trade, and the American Revolution.* New York: Simon & Schuster, 2006.

Resch, John. *Suffering Soldiers: Revolutionary War Veterans, Moral Sentiment, and Political Culture in America.* Amherst: University of Massachusetts Press, 2000.

Richard, Leonard. *Shays's Rebellion: The American Revolution's Final Battle.* Philadelphia: University of Pennsylvania Press, 2002.

Risch, Erna. *Supplying Washington's Army.* Washington, DC: United States Army Center of Military History, 1981.

Schlesinger, Arthur Meier. *The Colonial Merchants and the American Revolution, 1763–1776.* New York: Columbia University, 1917.

Sellers, Leila. *Charleston Business on the Eve of the American Revolution.* Chapel Hill: University of North Carolina Press, 1934.

Shachtman, Tom. *How the French Saved America: Soldiers, Sailors, Diplomats, Louis XVI, and the Success of a Revolution.* New York: St. Martin's Press, 2017.

———. *Gentlemen Scientists and Revolutionaries: The Founding Fathers in the Age of Enlightenment.* New York: Palgrave Macmillan, 2014.

———. *The Fourteenth Colony.* Lakeville, CT: *Lakeville Journal*, 2013.

Smith, Adam. *An Inquiry into the Nature and Causes of the Wealth of Nations.* London: 1776.

Smith, Barbara Clark. *The Freedoms We Lost: Consent and Resistance in Revolutionary America.* New York: The New Press, 2010.

———. "Food Rioters and the American Revolution. "*WMQ* 51, no. 1 (Jan. 1994): 3–38.

Steuart, James. *An Inquiry into the Principles of Political Oeconomy.* London: A. Millar & T. Cadill, 1767.

Sumner, William Graham. *The Finances and the Financier of the American Revolution.* Vols. 1 and 2, 1890. Reprint, New York: Burt Franklin, 1970.

Tyler, John W. *Smugglers & Patriots: Boston Merchants and the Advent of the American Revolution.* Boston: Northeastern University Press, 1986.

Unger, Harlow Giles. *John Hancock: Merchant King and American Patriot.* New York: John Wiley & Sons, 2000.

Van Cleve, George William. *We Have Not a Government: The Articles of Confederation and the Road to the Constitution.* Chicago: University of Chicago Press, 2017.

Wallace, David D. *The Life of Henry Laurens.* New York: G. P. Putnam's Sons, 1915.

Walters, Raymond, Jr. *Albert Gallatin.* New York: Macmillan, 1957.

Webster, Pelatiah. *Political Essays in the Nature and Operation of Money, Public Finances, and Other Subjects.* Philadelphia: Joseph Cruikshank, 1791.

Whitbeck, Paul Moore. *Jeremiah Wadsworth: Businessman-Patriot,* 1967.

Wilentz, Sean. *Chants Democratic: New York City and the Rise of the American Working Class, 1788–1850.* New York: Oxford University Press, 2004.

Wolf, Edwin, Jr. *John Dickinson, Forgotten Patriot.* Philadelphia: Dickinson Mansion, 1932.

Wood, Gordon S. *Empire of Liberty: A History of the Early Republic.* New York: Oxford University Press, 2009.

———. *The Radicalism of the American Revolution.* New York: Knopf, 1992.

Wright, Robert E. *One Nation Under Debt: Hamilton, Jefferson, and the History of What We Owe.* New York: McGraw-Hill, 2008.

——— and David J. Cowen. *Financial Founding Fathers: The Men Who Made America Rich.* Chicago: University of Chicago Press, 2006.

Index

List of Illustrations

1) John Hancock, by John Singleton Copley, 1765.
2) Henry Laurens, by John Singleton Copley, 1782. *National Portrait Gallery, Smithsonian Institution; transfer from the National Gallery of Art; gift of the A.W. Mellon Educational and Charitable Trust, 1942*
3) Boston Tea Party, by Sarony and Major (Currier), 1846.
4) Robert Morris, bust by C. W. Peale, n.d., approx. 1795. *NARA collection, #101, Revolutionary War images.*
5) William Bingham, by Gilbert Stuart, 1797. *ING Bank NV, London.*
6) 1776 Continental currency. *American Revolution Center.*
7) Elias Hasket Derby, *National Cyclopedia of American Biography*, J. T. White Company, 1893.
8) Jeremiah Wadsworth and son, by John Trumbull, 1784.
9) Pennsylvania's Constitution, September 28, 1776.
10) George Washington and Committee of Congress at Valley Forge, engraving from painting by W. H. Powell, 1866. *148-GW-184. NARA.*
11) Yorktown battle conference, Auguste Couder, 1836.
12) Daniel Shays and Job Shattuck, Bickerstaff's *Boston Almanack of 1787.*
13) Constitutional Convention, by Junius Brutus Stearns, 1856.
14) Alexander Hamilton, bust by Giuseppi Ceracchi, 1794.
15) First Bank of the United States, 1795. Architect, James Blodgett.
16) 1792 coin. *National Numismatic Collection, National Museum of American History.*
17) Thomas Jefferson, by Rembrandt Peale, 1800.
18) James Madison, by John Vanderlyn, 1816. *Association (White House Collection).*
19) Albert Gallatin, by Rembrandt Peale 1805. *Independence National Historical Park.*
20) Stephen Girard, Alonzo Chappel, 1862.
21) John Jacob Astor, by Gilbert Stuart, 1794.
22) The burning of Washington 1814. *Library of Congress, 1876.*